Francis King

was born in Switzerland and spent his childhood in India, where his father was a government official. While still an undergraduate at Oxford, he published his first three novels. He then joined the British Council, working in Italy, Greece, Egypt, Finland and Japan, before he resigned to devote himself to writing. Until recently he was drama critic of the *Sunday Telegraph*, and he reviews fiction each fortnight for the *Spectator*. He is a former winner of the Somerset Maugham Prize, of the Katherine Mansfield Short Story Prize, and of the *Yorkshire Post* Novel of the Year Award for *Act of Darkness* (1983). He lives in London.

From the reviews of *The Ant Colony*:

'Prodding into view a colourful variety of Anglo-Americans lodged in peeling palazzi, elegant villas or staid pensioni, King trains on them his ironic gaze. The pages crawl with freakish spongers and dilettantes subsisting in a tiny world that's seen as a termite heap humming to a never-ceasing drone of gossip . . . graphic evocation of place and period.'   *Sunday Times*

'Excellent . . . King has a marvellous ear for dialogue . . . a joy . . . a convincing portrait of human vanity.'   *Sunday Telegraph*

'A gallery of beautifully observed, sympathetically drawn characters swirl around [Jack and Iris]. There is violence, there are scandals and heartbreak, there is death. Through all this their education proceeds. In the end they lose something of their innocence but they gain a degree of understanding.'   *Scotsman*

'Francis King is a "pure" novelist who, faced with the complexity of people and their inter-relations, denies himself any idiosyncrasies of style or opinion in their presentation. The result of his sacrifice is a novel of great subtlety and a humane richness.'

New Statesman & Society

By the same author

NOVELS
To the Dark Tower
Never Again
An Air that Kills
The Dividing Stream
The Dark Glasses
The Firewalkers
The Widow
The Man on the Rock
The Custom House
The Last of the Pleasure Gardens
The Waves Behind the Boat
A Domestic Animal
Flights
A Game of Patience
The Needle
Danny Hill
The Action
Act of Darkness
Voices in an Empty Room
The Woman Who Was God
Punishments
Visiting Cards

NOVELLA
Frozen Music

SHORT STORIES
So Hurt and Humiliated
The Japanese Umbrella
The Brighton Belle
Hard Feelings
Indirect Method
One is a Wanderer
  (selected stories)

POETRY
Rod of Incantation

BIOGRAPHY
E. M. Forster and his World
My Sister and Myself:
  The Diaries of J. R. Ackerley
  (editor)

TRAVEL
Introducing Greece (editor)
Japan
Florence

FRANCIS KING

The Ant Colony

Flamingo
An Imprint of HarperCollinsPublishers

Flamingo
An Imprint of HarperCollins*Publishers*,
77–85 Fulham Palace Road,
Hammersmith, London W6 8JB

Published by Flamingo 1992
9 8 7 6 5 4 3 2

First published in Great Britain by
Constable and Company Limited 1991

ISBN 0 00 654471 1

Set in Monophoto Palatino

Printed in Great Britain by
HarperCollinsManufacturing Glasgow

TO
MICHAEL LITTLEMORE AND YOUNG-AM

1

Jack looked up, Iris looked down.

They stared at each other.

'Let me carry that for you.' He was on the platform; she, struggling with an outsize suitcase, was at the door of the train.

Late the previous night, when, his mouth sour and his temples throbbing, he had eased his way past the knees of the grossly snoring middle-aged Italian woman opposite to him and had swayed and staggered towards first a locked lavatory and then another awash with murky water, he had seen this girl standing beside an open window in the corridor of the next-door carriage – made up, unlike his, of sleepers. Her long, blond hair had been streaming in the wind. Her motionless body, the hands gripping the ledge of the window, had had about it a straining rigidity. 'Excuse me.' He had smiled at her as he had edged past; but she had at once looked away, without returning the smile. She was beautiful, he had decided, in a cool, classy way which simultaneously attracted him and made him uneasy.

'Oh, I can manage, thank you,' she now said.

'No, please.'

'No, I can manage. Really.'

Iris had no recollection of that late-night passing in the corridor. She was seeing this tall, muscular Englishman, a rucksack on his back and a canvas bag beside him, for what was, in effect, the first time. He was in an open-necked white Aertex shirt, its collar worn outside a hairy sports jacket in a dark-brown herring-bone pattern, grey flannels held up by a leather belt, one end of which was dangling loose, and blunt-toed, scuffed brown shoes.

Jack had now leaned forward, grabbed the handle of the suitcase and, with a single jerk and a grunt, had pulled it down on to the platform. 'Where are you going?'

Having jumped down from the train, Iris was peering anxiously over his shoulder. 'I don't know. Someone should be meeting me.'

'Someone should be meeting me too. The trouble is that I've no idea what my someone looks like.'

'I'm in the same boat. I've no idea what *my* someone looks like.'

Each gave an embarrassed laugh.

'You're from the North.'

'How did you guess?'

'Yorkshire?'

He nodded. He wished now that he had not helped her with the suitcase.

'I'm interested in accents. And good at them. I used to amaze my fellow ATS. I could almost always tell them where they came from.'

'Yes, I bet that amazed them!' He glanced down at the crocodile leather suitcase — no wonder it was so heavy! — and then said: 'You seem to have travelled everywhere. Even Shanghai. And — ' he peered — 'Acapulco.'

'Oh, the labels aren't mine. I've hardly travelled anywhere. I was unlucky in the War — Dundee was the farthest I was posted. No, the suitcase is — was — my mother's. She insisted on my bringing it. It's a beauty — every kind of fitting — but I'd much rather have brought something easy and light. Like that sack of yours.'

Sack! She knew at once, from the way in which he frowned down at his canvas bag, his lips sucked in between his teeth, that she had used the wrong word. But to correct it would only make things worse. 'My mother's always spoiled me. Perhaps that's because I'm an only child. It was she who paid the extra for me to have a sleeper.'

'Lucky you!'

'You sat up?'

'I sat up. Which is why I'd like to lie down now.'

'What's become of our someones?' The platform was now empty but for a group of elderly American tourists, vehemently arguing about something, and an Italian woman, her long legs bare and her right hand holding a cigarette up to her heavily painted mouth, also clearly waiting for someone — or even, perhaps, for anyone.

Then, simultaneously, both of them saw the plump, fortyish man, in a soiled white linen suit, bow tie, panama hat and white open-work shoes worn down at the heels, who was trotting towards them, smiling and waving a hand as he did so.

'That must be your someone.'

'Or yours,' Iris said.

It was, in fact, both her and his someone.

'Miss Crediton?' The man was out of breath.

Iris nodded.

'I thought it must be.' Grinning in relief, he held out a hand, nails savagely bitten, on which he was wearing a chunky wedding-ring and an even chunkier signet ring. 'Giles Conquest. Director of Studies. They probably told you about me in London.'

Iris merely smiled. 'They' had told her absolutely nothing about him. But 'they' had told her a lot about Mervyn Le Clerq, the art-historian Director of the Institute, much of it already known to her from friends of her parents who were also friends of his.

'And you must be —'

'Jack Prentice.'

The two men shook hands. Then: 'We'd better get hold of a *facchino*,' Giles said. The girl's expensive-looking suitcase must be as heavy as a ton of bricks, he'd decided at a glance, and he couldn't be sure that the boy would volunteer to carry it. '*Facchino! Facchino!* Oh, blast! Those Americans have taken him. I called him, he saw us first. But these porters invariably rush where they think the big money is. Let's hope he's made a mistake. American tourists aren't always all that generous, despite the popular belief.'

'I can carry the case as well as my own stuff,' Jack said. He was eager to oblige not this snooty girl but the man who was to be his immediate boss.

'Can you? Oh, in that case . . . I have to be careful of my back. A slipped disc . . .'

Giles kept turning round in the front seat of the battered little taxi to speak to them in the back. Iris wished that he would be silent, so that she could take in her first view of this city of which her pianist mother, who had known Vernon Lee, D.H. Lawrence,

Romaine Brooks, Norman Douglas and a host of other celebrities in the Florence of the years before the War, had told her so much; but Jack, who would often inform people 'I like to know where I am,' and who would often urge them 'Do put me in the picture,' was glad to listen attentively.

'You seem to have a lot of friends in Florence,' Giles told Iris at one point. 'Most of them *very* grand.'

'Not my friends, my mother's.'

'There are letters galore. And telephone messages. I'll give them to you when we arrive at the *pensione*. I have them in my brief-case.'

Iris would like the *pensione*, Giles went on. Many of the teachers had stayed there in the past; one of them – Miss Pryce – was staying there now. 'I think you'll take to Ethel Pryce. And I think she'll take to you.' He didn't sound sure. 'She's – interesting. And a really wonderful teacher,' he added.

'Shall I also be staying at the *pensione*?' Jack asked.

'Well, no. Actually, my wife and I thought you might like to stay with us. To begin with, at any rate. We'll charge you less than Signora Martinucci.' He gave an embarrassed laugh. 'Much less. Though our food may not be as good. My wife does a job, you see, at the Consulate – and so she has little time for cooking. And our skivvy – she's just a young girl from the country. Marvellous with the kids but . . . You did say in your letter that you wanted to stay somewhere cheap?' Giles had guessed that Jack was disconcerted by the news of where he was to lodge.

'Yes. Yes, I did.'

'Anyway, it needn't be a permanent arrangement. If you find something else – no obligation. None at all . . .'

'I'm sure I'll be very happy.'

'Well, at least I think you'll both be happy at the Institute.' As when he had spoken of Ethel Pryce, Giles did not sound sure.

Jack was left to wait in the taxi outside the grimed, late-nineteenth-century block, the ground floor of which was occupied by a bar, a hairdresser's and a leather shop. He would have liked to inspect the *pensione*, but he had not had the courage to say so when Giles, followed by the taxi-driver with the suitcase, had told him 'I'll only be a jiffy,' and then, returning as he was about to pass through the crumbling *porte-cochère*, had asked: 'You'll be all right, old boy?' 'Yes, of course.' Jack began to fumble through his rucksack for the ancient Baedeker which he had bought for sixpence in a second-hand bookshop in York.

Iris, Giles and the taxi-driver, a jolly, heavily moustached man stinking of garlic and wearing a grimy, dark-blue smock, all stood silent, looking up the lift-shaft as the ancient lift creaked downwards in a series of jerks. An attractive young woman, a faint moustache along her upper lip, and two small children, a boy and a girl, got out. '*Buongiorno*,' she greeted them with a smile.

'*Buongiorno*,' Giles replied, holding the lift door open for Iris to enter.

'You know her?'

'Never set eyes on her. But everyone here is much friendlier than in England. You'll find that. Not that it means much,' he added. He pressed the worn lift-button, and they began a laboriously creaking ascent. The taxi-driver, straddling the suitcase as though to protect it from a possible thief, in turn inspected Iris's ankles, her legs, her breasts, her bottom. Then he looked into her face and gave her a grin. His teeth were yellow and chipped, his nose was broken. But he had a roguish, battered charm. Iris looked away.

Pensione Dante. They had walked, in semi-darkness, down a long corridor with doors leading off it. Then there was the gleaming brass plate (once each week Signora Martinucci would polish it herself, just as each day she herself swept the area outside the front door), and there was the doormat also inscribed with the name of the *pensione*. As Giles rang the bell, the taxi-driver put down the case, raised a hand in a vague salute as he said '*Aspetto*,' and swaggered off down the corridor. 'I'll take it,' Iris said, remembering the slipped disc. But, as the door opened, Giles picked up the suitcase.

Signora Martinucci was so tiny that she was almost a dwarf. Dressed all in black as befitted a widow of her age and class, with her greying hair untidily bunched together inside a hair-net, she appeared to be overjoyed to receive her new lodger, putting out both her seamed hands to take both of Iris's in her own. She then proceeded to make an equal fuss of Giles — asking him about *la sua moglie* and *i due bambini*.

Iris could not resist at once throwing open the shutters of the small, high-ceilinged room into which they were ushered. As she did so, the light — they were up on the fifth floor — struck her in the face like a blow, so that she not so much recoiled as staggered backwards.

'That's the roof of the Pitti Palace.' Giles pointed. 'You know about the Pitti Palace?'

Iris nodded, although she didn't.

'That's the Casa Guidi. Did you know that when the Brownings were living there, Dostoevsky was living only a few doors away?' Iris hadn't known that either. 'A subject for an imaginary conversation. Between Browning and Dostoevsky. Or, even better, between Elizabeth B. and Dostoevsky.'

Signora Martinucci was slamming first one shutter and then the other back against the window. Then, standing on tiptoe, she jerked over the heavy metal fastener. Iris realized that she had already broken a rule of the house: shutters were only opened after sunset.

Giles pointed at the wash-hand stand, with its basin, jug and slop-pail. 'Sanitary arrangements are rather primitive. Not what you've been used to, I imagine,' he added with an emphasis on the 'you'.

'Oh, it was often far worse in the ATS.'

'Yes, I'd forgotten you were in the ATS. That was part of the info sent out to us. . . . Well, I'd better get back to that young man or he'll be wondering what's become of me.' Already he had forgotten Jack's name. Then a thought came to him: 'I wonder if . . .' He turned to Signora Martinucci to ask if *la Signorina Pryce* was *a casa*. He spoke Italian with an accent so markedly English that even to Iris, who knew virtually no Italian, it sounded comic.

Signora Martinucci hurried off.

'It's a good idea if you meet Ethel Pryce as soon as possible. Then, if you have any problems . . . I'm sure she'd be happy to help you.'

'You wanted to see me, Mr Conquest?'

Iris was surprised by the use of the surname; and she was even more surprised when Giles used the surname back: 'Ah, Miss Pryce! Yes, Miss Pryce. I wanted you to meet your fellow lodger and, er, colleague. Miss Crediton.'

'The Honourable Miss Crediton.' The 'H' was not merely pronounced but heavily exhaled.

Ethel Pryce, a woman in her late thirties or perhaps even early forties, stood in a curiously hunched way, long neck drawn down between sharply raised shoulders, as though to diminish her height. But it was this height which, with the fine-boned narrowness of her face and her body, gave her her distinction. Her black hair, parted in the middle and worn absolutely straight, was held back by tortoiseshell clips to reveal her long, narrow, pointed ears. Her white blouse, a plain gold pin at the throat, was as crisp as her voice.

'Just call me Iris.'

Ethel made no response to this invitation.

'I've told Miss Crediton that, if she has any problems, I'm sure you won't mind helping her.'

'No. Not in the least. My room's next door.' She raised a hand and pointed towards the wall behind the wash-hand stand. 'But Signora Martinucci will probably be better at solving most of your problems than I will.'

'I know so little Italian.'

'It's surprising how much English she understands.'

'Miss Pryce's Italian is, well, perfect. *Lingua Toscana nella bocca Romana*. Except' — Giles laughed — 'the *bocca* is *Irlandese*. Irish,' he translated. 'Miss Pryce comes from Ireland.'

'From the bogs of Ireland. A papist from the bogs of Ireland.' Ethel gave a small, jerky bow. 'Well, I'll leave you to it. You'll want to unpack.'

'And I must also leave you to it,' Giles said. Then he added, after Miss Pryce had closed the door behind her: 'She's a good sort. Don't hesitate to ask her if you want any help or, or advice. She has . . . that manner . . .' He turned away and then turned back. 'Anyway, my wife and I hope you'll have dinner with us this evening. This being Saturday, she can give her mind to preparing a meal. She's not at all a bad cook — even if by Florentine standards . . . Shall I call for you at about, well, eight?'

'Thank you. That would be lovely.'

As he was leaving the room, he suddenly returned. 'Oh, by the way . . .' He lowered his voice. 'Don't let on to Miss Pryce that we've invited you to dinner. You know how it is. One can't invite *everyone*.'

'I won't say anything.'

'Oh, and before I forget let me give you all those letters and messages. I can see that you're going to have a thoroughly social time in Florence.'

'I came here to work. And to learn Italian.'

13

But as, head bowed, he pulled the letters and a memo-pad out of his brief-case, he was not listening to her. He had already begun to think of all the things still to be done in the office.

Back in the car and now seated beside Jack, Giles began to ruminate aloud: 'You'd have thought that Ethel Pryce would have known better than to refer to Miss Crediton to her face as "The Honourable Miss Crediton". . . . And she pronounced the "H" in "Honourable". "*Honourable*",' he repeated, now pronouncing the 'H' himself. 'Well, she certainly knows better than that.' He paused, frowning as he tried to work it out. 'Unless, of course, she was being, well, snide. That's a possibility. She's not easy, Ethel, a pretty big chip on the shoulder. A war heroine, you know. Oh, yes! She was with SOE — parachuted into Italy. She speaks this wonderful Italian, far better than mine. Her mother was Italian, you see.'

Jack, who had been hardly listening, pointed: 'What's that?'

'That? That's one of the most beautiful buildings in Italy, one of the most beautiful buildings in the whole world. That's the Duomo — or, to be more exact, the Cathedral of Santa Maria del Fiore. You've heard of the Duomo, haven't you?'

'Nope.'

'Well, you'll certainly hear of it — often — now that you've come to live in Florence.'

Jack's indifferent shrug filled Giles with exasperation. 'Don't buildings interest you?

Jack shrugged again.

He'd learn, he'd learn. He, too, would eventually fall under the spell of the city. After all, Margot had done so — against all expectations. 'I'll drop you off with Margot — my wife — and then I'll have to leave you. The registrations are coming in and, although it's Saturday, I'll have to make a start on them with my invaluable Violetta — my secretary. I never have a moment.' Suddenly Giles began to unburden himself of all his pent-up grievances, as he often did to a stranger. 'We're hopelessly understaffed. I actually teach about fourteen or fifteen hours each week. No Director of Studies worth his salt should be expected to do that in addition to all his other duties. I even trek out once each week to the Aeronautica — the Air Force headquarters — to try to give bone-headed Air Force officers some grounding in

14

English. Deadly! *And*, in addition, I have to do a lot of things that Mervyn should be doing. Well, he should have met you, for example. But he's idle, bone idle. Oh, a world-famous art historian, of course, I grant you that. But there's more to being Director of the Institute than hobnobbing with B.B. and writing books about Caravaggio and Pinturicchio.' Bemused, Jack continued to stare out of the window beside him. He had no idea who was B.B. He had no idea who were Caravaggio and Pinturicchio.

Suddenly irritated by this lack of response, Giles asked: 'And what are your interests?'

'My interests?'

'Yes.'

'Well, I play the clarinet. I used to belong to a college jazz group. And I − I go in for pot-holing.'

'*Pot*-holing?'

Jack nodded.

'I don't know where you'll go in for pot-holing here.' Suddenly Giles felt tired. He had had enough of meeting these callow, uncultivated boys − and, from time to time, girls − sent out from London; of teaching them how to teach, how to behave, how even to carry on a conversation; of eventually, after a few months or a few weeks or (yes, it had happened once) a few days, losing them when they decided that they were bored, that they wanted to see another part of Italy, that they would go back to England to go into something more lucrative like advertising or publishing or stockbroking. 'My great interest is writing,' he said defiantly. 'Novels. Or, rather, a novel. A novel about Florence. I see the city as an extraordinary microcosm − a test-tube bubbling over with the bacilli of love, hate, envy, ambition, oh, all the human emotions . . .'

'That's interesting.' Jack meant it; and Giles, gratified, realized that he meant it.

'But most of it's still here.' Giles tapped his forehead with a forefinger the nail of which had been bitten to the quick, leaving a ridge of dried blood. 'Trapped. I can't get it out. Why? Because that famous art-historian won't get off his arse to get us more staff or get us more money or even get down to some hard work himself.' Moodily, wide, full mouth bunched, he stared out of the window. Then he pointed: 'The Ponte Vecchio. The Old Bridge. Have you heard of the Ponte Vecchio?'

'Can't say I have. Sorry. I'm going to make a start tomorrow.

With my Baedeker. I'm terribly ignorant. That's why I decided to take this job — to acquire some, well, general culture.'

All at once Giles felt touched by the youth's gaucheness and innocence. 'If I have nothing else to do, I'll take you round. I'd like to do that. I'll show you things.'

'Thanks. Thanks a lot.'

Having hung up his only suit in a wardrobe so tottery that when he had first tugged at its door, he had thought for a moment that it was about to keel over on top of him, and having stuffed the remainder of his possessions into the recalcitrant drawers of an equally tottery tallboy, Jack sat on the edge of the narrow bed, his jacket and shoes off, and felt the sweat pricking through his skin. On the day when he had left his home in Yorkshire, it had been cold and drizzly.

Suddenly, as he stared up at a small green lizard balanced motionless on the cornice, he was overcome with despair. It had all been a terrible mistake, he should never have come. He should have applied for a job in the Civil Service, as his father had wanted, or for a job with the John Lewis Partnership, as his mother had wanted. That girl Iris and that man Giles: they weren't his sort of people, and he would never be their sort of person. And the pay was a joke, a bad joke. And this room — it was even slummier than the room in which he had spent his last year, living out of college, in Oxford. Well, at least the room he could change. 'We've been meaning to have it painted,' Giles had explained. 'There was this girl here before you and frankly she was, well, a slut. She got hold of all these opera posters and she then stuck them up on the walls with innumerable drawing-pins — as you can see. And she had this absolute genius for spilling ink. I eventually suggested that she should confine all her writing to pencil. But she didn't listen to me. She never did. Then, all at once, she upped, gave up both the room and her job at the Institute, and went to live with a middle-aged American over here to study economics under the G.I. Bill. I except she's making *his* life hell, just as for all those months she made our lives hell.'

'I won't make your lives hell. I promise.'

Both of them had laughed.

Next door, Giles had explained, was the room of the skivvy of all work. 'Our Maria's quite an attractive little number. From a

16

village near Certaldo — Boccaccio's birthplace. She's engaged to this gigantic, extremely ugly woodcutter, who looks as if some modern Frankenstein had only just created him. So you'd better not get up to anything with her — despite the proximity.'

Jack, still a virgin, had felt affronted. But he had also felt vaguely flattered that Giles should suspect him of being capable of getting up to something with anyone.

He glanced at the Ingersoll watch which his older brother, employed by a firm of textile manufacturers in Bradford, had given him as a farewell present. Ten to six. He wondered what, allowing for the time difference, the family were doing now. It would be a slack period in the chemist's shop, so that his white-jacketed father would be sitting behind the counter, reading his *News Chronicle* or working at the crossword in the *Radio Times*. His mother, having said that she must get her head down (or her feet up) for half an hour, would be snoring on her bed. Ida would still be at work and Frank would still be at school. It was nine-year-old Frank whom, despite his jealousy of this Benjamin of the family, Jack would miss most.

This was the first time that he had ever been so far away from home; and when, in the past, he had been away from home — at university, at a scout camp in the Lake District, staying with an uncle and an aunt who had retired to Worthing — it had never been for the months and months which now uninterruptedly stretched before him, a long, straight, desolate road with not a single turning off it.

At that moment the door was flung open with such violence that it banged against the wall, its handle gouging an even deeper wound in the plaster. A handsome boy of seven or eight, unmistakably Giles's son, and a younger girl, skinny and sallow, rushed in. Seeing Jack, both of them froze.

'Hello!' Jack greeted them.

'You've arrived on the wrong day,' the boy said.

'No, I've arrived on the right day.' Jack got off the bed.

'Daddy said you were coming on Sunday.'

'He couldn't have said that. Today's Saturday and he met me today.'

'When no one's living in this room, we're allowed to play in it,' the girl said.

Why should any child wish to play in a room so gloomy?

'Well, I'm sorry. I'm living in it.'

The boy was pulling open a drawer. 'Is that your camera? May I see it?'

'It's only a Box Brownie.'

'Daddy used to have a Leica. Then he had to sell it. He needed the money.'

'I don't think I'd get much money for that Box Brownie.'

'What's your name?'

'Jack. What's yours?'

'Piers. And this is my sister, Prunella. At the International School everyone calls her "Prune" or "The Prune".'

The girl laughed, happy with her nickname.

'Have you met Maria yet?'

'Nope.'

'You'll like Maria. She's very pretty. When Mr Chantry was living in this room, he fell in love with her.'

'Children! Children!' Margot could be heard calling from the farther end of the corridor, in a high, exasperated voice. 'Where are you? Children! Maria! Children!'

Piers put his head outside the door. 'We're here. With the new bug.'

'How dare you speak of Mr Prentice like that!' Her round face flushed, a kimono wrapped around her, Margot had appeared in the doorway. Her feet were bare. 'I'm so sorry, Mr – er –' She, too, had forgotten his name.

'Jack.'

'These two children are completely out of hand. Ever since they got a new, Swiss headmaster at the International School, discipline has gone to pot. And Giles and I have to spend so much time at work that there's awfully little we can do about imposing discipline at home.' She turned to Piers. 'Where's Maria got to?'

'She said she was going out to the post office.'

'You bet! We know all about those visits to the post office. And those visits to that sick aunt of hers. Now scram!' Reluctantly, the boy looking back over his shoulder to give Jack a grin, the children left the room. 'Sorry about that. You mustn't put up with any nonsense from them. When you've had enough of them, just tell them to beat it.'

'They're nice.'

She gave him a grateful, if tired, smile. 'You seem nice, too.'

He was not sure how to take that. 'Thank you.' He shifted awkwardly from one foot to the other.

18

She put a hand up to her hair and pushed it up and away from her damp forehead. 'I'd love to have a long, long siesta. But I'd better make a start on the evening meal. I only hope Maria gets back in time to lay the table.'

'Doesn't she have Saturday off?'

To Margot the innocent question was an accusation. 'Every other Saturday, not every Saturday. But she has lots of time off all through the week. She has an easier time of it with us than she would with any Italian family, I can assure you of that.'

'Can I do anything to help?'

One hand holding together the top edges of her kimono, she stared at him. Then she threw back her head and laughed. 'In the kitchen?'

'Why not? I've nothing to do.'

'Giles never helps me. Never, never once. He's far too busy, you see. Oh, far, far too busy.'

'I often have to help my mother at home.'

'But you're not at home here. You're a lodger.' Then she relented. It was a shame to take out on this harmless boy all her irritation with Giles. 'Come and talk to me while I'm working. You can do that.'

It was a large, untidy, murky kitchen, its cobwebby window too high for anyone sitting down to see the garden. When she caught him looking round it, she said: 'Primitive?'

'It's rather like our kitchen back at home.' He might have added: 'Except that my mother keeps ours tidy and clean.'

'Ever seen a refrigerator like that?'

The vast refrigerator, which was keeping up a constant low crooning, was surmounted by what looked like the two funnels, yellow with brine, of a yacht.

'An antique!'

She laughed, as she reached under the sink for a wicker basket of potatoes. She held up a potato: 'Do you think it matters that these potatoes are sprouting?'

He had no idea. But he replied: 'Oh, I shouldn't think so. Not if you remove the sprouts.'

'Sit.' She pointed to one of the four wooden chairs ranged round the table.

'Wouldn't you like me to peel those potatoes for you?'

'No.' She began inexpertly to peel one herself. Then she broke off: 'Shall we have a drink?'

'Not for me, thank you. I — I don't drink very much. Just the occasional beer.'

'Perhaps you're right. Giles won't like it if he comes home and finds me stinking. It's so cheap and easy to get stinking out here. The colony is full of alcoholics.'

'Have you been out here long?'

'Too long. Three years. Almost. We came here from Egypt. Giles was teaching in Cairo through the War. His war work,' she added derisively. 'All that time he was trying to write his Cairo novel. Now he's trying to write his Florence one. When we go back to England — *if* we go back — then he'll start trying to write his London or Birmingham or Manchester one.' She cocked her head and sniffed. 'Can you smell something?'

Jack also sniffed. 'I think something's burning.'

'Of course something's burning!' Her anger with herself and all the circumstances of her life now became also an anger with him. She scurried over to the huge kitchen range and jerked down the door of the oven. Smoke, acrid and thick, billowed out. 'Oh, fuck, fuck, fuck! This bloody stove! There's absolutely no way of controlling the heat.' She grabbed a cloth from a hook, stooped and then eased out a casserole. Setting it down on the table, she plucked off its lid. 'Oh, no, no, *no!*'

Peering through steam, Jack was unable to make out what it was that had been reduced to a black, glutinous mess.

'Oh, *no!*'

She sank on to a chair, the casserole in front of her. Then, having placed her elbows on either side of the casserole, she rested her chin on her palms. Tears began to spill out of her eyes, some catching on her lower eyelashes and some coursing down her cheeks. Otherwise her face was motionless.

Jack stared at her, dumbfounded. Then he ventured: 'I shouldn't worry about it. There must be something else . . .'

'Oh, please, please, please!' Now she began to sob.

2

There was a rap on the door and a man's voice sang out falsetto: *'La cena è servita, signorina.'*

Although she did not understand the words, Iris guessed that she was being summoned to the evening meal. Calling out 'Thank you!', she got up from the rickety desk strewn with the letters handed to her by Giles the day before. She had asked her mother not to write to all these ancient friends to warn them of her coming, but her mother, anxious that she would get in with the wrong people or even with no people at all, had disobeyed her. Most of the letters were written on stiff, heavy paper, embossed with the kind of .succinct address — *'Le Fontane, Bellosguardo', 'La Villa Favorita, Fiesole'* — which indicates a house of size, an owner of importance, or both of these things.

Since she had had her breakfast that morning brought to her room, and since the man who had summoned her had already disappeared when she emerged into the corridor, Iris followed behind an elderly German couple whom she assumed also to be on the way to the dining-room. Clearly they both had changed for dinner; the man's hair, grey and shaggy around the neck, was even still damp from a bath or shower. Iris wondered if she ought to return to her room also to change; then she decided that it would probably be more reprehensible to arrive late in a silk frock than to arrive on time in the cotton blouse and linen skirt in which she had spent the whole day wandering round Florence.

The worn, red velvet curtains of the high-ceilinged room had already been drawn, enclosing the seven tables in an airless gloom. Two Art Nouveau electroliers, their serpentine brass-work tarnished, disseminated a thick, yellow light through opaque glass shades. The man who had summoned her, elderly, with a bushy grey moustache, scuttled crab-like towards her, a steaming bowl of pasta held in both his hands. He gave her a brilliant smile — Giles had been right, after the sombre austerity of England in the immediate aftermath of the War, everyone here was so friendly and cheerful — and cried out in his piercing falsetto: '*Buonasera, signorina! Lei è di qua! Di qua!*' He used his narrow, pointed head to indicate the direction in which she should come. Later, Iris was to learn that he was some distant relative of Signora Martinucci, whose limp was due to the shattering of his leg in the final artillery duel before the surrender of the city by the Germans.

As Iris passed between the tables to the one, at the far end of the room beside a hatch laden with piles of plates, which his head had seemed to indicate, the diners already seated looked up to watch her. An elderly Italian woman in a large black straw hat, its brim dipping down so low that it all but concealed one of her heavily made-up eyes, gave a brief nod, and her even more elderly husband, a fork dripping strands of pasta, then grunted, '*Buonasera, signorina,*' before lowering his head to suck them into his mouth. The Germans, still waiting to be served, leaned towards each other, their eyes on this newcomer. The man muttered something to the woman, and she gave a quick nod.

Ethel Pryce glanced up from her book. Then, taking up a fork and placing it between its pages, she reluctantly closed it. 'It seems we're to sit together.'

'Oh, how nice!'

'I'm glad you don't mind.'

Signora Martinucci's distant relative was rushing, single-handed, about the room with falsetto cries of '*Ecco! Ecco!*' as he set down a plate or '*Vengo! Vengo subito!*' when one of the diners attempted to attract his attention in order to ask for something.

'You didn't come in to dinner last night.'

Iris remembered Giles's injunction. 'No. I decided to take myself out to a restaurant.' She began to blush at the lie.

Ethel picked up the bottle beside her. 'Would you like some of this? You'll think it putrid, but at least it's cheap. The drill is that we each have our bottles, we drink what we want, and then what's left is kept for the next meal.' She pointed to the label. 'We initial our bottles.'

'Then perhaps I should order a bottle of my own.'

'Well, for this evening . . . A bottle costs so little.' Her hand went out to her book, rested on it, almost opened it. The movement seemed to be telling Iris that she would really much rather be reading than talking to her.

'What's the book?'

'It's the first of a new series of text-books. By someone called Eckersley. Heard of it?'

How could anyone choose to read a text-book at dinner? Iris shook her head. 'I feel an awful fraud. I know awfully little about English-language teaching.'

'Then how did you get the job?'

Iris shrugged. She suspected that she had got the job partly because, at her interview, two of the members of the all-male board had blatantly flirted with her, and partly because her mother was a friend of the chairman. She had no academic qualifications other than a Higher School Certificate.

'It's really rather good.' Ethel patted the book. 'I think I'll suggest to Conquest that we use it. Not that he'll agree. He's so obstinate. If he hasn't thought of an idea himself, then he decides it's not worth taking up.'

The two of them began to eat their pasta in silence.

'I'm so clumsy at this,' Iris said at one point, as strands of spaghetti slithered off her fork.

'You'll learn.' Evidently Ethel was not prepared to teach her.

A young couple, he in a shimmering pale-grey suit, the jacket pinched in at the waist, and she in an elegant beige silk coat and skirt, sheer nylons and lizard-skin shoes with immensely high heels, breezed in, laughing at something which one or other of them had said outside the room. When they had seated themselves at the next-door table – with a deep bow, the man had drawn out the chair for his wife – Ethel said something to them in her impeccable Italian and they both then answered simultaneously. Ethel said something else and they threw back their heads and laughed. Iris at once took to them, as she had at once taken to Signora Martinucci and her falsetto-voiced, limping relative.

'You're fluent in Italian.'

'I ought to be.'

Later, as she was spooning up her zabaglione, Iris confessed: 'I feel terribly nervous about tomorrow.'

'Tomorrow?'

'Being thrown in at the deep end. I've never taught a class before.'

Ethel put down her spoon and stared at her. Then she gave a small, contemptuous smile. 'Well, then, things have been easy for you, haven't they?'

'I suppose they have. But they're not going to be easy now.'

'I only got my job because a twit at the Institute broke his contract and went off to Greece with a Dutch girl he'd picked up in the Loggia. And *I* have a degree and put in a year at the Institute of Education. Well, that's how things go.'

Iris felt guilty and embarrassed.

'I was living off — or trying to live off — private lessons before I got the job,' Ethel went on relentlessly. 'Not at all easy. The richest people were the worst payers. I had the greatest difficulty in getting anything out of the Caparettis — and he virtually owns the whole of the Italian film industry. I think that they took the line that it was a privilege for me to teach their moronic son.' She reached for her book. 'Anyway, there's no need for you to worry. Most of the pupils at the Institute are girls from rich and/or aristocratic families. They're not supposed to work, that wouldn't do at all. So, until they get married, they study art or music or French or English. They'll all be thrilled at having a teacher with a title. And their parents will be even more thrilled. Oh, you'll be all right. In fact, you'll be a great success. Nothing to worry about. Nothing at all.'

She got to her feet, although Iris had not yet finished her zabaglione.

'Well, I'd better return to Eckersley.'

'Eckersley?'

'The new text-book.' Then, suddenly and inexplicably, she gave a friendly smile. It was as though, after an hour of confinement in a wintry room, a shaft of warming sunlight had suddenly struck Iris through the window. 'Don't worry. You won't have any trouble. But if you do — and if I can be of any help . . .'

Her low-heeled shoes clicked over the worn linoleum as she hurried off.

3

'How did you get on?' Jack asked.

'I've no idea,' Iris answered. 'It's called a conversation class. But how do you teach people to converse? Most of them were girls, so most of the time we conversed about clothes and the smarter shops in Florence and London. It must all have been terribly boring for the men. And you?'

'Mine was a class in business English. I never knew that there was a special kind of English for business. We use a text-book first published before the First World War. Did you know that the business English for a letter is "a favour" and that if a favour is "to hand" it means that it's been received?'

Iris laughed. 'No, I didn't.'

'My pupils are clearly different from yours. All men. All terribly serious. All in business, I suppose. Or about to go into business.'

Across the long table of the common room, a half-drunk cup of coffee at her elbow, Ethel was correcting a pile of exercise books. With extraordinary rapidity she used her red pencil now to cross something out and now to write something in. From time to time she looked up, frowning, as Jack and Iris chattered. Then she put down the pencil and turned her head towards them. She stared. Finally, she said: 'I wonder if you could talk a little less loudly. Or somewhere else.'

'Sorry,' Iris said. Then she whispered to Jack: 'Let's move over there.'

An elderly woman, the gold chain on her pince-nez pinned, incongruously, with an ordinary safety pin to her voluminous blouse, was seated in a corner, a hand on either massive knee, staring out of the window. From Giles's hurried introductions that morning – he had all but pushed them into the room ahead of

25

him and had then rattled off the names of the members of the staff who were there — they knew that she was Miss Sweeney. There were two empty upright chairs beside her.

'Would we disturb you if we sat here?'

'Not at all.' Miss Sweeney shifted over to the edge of her own chair, as though to make room for one or other of them on it. 'Perhaps you'll cheer me up. I'm just a little *giu* at present.'

From across the room a young man called out: 'That reminds me of a story I heard about Berenson. Percy Lubbock asked him why he was looking so depressed, and he replied "I'm just a little *giu*." He gave a braying laugh; Miss Sweeney smiled with a weary patience; Iris and Jack merely looked bewildered. 'G-I-U, J-E-W,' he spelled out. 'Got·it? Pronounced the same!'

An elderly man looked up from the copy of *The Times*, more than a week old, which he had spread across the table: 'When I first heard that story — which was years before the War — it was told about Toscanini and Rubinstein. *Plus ça change* ...' He leaned across the table. 'And what, if one may ask, Miss Sweeney, is making you feel *giu* on a day as beautiful as this?'

'My neighbour's been complaining about Mr Perkins. He doesn't like the way he jumps over the fence to use his garden for his business. But he can hardly expect me not to let the poor boy out, and in any case I do so hate trays. They're so insanitary.'

'Perhaps, my dear Miss Sweeney, your landlord feels that it's insanitary for your, er, poor boy to do his business in his rose beds instead of in yours.'

'Oh, but he always covers up! He's most particular about that.'

'I sometimes wish that our own, er, facilities were a little less insanitary. One all too often has to, er, cover up there too.' He gave a little laugh that sounded like a door creaking open.

'If niggers start at Calais — as some johnny or other once sagely remarked — then decent plumbing ceases there. One just has to face the fact.' It was again the young man.

'Oh, Tim, you really are so insular,' Miss Sweeney protested. 'I often wonder why you ever decided to come to work abroad.'

'You know perfectly well why I did. I met this Italian girl when I was in Florence in the army. I fell madly in love with her. I wanted to see her again. But by the time I got back here she'd married an accountant.' He tipped his chair backwards, smiling at them. 'Sad. But as they say, *La vie est comme ça*. Or, if you like, *Così è la vita*.'

Ethel slammed shut the top exercise book on her pile and jumped to her feet. She then picked up all the exercise books and put them under an arm.

'Sorry, Miss Pryce!' Tim called out.

'Sorry? Sorry? Why?'

'I can see that our inane chatter's disturbing you.'

'Not at all. The bell's about to go. Not that that's likely to worry *you* over-much.'

'*Touché!*' Tim pulled a face at Ethel's retreating back. Then, when she had shut the door behind her, he remarked to the company at large: 'She *does* take life seriously, that one, doesn't she?'

'Which is why she's a better teacher than any of us,' the old man said severely. 'And why there's always a waiting list for her classes.'

Tim sighed. 'Well, I must admit there's never been a waiting list for any of *my* classes. They have an alarming way of *dwindling.*'

4

From the lavatory of his penthouse flat on the top floor of the *palazzo* which housed not merely the Institute but a bank and a South American consulate, Mervyn Le Clerq could always hear the whirr of the lift as it ascended. Hearing it now, he dashed out, hands feverish at his fly-buttons, and bounced on to the stool before the grand piano in the vast but meanly low-ceilinged drawing-room. His hands descended. Then he pulled a face. Nowadays he always had trouble with the arpeggios at the opening of the 'Moonlight'. He should have stuck to the Chopin nocturne, the score of which was propped up, open, before him.

His Swedish wife, Karen, shouted from the *salottino* in which, still in her dressing-gown, she was writing out some invitations in her large, erratic hand: 'Too early! Too early! Stop it! Stop it, Mervyn!' Mervyn pulled another face and, tip of tongue stuck out between teeth, went on playing.

Almost immediately the door opened and the grey-haired manservant, Carlo, in black trousers and a striped black-and-white waistcoat, put his head round the door to announce that the signorina had arrived.

Mervyn bobbed up from the stool. 'Miss Crediton! I really am *delighted* to see you!' His left hand went round her right wrist, as they shook hands. Then he stepped back and, head on one side, smiled at her. 'Amazing! You look so like your mother in the days when there was scarcely a house-party of young people at which we didn't play duets together. The gramophone and the wireless have changed all that,' he added. 'Although' — he pointed towards the grand — 'I still try to keep up with my music. Do you play?'

Iris shook her head. He was smaller and rounder and much less impressive than she had envisaged from those blurred, sepia-coloured snapshots. 'No, I'm terribly unmusical. A great disappointment to my mother.'

'Yes, I'm sure. Your father was unmusical. You must get your unmusicality from him. Come and sit down.' This time his hand closed not on her wrist but her arm, as he guided her across the room and into a chair. Once again he pointed towards the piano. 'Do you know who was seated at that piano the week before last?'

Iris shrugged.

'Benjie Britten! Yes, we even played some duets together. He was over here to give a concert with Peter. You must have met them of course.'

'Well, they did once . . .'

'Yes, of course you've met them. Oh, this *is* fun! I was so delighted when I heard that you'd been recruited. That board back in England has a way of sending us totally unsuitable people. With all the necessary academic qualifications, needless to say, but in every other respect . . . In short, not' — he gave a merry laugh — 'exactly the sort of guests one would wish to see at one's dinner table.'

The manservant came in with a silver tray with two glasses and a decanter on it. 'You'll join me in a glass of sherry wine? Or would you prefer some coffee?'

'Nothing for me, thank you.'

'Nothing!'

'Well, some sherry then.'

When each of them held a glass of sherry and the manservant had left the room, they looked at each other in swift but comprehensive appraisal. Mervyn liked what he saw more than Iris did.

'Are you comfortably lodged?'

'Thank you, yes. It's a *pensione* on the other side of the river. The Pensione Dante.'

'Oh, is *that* where Conquest has put you?' He wrinkled his nose. 'He — and you — could have done better than that, I'd have thought. Isn't that where that disagreeable woman boards?'

Iris looked at him in interrogation.

'Miss — Miss Pryce.'

'Yes, she's there.'

'She's all but started a trade union among the teachers. Constantly asking for more pay. We'll be having a strike next!' He sipped at his sherry, smiling at her over the rim of his glass. He had always liked tall, cool, aristocratic young women with long legs, neat ankles and a sense of how to dress. He had once been in love with her mother, who had been just such a young woman. Perhaps — the daring, intoxicating idea suddenly came to him — he would now fall in love with her. It was several months since he'd been in love with anyone.

'Well, the pay isn't *all* that good, is it?' Iris ventured. 'I'm lucky, I have an allowance. But for someone who —'

'Oh, don't let's talk of money! It's so sordid. Conquest was nagging me about it earlier this morning — the rent, the repairs to the roof, books for the library. Money — or the lack of it — seems to fill all that man's days and most of his nights. Let's talk about Florence and you. Both so beautiful!' he recklessly added, wondering if from the *salottino* Karen could hear him. 'The one so old, the other so young!' The recklessness had been a mistake; Iris looked embarrassed, even cross. 'Have you seen anything of the glories of the city?'

'Very little as yet.'

'Well, it takes time to settle in. You've only been here — what? — three days.'

'Most of those three days have been spent in preparing my classes.'

'Teaching is such a wretched profession. I once taught at the Courtauld. Hated it. I only did it to earn some pennies . . .' He did not add that it was Karen's kronor which had eventually freed him from this drudgery. 'Have you read any of my books?'

'Sorry. No.'

'Not my book on Caravaggio? But it's generally agreed to be the best book ever written on the subject. Even the Italians agree on that. Even B.B. — Bernard Berenson — does!'

She shook her head.

'Oh, my dear girl! Your education has — in some respects at least — been sadly neglected.' He was half joking, half in earnest. 'Let me lend you a copy.' He rose to his feet. 'No, let me *give* you a copy.' He crossed over to a bookshelf, hunted along it, and then found what he was looking for. 'Shall I sign it for you?'

'Well, that would be . . .'

'Have you got a pen?'

Pen in hand and the book open at its fly-leaf on the top of the grand piano, he deliberated. Then he inscribed in a cramped italic script: '*To Iris Crediton, beautiful and talented daughter of a beautiful and talented mother.*' As he signed it, he wondered: Talented? He had seen no indication of talent. But − well − no matter.

He handed her the book.

'Thank you. I'll treasure that.'

'The inscription and signature may give it a small additional value,' he said, beaming down at her. For the first time she was aware of the tininess of his feet in their black patent-leather pumps and the similar tininess of the hands which were now clasped under his swelling stomach.

'I know nothing about Caravaggio.'

'Well, if you read that' − he pointed − 'you will eventually know a lot.' He returned to his chair, crossing one leg high over the other. 'I've also written what is generally regarded as the definitive work on Pinturicchio. I'll give you a copy of that, too − just as soon as you've provided me with convincing evidence that you've got through the Caravaggio.... Oh, I do so envy you coming to this city for the first time! I remember its first impact on me, when I was a skinny, spotty undergraduate, totally uninterested in art. That was what inspired me − that and a letter to B.B. from my godfather. Otherwise − well, I might easily have gone into my father's business. Fireworks,' he added. He ruminated for a moment, repeated 'Fireworks' and then tossed back his head and laughed. 'Well, I suppose I *am* − in a sense − in the business of fireworks. Letting off verbal fireworks for my readers. Putting firecrackers under the seats of the sillier and stodgier members of the art-history fraternity.' He sipped again at his glass: 'Not bad, this sherry wine.'

'It's very nice.'

'Tell me, Iris − I may use the Christian name, mayn't I, since your mother and I were once such close friends? − tell me − what are your *interests*?'

Iris considered, head on one side, with none of the embarrassment that a failure immediately to answer that question might have been expected to bring. 'I don't know that I have any particular interests. Perhaps I'm still too young. I used to be interested in horses.'

'*Horses*?'

She nodded.

'Oh, gosh! That must have been the influence of your dear father. And what else?'

'Reading.'

31

'Reading? I never know what that means. Does it mean the reading of Jane Austen or Proust or James? Or does it mean the reading of the *News of the World* and the back of cornflakes packets? Or — yes, why not? — the reading of gas and electricity meters?'

'In my case, somewhere between the first two of those.'

'Well, we'll have to do something about that, I think.' He put his small hands between his knees and then pressed the knees together. He smiled roguishly at her. 'Shall we do something about it?'

'I came here — I came to Florence . . .' But she could not confess to him that she had come to Florence precisely because she wanted to find those 'interests' about which he had asked.

'I'm going to be your mentor. Even though you say that you're unmusical, I'm going to take you to the opera. And I'm going to take you to the Uffizi and the Pitti — just for a start. And I'm going to draw up a reading list for you. Now how about that?'

'Well . . .' She smiled. 'What about my work?'

'Your *work*? Oh, don't bother about that. You mustn't make the mistake of being too conscientious about things of no importance. Otherwise you'll become like our Miss Pryce. And you wouldn't want that, now would you?'

Late that afternoon, Iris and Ethel Pryce made their way back to the *pensione* together. Did Ethel really want her company? Iris could not be sure. She had emerged from the Institute and there Ethel had been on the steps, talking to a dumpy, harassed-looking woman who, a text-book and a note-pad under an arm, was clearly a pupil. When the woman had backed off with a repeated '*Grazie, signora*', Ethel, seeing Iris, had remarked: 'I don't know why that woman persists in calling me "signora", although I've repeatedly corrected her. Perhaps she feels that teachers, like cooks, should be given an honorary "Mrs".'

Iris had laughed although, as so often with Ethel, so dry and even sharp in her tone, it was difficult to tell whether she was joking or not. 'Are you walking back to the *pensione*?'

'Yes, I suppose I am. I thought of having a coffee and a snack — I missed having any lunch because of a private lesson — but then it all seemed too much bother. This is the hour when every café in Florence is full of idle, middle-aged women gorging themselves on cakes. Apart from the lengthy wait to be served, it's a pretty repulsive spectacle.'

As always at the close of a day of strenuous, often non-stop teaching, there was an air both of elation and of fatigue about Ethel, as about a mother after childbirth or about an athlete after victory. Her eyes behind their glasses were abnormally bright, even feverish; but under each of them there was a silvery, almost luminous sheen.

'Do you mind going this way?' Ethel pointed to a narrow pathway between mounds of rubble. 'It's quicker and so I usually take it. I seem to live in a state of constant hurry.'

'What's that?' Iris pointed.

'*That*? Don't you know what that is?' Ethel gave a scornful laugh. Then, relenting: 'Well, why should you? That's the Ponte Vecchio. We're walking through all this mess because the Germans blew up the approaches on either side of the Arno in order – as they hoped – to prevent the Allies from crossing it.' She scrambled over a jagged slab of masonry and then turned, holding out a hand. 'My shoes are more suited to this kind of mountaineering than yours.'

Iris did not take the hand. 'I'm all right,' she gasped, heaving herself up.

'I gather that you had a royal summons today.'

'A royal summons?'

'To see the big white chief. Mr Le Clerq. Mervyn.'

'Yes, that's right.'

'Did he offer you some "sherry wine"?'

'Yes. As a matter of fact, he did.' Iris laughed at the recollection. 'Sherry's something I don't really like. Not unless it's really sweet and sticky.'

'Oh, Mervyn wouldn't have sherry like that in his household! Except, of course, for the cook to make *zuppa inglese* – which is not, as you may imagine, Brown Windsor soup but trifle. I remember that, at the end-of-term staff party, he asked me what I wanted to drink and I said "A sherry". He then said: "A *glass* of sherry wine," and repeated to that man of theirs, "A *glass* of sherry wine for la Signorina Pryce." Later, Mr Greville – you know, that rather sweet old boy who spends all his free hours reading copies of *The Times* passed on to him, days late, by the Consul – told me that it was "not really quite the thing" – his phrase – to speak of "a sherry". To me that's all so absurd. But

33

perhaps to you, with your background, shibboleths like that still have an importance . . .'

'Absolutely none.'

'It's interesting that Mr Le Clerq' – it was with irony that Ethel used the Mr and surname, since in the conversation of the staff he was usually 'Mervyn' or even, jocularly, 'Merv' – 'decided to see you on your first day at work. He didn't ask to see that young man – that Prentice – who came with you, did he?'

'No,' Iris frowned. 'I did wonder about that.'

'But then I don't imagine that Prentice arrived with introductions to all and sundry. You know, when I began to work at the Institute, I might never have existed as far as Mr Le Clerq was concerned. So far from summoning me to his "apartment" – as his wife likes to call that grace-and-favour flat of theirs – for "a glass of sherry wine", he didn't even greet me when we ran into each other in the Institute. Then, when I had translated an article written by the director of the Accadèmia for the *Burlington Magazine*, he at last deigned to speak to me. "That was a very *serviceable* translation, Miss Pryce." No doubt Prentice will also have to do something like producing a serviceable translation of an article by some distinguished Florentine, before the big white chief deigns to notice him.'

Suddenly, from high above them, a voice shouted: '*Signorina! Signorina Pryce!*'

Ethel raised a hand to shield her eyes from the setting sun. Iris also looked up. In ragged shorts, a torn shirt, canvas shoes and a cocked hat folded out of newspaper, a stocky young Italian, clearly a builder working on the restoration of the half-demolished *palazzo* on their left, was waving at them.

'Oh, it's Guido Antonini,' Ethel said. She raised an arm and waved. '*Come sta, Guido?*'

'*Bene, bene! Grazie, signorina.*'

For a while the two of them, incomprehensible to Iris, continued to shout at each other. Then with '*Domani, domani! Alle sei e mezzo!*' Ethel began to walk on.

Iris wanted to ask 'Who was that?' but decided not to. Then, after several seconds, Ethel spontaneously provided the answer to the unspoken question. 'Guido is – believe it or not – one of my brightest pupils. I used to lodge – in some squalor and discomfort, miles and miles out beyond the Cascine – with his aunt before I got the Institute job. She asked me if I'd give him

34

English lessons in lieu of part of my rent. He has a real flair for languages and a real thirst for knowledge. Picked up the rudiments of English grammar in a matter of weeks. An accent far better than that of many of our classier pupils, who tend to have acquired ineradicable Cockney accents from their English nannies. Yes, Guido is going to go places, I'm sure of it. He's not going to be a labourer forever. I still give him lessons,' she added after a moment. 'Private lessons. He couldn't afford the Institute fees. Sometimes he pays me, sometimes – well . . .' She shrugged.

'I think that's awfully good of you. When you already have so much work.'

Again Ethel shrugged.

They were now trudging up the cobbled street to the building which housed the Pensione Dante. '*Bollito misto*,' Ethel said.

'Sorry?'

'How do I translate that? "Mixed boilings"? Anyway that's what Signora Martinucci always gives us on Mondays. Not at all bad. I'm hungry, aren't you?'

'Not all that hungry.'

'Well, unlike me, you didn't have to miss your lunch in order to give a private lesson.'

'You make me feel guilty.'

Iris was to learn that to make others feel guilty was something for which Ethel had a gift.

5

Swinging his legs as he sat perched on the parapet overlooking the Arno, Jack examined the Box Brownie. Given to him by his grandfather when, at the age of fourteen, he had scored a century in a school cricket match in which he had been the youngest player, it had a worn, battered look, the chromium rubbed off the winder to reveal the brass beneath and the metal casing of the lens dented in many places. He had once thought, examining some Angus McBean studies of ballet-dancers in dramatic chiaroscuro in a magazine in a dentist's waiting-room, that he too would like to become a professional photographer. But the results with the Box Brownie had not encouraged him.

Nonetheless, he still persisted with the simple, sturdy camera, just as he still persisted, now that he was so far away from home, with the patiently detailed letters in which he tried to capture for his family the people whom they would never meet and the places which they would never see.

Click. Across this photograph, taken in the slanting sunlight of late afternoon, his elongated shadow would also slant, filling him, many years later when he came on a pile of yellowing snapshots pushed to the back of a drawer, with a vague ache of loss. This was all that remained of his youthful self: a blurred finger of blackness across a white ridge of mud. Beyond the finger, three urchins in bathing costumes, the girl with her arms clamped to her sides, one of the boys raising a hand, the nails rimmed with engine-oil, up to his forehead to protect his gaze, and the third boy tilting his body sideways and his head downwards and away, held their rigid poses. It was the smaller and younger of the two boys, the navy-blue wool of his over-large bathing-trunks knotted at the waist to prevent them falling down, who had urged him to photograph them. Later, after Jack had thanked

36

them ('*Grazie, grazie tante,*' learned from a phrase-book lent to him by Margot) and had then begun to wander off along the shrunken mud flats back towards the city shrouded in a haze, it was this same boy who had scampered after him, shrilly calling, 'Johnny! Johnny!'

'Yes?' He stopped and turned, camera still in hand. Did they want to be paid for having allowed him to take the photograph?

The boy grinned impudently. 'You go hotel? Excelsior, Kraft, Croce di Malta, Baglioni, Majestic?' He rattled off the names of the most expensive.

'No, no. No hotel.' Jack began to walk on.

The boy touched his arm, the fingers cold and corrugated from day-long immersion in the waters of the river. 'I come with you, I come to hotel.'

'No, no!' Jack walked faster.

For a while the boy kept up with him, then he halted. He shouted something incomprehensible in a voice suddenly strident and crude. What was it all about? What did he want? Why did he suggest coming back to the hotel? In his innocence, Jack had no idea. At all events, it must have something to do with money, he decided.

Click. In the Piazza della Repubblica another boy, far smaller than either of the boys beside the Arno, with strands of lank hair sticking to his abnormally high, narrow forehead and his scrawny, pigeon-chested body hunched inside a tattered tweed overcoat so big for him that it slumped off his shoulders and reached almost to his ankles, hissed: 'Cigarette! Cigarette!' Then he used his hands, placed in its pockets, to jerk the overcoat open and once more to jerk it closed around him. In the second during which the overcoat was open, Jack glimpsed the packets of black-market English, French and American cigarettes sticking out of makeshift pockets tacked to its threadbare lining. The boy grinned. 'Cigarette, *signore*? Cheap, very cheap!'

'I don't smoke. No smoke!' Jack shook his head vigorously. After a moment of hesitation, he then indicated, in invitation, first the camera, then the boy.

The boy seemed dubious. He frowned, shook his head, even began to edge away. But eventually he turned back, nodded, posed before a café table, with one foot in its soiled white canvas shoe resting negligently over the other. He held a fixed smile.

Jack lowered his head, to peer into the view-finder. As his hand

37

went to the shutter-release, the boy once again whipped open the coat, so that years later the photograph would show him with his illicit merchandise draped all around his fragile body. As quickly he closed it again. The two of them laughed.

The boy wandered off, while Jack wound on the film; then suddenly the boy was back. Scowling, he put a hand on the camera and said something, rapidly and indistinctly, in Italian. Was he afraid that Jack might pass on this evidence of his black-market dealings to the police? Or did he wish to be paid a model's fee? Jack felt in his trouser pocket and found a few coins. He held them out. The boy stared down at Jack's palm; then spat out a single word and hurried off. Too little? Not what he wanted? There was no way of knowing.

Click. The sun was now so low that it rested, a disc yellow at its centre and orange round its rim, on the far horizon. A young Italian couple leant across a café table, one of four set out on the narrow pavement which ran beside the river, with their small, empty coffee-cups beside them. Her elbow rested on the table, and against her upraised arm (a dangling bracelet glinted) the back of his hand lolled motionless. Then the hand moved up and down in a slow, prolonged caress. They gazed into each other's eyes. They smiled.

Jack was suddenly thrilled both by their beauty and by the charge of emotion which he felt to be surging, constantly renewed, between them. Then, as though that same charge had suddenly jolted through him, he was embarrassed by an importunate movement in his khaki shorts. *Click* again. They paid no attention. Either they were too much distracted to notice him or else they did not care.

Developed and printed by the small, friendly man, a cock's comb of white hair sticking up from his spherical head, whom Giles had recommended, the snapshots — they hardly qualified to be called photographs, Jack ruefully decided — eventually arrived in Yorkshire, to be examined with the same perfunctoriness and puzzlement with which his letters were read. 'The lad finds some odd things to photograph, doesn't he?' 'It beats me why he chose to go there.' 'Well, it looks a nice place.' 'I suppose he's happy.' 'Yes, he must be happy.'

Was Jack happy? He did not know if this constant alternation of bewildered surprise and wary anticipation was happiness or not.

6

When, on her way out, Iris opened the door of the *pensione*, it was
to find herself face to face with a handsome young man, with
crinkly, heavily brilliantined black hair, a carefully trimmed
moustache, and hands and feet which, like those of Michelangelo's David, seen by her for the first time that afternoon, seemed
over-large for his athletic body. From the white of his open-
necked cotton shirt the column of his neck rose straight, thick and
sunburned. Somewhere she had seen him before, but she could
not remember where. Did he perhaps work for Signora
Martinucci?

He smiled at her, at once friendly and awkward. '*Scusi, scusi. La
Signorina Pryce?*'

Now she remembered. Yes, of course! He was the builder,
Ethel's pupil, glimpsed perilously high up on a jagged escarp-
ment of a half-demolished *palazzo* beside the Ponte Vecchio.
Guido: that was his name.

She nodded and pulled the door further open. 'Come in.'

He edged past her, saying in English: 'Thank you, signorina.'
Then he halted and turned, once again smiling.

'Do you know the room?'

He shook his head. 'Sorry. *La prima volta.*' He thought, head on
one side and forehead creased, and then continued, carefully
enunciating the English: 'This is the first time I come here.'

'This is the first time I've come here,' she corrected. Both of
them laughed. 'I'll show you then.'

He tiptoed down the corridor behind her, as though on some
clandestine errand. Iris knocked at Ethel's door.

'Guido?'

'Yes, he's here. He didn't know the way, so I . . .'

The key turned in the door – Iris herself never thought of

39

locking herself into her room – and Ethel's face appeared around it. 'Oh, thank you. Why didn't one of the staff answer the bell?' She was brusque.

'He hadn't had time to ring. I opened the door just as he was about to do so.'

'*Buonasera*, Guido. Good evening, Guido. You're' – she looked at her watch – 'seven minutes early. But never mind. The sooner we start, the sooner we finish.'

Guido edged past Iris into the room as he had edged past her through the front door. He smiled back at her and nodded. '*Grazie, signorina.*'

'Thank you,' Ethel said abruptly, closing the door.

Iris had had time to notice that Ethel had changed out of the cotton skirt and blouse in which she had been teaching and was now wearing a dress in an attractive pattern of small green oak-leaves on a background of darker green. Her lips were bright with lipstick and, just above them, tiny beads of sweat glistened through a heavy-handed application of powder.

Out in the sunshine of early evening, Iris strolled along the Arno. She had plenty of time, she did not wish to be the first arrival. Had any other member of the staff been invited? Clearly Ethel had not. It would be embarrassing if she herself were to be the only one. Couldn't Merv – that was how, having heard her colleagues so often call him that, she herself now thought of him – see that? Or did he just not care? The second of these alternatives seemed the more likely.

A young man high on an ancient bicycle was weaving beside her, from time to time turning his head to flash her a smile. Eventually he spoke: '*Buonasera, signorina.*' Without answering, she walked on. '*Bonsoir, mademoiselle.*' Again she ignored him. 'Good evening, lady.' He rang his bell to attract her attention. Now he was a few feet ahead of her. His bicycle weaving even more abruptly from side to side and progressing so slowly that, with each weave, it all but tipped over, he again swivelled his head round to flash the same inane, good-natured smile. Then there was a crash, as he rode straight into a pile of gravel on the side of the road. He fell off.

As he extricated himself from the fallen bicycle and began, frowning in concentration, to dust down his clothes, Iris could not help laughing. Hearing her do so, he himself began to laugh. Looking at each other, they laughed together. Then she walked on. All at once the trivial, silly incident had made her feel happy. It was the first time that she had felt really happy all that day.

Someone, Mervyn reminded himself, had once said that it was the moot guest who always arrived first; so it was hardly surprising that, at exactly seven o'clock, as the grandfather clock was striking in the hall, Carlo should show in that boy. It was even less surprising that Carlo, so quick to notice such things as unpolished brown shoes with a crumpled blue suit, should look so disdainful. For a long time Mervyn had dithered whether to issue the invitation or not. It was Karen who, as so often, had ended his dithering. 'Yes, of course you must invite him. After all, you had the girl in for a drink *days* ago.' 'Four days ago.' Unwisely, he had been far too enthusiastic about Iris to Karen – so like her mother, so elegant, so attractive, he had burbled – and the result was that now Karen had it in for the girl, as for so many other young and pretty girls in the past. Not that he would ever *get* anywhere with this one, Karen should know that. After all, he had nothing to offer her other than some instruction in, well, the culture she so obviously lacked.

'Prince! How nice to meet you at long last!'

'Prentice.'

'Sorry?'

'I'm Jack Prentice. The new teacher. Were you expecting a Mr Prince?'

'Good heavens no! I was expecting you, dear boy. It's the onset of senility. I simply cannot remember names. The other day I gave a lecture on sixteenth-century Italian art and I kept saying Sogliari instead of Solari. The audience didn't notice, of course. But afterwards I felt so embarrassed. One day I'll be saying Monet instead of Manet, or Pissarro instead of Picasso.'

Jack could feel the sweat breaking through on his forehead. He wished that he possessed a lighter suit and that he had not jogged up the Via Tornabuoni in his fear, now all too clearly unjustified, of arriving late. 'You have a lovely home,' he ventured, looking around him.

'Well, it serves its purpose. Although I wish I had more room for pictures and books.'

41

Jack again looked around him. 'There seem to be an awful lot of pictures and books here.'

'Has someone arrived?' Karen called from the passage. Then, still struggling to pin a sheaf of gardenias to the top of an electric-blue dress which reached almost to her puffy ankles, she swept into the room. 'Oh! Now who are you?' she asked, looking Jack up and down. Then she cried out: 'I know! You're the new one!' She shook his hand, making him embarrassingly conscious of the heat and dampness of his palm against the coolness and dryness of hers. 'Carlo!' she called. 'Drinks! Drinks!'

'My wife refuses to speak Italian. And Carlo refuses to understand English. But, despite that, they manage to get on.'

Soon other guests were arriving. At first, Mervyn or Karen would introduce Jack – 'This is our new, er, lecturer,' Mervyn would say, having decided that a lecturer would be more acceptable than a mere teacher in such a gathering; but after a time both of them had forgotten him. 'Is this your first visit to Florence?' those to whom he was introduced invariably asked, and then, hardly waiting for his answer, they would turn away from him with a cry of: 'Daisy darling, where have you been all this long, long time?'; or '*Carissimo*! We expected to see you at Max's!'; or 'Dearest heart, what have you done to yourself? You look so *slim*!' Eventually, having spent minutes on end standing by himself, icy glass in hand, he wandered out on to the terrace where, alone, he stared down moodily over the rooftops of Florence. How soon could he go without giving offence?

'*Prego, signore.*' It was Carlo, holding out a silver entrée-dish full of prunes wrapped in bacon.

Clumsily, Jack took one and popped it into his mouth. He felt a searing on his tongue and the roof of his mouth. He raised a hand, opened his mouth behind it, drew in a breath, all but spat out the morsel. Carlo looked at him with a glint of sardonic malice. Then he vanished. Jack spat into his palm. As he did so, Giles appeared. Hastily Jack put his hand, the morsel still in it, behind his back, hoping that Giles had not seen him spitting.

'I'd no idea you'd been invited. You could have come along with us,' Giles said.

'Oh, I wanted a walk.'

'You're lucky to have time for one. I've not put in a moment at the novel since the day you arrived.' It was almost as though he were blaming Jack for the deprivation.

Margot appeared at the open glass doors. 'Oh, hello, Jack,' she said perfunctorily. Then she turned to Giles: 'Darling, you must come and talk to that Marchese Thingummy-bob. The one with the son who failed to get his Certificate of Proficiency. She thinks it all the fault of Tim.'

'Probably was.'

The two of them vanished, Giles indignantly muttering, 'Thingummy-bob, Thingummy-bob!' No doubt Margot had called the woman that to her face, he was thinking.

Jack threw the chewed morsel in his hand in a wide arc over the balustrade and out across the rooftops. He watched it descend. Then he made up his mind; he had had enough of all this.

'So soon!' But Mervyn really did not care if the boy stayed or not. At least he'd done his duty by inviting him. 'Well, if you must, you must. Can you see your way out?'

'I'd better say goodbye to Mrs Le Clerq. Hadn't I?' he added dubiously, unsure of what etiquette demanded.

'Oh, don't bother about that. She's busy with the Mayor. You haven't seen Ivor Luce, have you?' He peered around. 'No, you wouldn't know him. We asked him and he said he'd be coming.'

When the lift arrived in answer to Jack's summons, Iris stepped out of it.

'You're not *leaving*, are you?'

He nodded. 'Couldn't take any more.'

'But you can't have been here more than' – she glanced at her watch – 'half an hour.'

'It seemed like hours and hours.'

'I was wandering up the Via Tornabuoni and then I somehow just got lost.' She put a hand on his arm. 'Come back in. Come back in with me!'

He hesitated. Then he said: 'Can't. I've said my goodbyes. It would be too embarrassing.'

'Who cares about embarrassment?'

But Jack cared.

'Ah!' Small hands outstretched, Mervyn hurried across the room to greet Iris, while Karen, perched on the arm of a chair as she pretended to listen to an Italian antique-dealer hold forth about recent bargains which he had picked up in Calabria, watched him balefully. 'Iris! I was afraid you'd forgotten – or decided not to come.'

'I wouldn't do either.'

43

'No, you're right. Your mother brought you up far too well.'

'Not so much my mother. The nuns.'

'Yes, the nuns, the nuns!' He spun round, away from her. 'Donald! Beatrice! You must meet Iris Crediton.'

'Fiona's daughter?' Beatrice, an Italian, asked.

'The same.'

'But why, why, my dear, does your mother never come to Florence? The War is far behind us.'

'She's been giving a lot of concerts in America.'

'Making oodles of money!' Donald, a middle-aged South African, put in.

There were other friends of her mother; there were even more friends of friends of her mother. Some were among those who had sent her letters and left telephone messages, most of which she had still to answer. To these she kept saying how sorry she was not to have got in touch; her first days at the Institute, she explained, had been so busy, she had really had little time for anything but work. But she must, must come to visit them, all of them then insisted – at Fiesole, or San Domenico, or Lucca, or Siena. Those of them who had unmarried sons thought what a good match she would make. Those who had unmarried daughters thought of possible invitations to England.

'You haven't seen Ivor Luce, have you?' Mervyn had joined the latest group of people to whom Iris was chatting.

'Ivor who?'

'No, of course, you don't know him, my dear.'

'But you will, you will,' an elderly, dandified Frenchman, leaning on a stick, assured her. 'In the end everyone knows Ivor. He's ubiquitous.'

'Well, not so ubiquitous that he doesn't from time to time accept an invitation and then fail to come.'

'I expect he has one of his migraines,' a woman put in, in a rasping voice. 'I used to think that it was only women who used migraines as excuses for not doing what they didn't want to do.'

'Do you use migraines as excuses for not doing what you don't want to do?'

In years to come Iris would often say of the bass, vibrant voice now behind her that it always gave her goose-pimples. It was as if a bow had been drawn across a cord deep within her body, to resonate on and on. She turned and at once felt astonishment. Who would ever have supposed that a voice of that kind would

44

emerge from someone so delicate, even fragile?

'No. I'm happy to say I've never had a migraine in my life.'

'Yes, you do look wonderfully healthy. I wish I could say the same.'

'You know Dale – Dale Somers?' Mervyn asked. He did not care for this Yankee, whom he had asked only because he had asked Pippa Lavery. But at the last moment Pippa had telephoned to say that she could not come because of 'a bilious attack' (her usual euphemism for a hangover), so here was Dale on his own.

Iris shook her head. Like many excessively tall people, this Somers was standing, head tilted forward and knees slightly bent, as though in a deliberate effort to reduce his stature. Ethel also stood like that, Iris suddenly recollected. His hair, so blond as almost to be white, was parted in the middle and then fell, straight and unusually long, on either side of his pale, narrow face, to just above his shoulders. 'This is the daughter of a very dear friend of mine. Her name's Iris Crediton and she's come to teach for us here – among other things.'

Dale Somers gave a little, hiccough-like laugh, looking not at Iris but down into his glass. He then glanced up at her and at once glanced away, over her shoulder. 'And what are those other things?'

'She's going to discover Florence,' Mervyn announced. 'With some assistance from me and no doubt with some assistance from all of you. In discovering Florence she may – who knows? – also discover herself.'

'How do you know that she hasn't discovered that already?' Dale asked, again with that little, hiccough-like laugh.

'People rarely succeed in discovering themselves when young,' Mervyn said. 'I'm not sure that I've fully discovered myself even now.'

'If that's the case, should you sound so proud of it?' Pursing his lips, Mervyn moved off with a muttered: 'Excuse me . . . I must just . . .' Through the door to the kitchen, he had seen one of the hired waiters gulp at a tumbler of gin and tonic from the tray he was about to carry in.

'It's so hot in here.' Dale put a hand up to the paisley-patterned cravat which he was wearing with a beige silk shirt and a navy-blue blazer. Ignoring the other people in the group, he then said to Iris: 'Why don't we go out on to the terrace?'

'Yes, why not?'

The sun had now sunk, and the heat, unusual for late September, had at last relented. The terrace was empty except for a forlorn old woman at its far end, who was feeding a pigeon with a crumbled cheese straw held out on a trembling hand.

'Beautiful,' Iris said, looking out over the rooftops.

He nodded. 'I spent the morning painting those rooftops from my bedroom window. But somehow – it never quite worked.'

'You're a painter then?'

'In an amateur way. I do a lot of things in an amateur way,' he added.

'You live in Florence?'

'For the moment, yes. I – er – work for someone called Pippa Lavery. You may have heard of her?'

'The name seems familiar. I think my mother . . . Isn't she very rich?'

'Very, very rich.'

'The daughter of a Greek shipping magnate?'

'Exactly. Now a widow. Who collects pictures. I'm supposed to be her secretary. But I can't take shorthand and I type with two fingers! She's rented this *palazzo*, but God knows how long she'll stay. Last year she rented a house on Capri and then, after less than a week, she decided the place was just too vulgar and crowded for words . . . You must meet her.'

'Would she want to meet me?'

'Of course! Why not? You must come over.'

Carlo appeared. '*Scusi, signore. Il telefono.*'

Surprised, Dale placed a narrow, long-fingered hand on his chest. '*Per me?*'

'*Si, signore. Per lei.*'

'I've got to go to the telephone. Excuse me. I'll be back in a moment.'

Iris wandered down towards the woman who had been feeding the pigeon. They smiled at each other. 'They're said to be vermin,' the woman said in a transatlantic accent. 'But they always strike me as being superior to the majority of humans. So industrious, cheerful, spunky. Why does one come to these parties?' she went on. 'One would so much rather be curled up in bed with a good – or even a bad – book. Well, you wouldn't!' she went on. 'You're young. And when one's young, one thinks that at every party to which one goes one's going to meet the most exciting people – or the most exciting person – in the world.

46

Talking of which, I saw you with Dale Somers.'

'Is he the most exciting person in the world? I hadn't time to discover.'

'Pippa Lavery must think that he is. The story is that she met him in some New York gallery when he was trying — unsuccessfully — to sell her a picture. In my youth the euphemism "secretary" used to be applied only to women,' she added, with a broad smile and a gesture of smoothing down her dress over her ample thighs. Iris was too innocent to understand precisely what it was that this elderly woman was attempting to convey. But she received a sense of something dank and corroding oozing out of her, for all her apparent friendliness and benignity.

Dale returned. He was flushed and clearly harassed as, a hand fiddling with his cravat, he told Iris: 'It's Pippa. She wants me back because she says she can't find some invoice or other. I ask you! An invoice! Can't she wait till tomorrow?'

Iris shrugged in resignation.

'But we'll meet another time. Won't we?'

'Why not?'

'How do I find you?'

'Pensione Dante. Do you know it?'

'Yes, I know the Dante. It's a favourite with students over here on the G.I. Bill.'

'There are no students like that now at the Dante.'

'Perhaps it's become too expensive.'

After he had gone, the American woman, her head on one side and a small smile twitching one corner of her mouth, remarked: '*Il a du chien*. Definitely. If one had the money, one could certainly do worse.'

Iris left her. Suddenly she had realized what the woman had been trying to convey. Suddenly she felt tired and deflated.

Giles was just inside the room, staring moodily at one of the extravagant flower arrangements on which Karen expended so much of her time. 'What is your school?' a visiting Japanese scholar had once politely enquired of her when being entertained in the flat. 'Constance Spry,' she had answered mischievously. 'Ah! Constance Spry!' With fresh interest he had re-examined an arrangement which had previously struck him as vulgar in its multi-coloured profligacy.

'Time we beat it,' Giles told Iris. 'Mervyn never likes people to stay after half-past eight. Have you noticed how lazy people are far more obsessed with time than active ones? Where's Margot?' He stood on tiptoe to gaze across the room. 'What are you doing about dinner?'

'I hadn't planned anything. I'm too late to eat at the Dante. Perhaps I'll go to that Ristorante Popolare which Tim showed to me at lunch-time.'

Giles pulled a face. 'Oh, you can't do that. It's the Italian equivalent of one of those British Restaurants during the War. The food is awful. And the people . . . Why not come with us to a little trattoria which we frequent? We were planning to ask Jack, but he's already done a bunk. He's not all that sociable, is he?'

'He's shy.'

'Anyway – come with us. It's not the kind of place of which Merv would approve, so perhaps you won't approve of it either. But let's risk that.'

'Why do you imagine that Mervyn and I have the same tastes?'

'Well . . .' He shrugged.

'You're not *leaving* are you, dear girl?' Mervyn said aghast, when Iris approached him to say goodbye.

'Must. It's getting late.'

'But I intended you to stay on for a small *goûter*. Just the two – er, three – of us. Something light. Some champagne. Yes?'

'I've already been invited to a trattoria by Giles.'

'Oh, you needn't bother about that. Just tell him you've changed your mind.'

'I couldn't do that.'

'Those nuns *did* bring you up strictly!' All at once he sounded cold, even hostile. 'Ah, well. No matter.' He turned his back on her and hurried away.

In the lift, Giles asked Margot if she had managed to have a word with 'the Corsini aunt'.

Margot shook her head angrily. 'You should have had a word with her – if anyone was to have a word.'

'The Corsini are the landlords of the Institute,' Giles explained. 'And the drains keep smelling – as you may have noticed,' he added.

'They also smell in the Palazzo Corsini,' Margot remarked, although she had never been there. 'Not that that's any consolation.'

As they stepped out of the lift, a typewriter was making a distant clatter in the front office of the Institute. Giles halted, his head cocked on one side. 'Violetta must still be working,' he said. 'At this hour.'

'Oh, come on!'

Giles ignored Margot's command. 'Surely she *must* have finished those lists by now. That woman's so conscientious.'

'Oh, *do* come on, Giles!'

'I think I'd better just pop in and see what she's up to. Hang on a moment!' He strode off.

'Really! He has Violetta and the office all day.' Margot pulled a handkerchief out of her bag and dabbed her forehead with it. 'Why not just leave her to it? If she's so slow that she can't get things done in office hours, then that's just too bad. Why should it be any concern of his?'

The two of them then stood in silence. The typewriting had stopped.

Eventually Giles emerged, followed by a wispy, wan, thirtyish woman with a pronounced stoop.

'Hello, Violetta.' Margot was off-hand.

'I've persuaded Violetta to stop working and to come out to dinner with us.'

'Well, let's get going.' Margot walked towards the door which led out into the courtyard.

'Iris — this is Violetta Ocampo.' Violetta peered up at Iris myopically through horn-rimmed glasses which seemed to cover half her cheeks. She gave what was, in effect, a little bobbing curtsey, as she held out a hand, muttering '*Molto piacere.*'

'This is Miss Crediton.'

'Yes, I guessed that. I saw her coming into the Institute this morning with Miss Pryce.' Violetta's English was almost perfect.

'Oh, Giles, do come on! I'm famished.'

'Sorry, darling. Sorry!'

Iris found herself walking in silence with Margot, while Giles and Violetta, chattering in Italian — from time to time Violetta would emit a surprisingly shrill laugh — followed behind.

Eventually Margot said: 'I wonder what he's found to say to her that's amusing her so much. She's never shown any sense of humour in the past.' After a pause, she went on: 'She was engaged to some Welsh corporal, posted out in Prato. But then he thought better of it and, as soon as he'd got his demob, scurried back to

Aberystwyth or Abergavenny or somewhere like that. I can't say I blame him.'

When they had stepped down into the basement in which the trattoria was located, a stout, beaming Italian woman, evidently the proprietress, rushed over to greet them. Most of her attention was channelled to Giles, whom she repeatedly addressed as 'Bellino'. Giles reciprocated by a show of flirting with her.

'Oh, do let's go to our table,' Margot eventually said crossly. Then, as she lowered herself on to a banquette from which she had first shooed off a somnolent tabby, she said to Iris: 'All this "Bellino" business! It really is so silly.'

'What does "Bellino" mean?'

'Oh, don't you know? Well, why should you? "Bello" is "beautiful". And "-ino" is the diminutive. So "Bellino" means "little beauty". But as Giles is neither beautiful nor little . . . The Italians are so insincere.'

Since Violetta must have clearly heard this last generalization, Iris felt embarrassed.

Fortunately, as soon as Margot had embarked on the excellent tagliatelle al pesto which the proprietress had insisted that all of them must eat, she at once recovered her humour, and Iris began to like her. She was knowledgeable, shrewd, occasionally even witty. Giles drained one glass of Chianti Antinori and then finished off another in a few, rapid gulps. It was not long before his face grew flushed, his eyes glazed and his speech indistinct. 'Oh, I *am* enjoying myself!' he announced at one point. Then he turned to Violetta: 'Are you enjoying yourself?'

'Thank you, yes, Mr Conquest, I am having a very nice time. This lamb is delicious.'

'Good! We must all enjoy ourselves. That's what we've come here for. We must all be happy and jolly and gay.'

'Oh, Giles, do shut up!' But Margot said it indulgently. 'Don't be such an idiot!'

The proprietress came over to the table: '*Tutto va bene, Bellino?*'

'*Magnifico! Stupendo! Grazie, signora.*'

'Oh, all this "Bellino" nonsense!' Margot laughed.

'You're just jealous because she never calls you "Bellina".'

'I should hope not! If she did, I might begin to suspect that she was a friend of our Eva.'

'Eva?' Iris queried.

'You'll no doubt meet Eva in due course. Sufficient unto the day is the Eva thereof.' By now Margot herself was getting tipsy.

Iris tried to engage Violetta in conversation, first asking her questions about her work and where she came from, and then, when she had proved singularly unforthcoming on both these topics, seeking advice about what should be her priorities in sightseeing. To this last question, Violetta replied with a little shrug: 'I'm sorry. Although I am from Florence, I know so little about its history and its architecture and art. Mr Conquest knows far more than I do.' As she looked across at Giles, not merely her eyes but her whole person seemed to glow. 'He will advise you better. He is an expert.'

'Oh, nonsense, my dear!' But Giles was clearly pleased. He turned to Iris: 'When I take Jack sightseeing, as I promised, I'd better take you too.'

'Thank you. That would be nice.'

'He never offers to take *me* sightseeing.' But again there was no real acrimony in Margot's complaint.

When, after innumerable requests for it, the bill eventually came, Iris offered to pay her share. But, waving his napkin in the air before her, Giles refused. 'I wouldn't dream of it, my dear. No, no! It's an honour. It's not often that I have the opportunity to give a peer's daughter dinner in a humble trattoria.'

'Can't we drop that?'

'Drop what?'

'All this business about my father's title. *His* father – my grandfather – was a self-made man, you know. A mill-owner. He was a supporter – a financial supporter – of Lloyd George. Nothing very grand or glorious in that. So, I'd really prefer it . . .'

'Your wish is my command. Definitely. Quite definitely.' Suddenly Giles sounded not tipsy but very drunk.

'Anyway – thank you for treating me.'

'Not at all! Not at all! Not another word!'

'Oh Giles! *Please!*' Angrily Margot reared up from the banquette. 'Come on! Let's get moving!'

7

Over a glass of grappa in the tiny, murky bar, little more than a cellar, into which they would sometimes slip on their way home after work, Giles had once remarked to Jack that the wattage of the average Italian personality and the wattage of the average Italian electric-light bulb were in inverse proportion to each other. He had then proceeded to elaborate on this facile and fragile conceit. The glare of the one and the dimness of the other had, paradoxically, the same effect: it was awfully difficult to make out what was going on. Of course – he was now twirling his glass by its stem between middle finger and thumb – a people who always preferred to show off to the world by talking than to retreat from it by reading would naturally opt for the sort of light which encouraged the first of those activities while discouraging the second. Perhaps – who knows? – it was the inadequacy of the candles at the time when Milton visited Italy which had eventually led to the blindness of someone who, unlike the Italians, read prodigiously. And could it not be that Goethe's cry for 'More light!' had been uttered not on his death-bed as was generally thought but, more prosaically, while he was pursuing his botanical researches in Padua?

It was odd, in view of these remarks, that both bedside and overhead light in Jack's room should be so feeble. Was the reason a wish for economy in a household in which, despite the fact that both master and mistress were employed, money was so constantly an occasion for arguments and even quarrels between them? Or a fear of fuses in a system so antiquated that wires wound and dangled everywhere? Or a laziness which had prevented the substitution of new bulbs for those already in place when the furnished house had first been rented from its impoverished owner, a widowed contessa who had moved into an even more dilapidated *villino*, belonging to her son, far out in the Tuscan countryside?

Now, because of that general dimness – dare he buy a couple of bulbs without first asking permission? – Jack had stopped reading the *Collected Poems* of Coventry Patmore, picked up on a barrow outside the Pitti Palace, and had instead relapsed into a state of glum rumination. It was that volume which was fortuitously to impel him in the direction in which his career as a redbrick academic was eventually to meander.

Because of the extraordinary heat of that late autumn – Miss Sweeney had even taken to lugging a fan into her classes, as much (she confided in Jack) to dispel what she called the *esprit de corps* of her pupils as to keep her own *corps* cool – he was in underpants and vest, his feet stretched out bare ahead of him, when there was a knock at his door.

'Just one moment!' he called, as he snatched out for the trousers that he had thrown across his bed. But before he could rise, much less struggle into them, Margot had entered. Paying no heed to his state of undress, she said briskly: 'Sorry to burst in on you. But I wonder if I might just get something out of the top of that cupboard for Piers. If, that is, it's there, as he says it is.' Without waiting for his permission she dragged towards the cupboard the only chair other than the one on which he was seated and clambered on top of it. 'I've got no head for heights,' she said as she teetered dangerously.

'Can I get it for you?'

'It's all right.' Still teetering from side to side, she raised a hand and tugged at the door, set high above her head. 'Last birthday old Audrey Heaton – she's the one next door, you may have glimpsed her feeding all those mangy cats on spaghetti and risotto – gave him this mouth-organ, far from new. No doubt it once belonged to her beloved Johnny. Piers was totally uninterested in it. But now, suddenly, he's decided he wants to learn how to play it.' Some cricket pads, a volume of the *Children's Encyclopaedia*, a box of paints and another box containing a xylophone slithered past her – the last of these bursting open on hitting the floor. 'Oh, hell!' she cried out. Then, as Jack leaned down to retrieve what had fallen: 'Oh, here it is!' Having jumped heavily off the chair, she began to examine the rusty mouth-organ, turning it now one way and now the other under her gaze. 'D'you think it's quite sanitary? Not that

Audrey's Johnny died of anything disgusting. But even so . . .'

Fearful that his skimpy underpants might be revealing too much, Jack had hurriedly once again sat down. 'I should think it's all right.'

She nodded. 'I suppose so.'

Mouth-organ in right hand and left hand on hip, she stared down at him. Then she put out the left hand and rested it on the back of his head, in a maternal, wholly asexual, gesture. Suddenly she had intuited his mood of shut-in, stoical depression, and had felt an intense, albeit brief, compassion. 'A little down?'

He looked up at her momentarily, then looked away, shaking his head. He wanted to say: 'Yes, I'm more than a little down,' but somehow he could not do so.

'Cheer up! Things are never as bad as one thinks.' As she came out with the worn, comfortless words, she was already thinking of something else: would Piers now make their lives hell with the mouth-organ as he had done a few weeks before with the xylophone? She prepared to leave, then turned back: 'You know, if you want to sit with us in the *salone*, do feel free to do so. Any time.' But she wondered if Giles, isolated in a corner of the *salone* as, head bowed over a school exercise book, he dashed down a paragraph here and a paragraph there of his novel, would welcome an alien presence. As it was, he would often ask her impatiently: 'Do you think you could possibly manage not to rustle the pages of that newspaper quite so loudly?' or angrily protest: 'Oh, please, please stop that fidgeting about!'

After Margot had gone, Jack once again rose from the chair and crossed to the window. The wire-netting tacked to the frame had rusted away in places, with the result — since in this heat it was impossible to keep the window closed — that mosquitoes would constantly whine around him and even, while he was sleeping, feed off his blood. He looked out. The children, Maria and he slept in three adjacent rooms in a one-storey oblong of a building added to the original house to provide servants' quarters. All four of them shared a bathroom, its tiled floor uneven and even cracked in places, and a dank lavatory, with a stained bowl into which water perpetually lisped. Jack looked out. Across the blackness of the overgrown garden there fell three yellow rectangles of light, fuzzy at the edges. The first of these rectangles was empty; the second showed his own shadow, his back oddly humped, as though from a deformity; the third showed — suddenly he felt a quickening of his heart-beats and a thumping in his temples — the shadow of Maria. She must be gazing out of her window, just as he was gazing out of his. He could make out her nose, bizarrely elongated, and the slope of a shoulder.

On an impulse he struggled into his trousers and then, his feet still bare, crept out of his room into the corridor, walked down it and passed through its door, left open, presumably by one or other of the children, into the garden, acridly scented, beyond. The grass was so dry and sharp that he wondered that its blades did not cut his feet. He carefully avoided the three rectangles of light. From somewhere in the undergrowth on his right there came a rustle; then a sustained squawk, as one cat chased another out across the lawn and up on to the wall which separated the property rented by the Conquests from that of the woman to whom Margot had just referred as Audrey Heaton and whom he had once seen, in a floppy peasant's straw hat, espadrilles and a voluminously skirted cotton dress, making her way, basket in hand, down the lane which led to the nearest shops.

Jack seated himself on the swing which, at the height of the summer, Giles had put up for the children and which, ungratefully, they had since hardly used. With a kick, he propelled himself forward and then, with another, propelled himself back. As he now creaked backwards and forwards, he stared at Maria, as she stood absolutely motionless at her window, her arms along its sill. Her hair, usually worn in a plait, was hanging loose around her bare shoulders. A pink brassiere uptilted her full breasts.

Had she heard him moving across the garden? Seen him? Could she see him now? Could she not hear the creaking of the swing? That he could not be sure of the answer to any of these questions only intensified his excitement as, motionless now and hunched forward, hugging himself as though to appease some intense, internal pain, he stared and stared.

Suddenly he was pierced by the recollection, startlingly vivid, of that couple whom he had seen, three weeks ago now, leaning towards each other across a café table, while the man moved his hand slowly up and down the woman's forearm. Then, more insidiously, there crept up recollections of the many occasions when he would catch Maria glancing briefly at him, with what appeared to be surreptitious calculation, from under those heavy

55

lids of hers. When he smiled at her, she would never return his smile. Sometimes she would even scowl, as though in displeasure. 'Buongiorno, Maria.' 'Buongiorno, signore.' It was as though he and not Giles were her master. To Giles she did not speak with that almost hostile deference. With Giles she even sometimes ventured a cheeky retort.

Suddenly she jerked down the blind and vanished.

Jack continued to stare at its blank rectangle, willing her to return, to raise it once more, once more to reveal herself to him.

Then the light went out.

8

That afternoon the elderly teacher, Mr Greville, had gently chided Iris in the common room: 'Forgive my saying this, Miss Crediton, but do you really think that you should *do* your face in public for all of us to watch?' Now, in the privacy of her bedroom, she was once again 'doing' her face, before going out to meet the young American, Dale Somers, for a drink.

From the corridor outside her room, she could hear the voices of Ethel and Guido. By now her Italian was already good enough for her to understand something at least of what was passing between them. It was clear that Ethel was telling the Italian that he owed her for three lessons, and that he in turn was assuring her that the next morning, very early, on his way to work, he would bring round the money without fail – *senza fallo*. 'Well, if that's a promise, Guido . . .' Ethel said in a resigned voice in English; and Guido then replied fervently, also in English: 'I promise, I promise.'

How hard Ethel worked! After a long day at the Institute, where she was always prepared to earn extra money by deputizing for any teacher who was absent, she would hurry back to the *pensione* to take her private lessons.

'Does she need the money so badly?' Iris had on one occasion asked Miss Sweeney.

'Well, yes, she does,' Miss Sweeney had answered severely, almost adding: 'I don't imagine that *you've* ever needed money badly, have you?' She had then sucked pensively on the end of the red pencil with which she had been correcting a composition ('How I Spent My Summer Holidays'), while she had wondered about the propriety of gossiping about a colleague. Finally, unable to resist, she had gone on: 'You see, she has this sister. A younger sister. Who's, well, not quite normal.'

'Not quite normal? How do you mean?'

'Well . . .' Miss Sweeney, head on one side, had pondered. Then she had answered: 'I'm not conversant with the details. It's not something about which I should, er, wish to catechize poor Ethel. Or indeed speculate over-much. But she has to earn all that she possibly can in order to keep the sister in some kind of home. I call that gallant,' she had added.

Iris had also thought it gallant; and she had at once felt for Ethel a warmth hitherto absent in their relationship. But the warmth had not lasted; Ethel's behaviour to her had been too chilling in its formality and remoteness for it to do so. That her behaviour to Tim, to Jack, to old Mr Greville and to all the Italians on the staff was similarly chilling (only to Miss Sweeney and to another elderly female colleague did she show any friendliness) was little consolation.

Almost five weeks had passed since, at Mervyn's party, Dale had asked Iris where she was staying and had told her that he would soon get in touch. What had become of him? Well, she didn't really care, she had told herself. But each time that she had gone to the house or flat of some friend of her mother, it had been in the hope that — yes, she had to admit it — she would see him. Sometimes there would be talk about Pippa Lavery — she had this crazy idea of buying one of the towers in San Gimigniano and turning it into a gallery of modern art; drunk, she had toppled down the steps of the French consulate and cracked two of her ribs; she and Ivor Luce had embarked on another feud. But Dale was never mentioned. Eventually, when at one of his frequent dinner-parties Mervyn had recounted the story of how Pippa had cheekily pointed at a Tiepolo drawing at I Tatti, had demanded of Berenson, 'How much do you want for that?' and then, having been glacially informed that none of his pictures was for sale, had burst into derisive laughter and told him, 'Come off it! If the price is astronomical enough, you know that anything and everything here is for sale — and that includes a dud authentication,' Iris had had the courage to ask, 'What's happened to that secretary of hers?'

Mervyn had turned towards her a face which, after a spasm-like grimace, seemed to have acquired the greyness and hardness of concrete. 'Secretary?'

'That — that . . . What was his name?' Iris had pretended to be vague. 'Dale — oh, something or other . . .'

'I've no idea, my dear. Absolutely no idea. But my guess is that by now Pippa has traded him in — like that Alfa Romeo she used once to have — for a model both less shop-soiled and more reliable.'

It was at Doney that Dale had told Iris to meet him. 'Doney?' she had queried, thinking of the hatted and bejewelled women, friends of her mother, of the sleek, scented young men of whom her mother would certainly disapprove, and of the gawping tourists debating whether to splash out on a Negroni or an Americano or to settle for an espresso or a capuccino.

'Yes, Doney. Where else? Unless you'd prefer Giacosa?' Clearly these were the only two cafés to which he was accustomed or willing to go.

He unwound his long legs and rose to greet her. 'Iris! You look terrific. Marvellous! Even more beautiful and more elegant than on that terrace — how many weeks ago?'

Not realizing that it was social insecurity which made him gush in this way, Iris felt irritated. 'Oh, I don't know,' she lied, sitting down on the chair which he had pulled out for her. 'Four, five?' Yes, she had been right: the café was full of precisely the sort of people whom she had expected. Over there, sitting alone near the bar, was that American woman who had been so bitchy about Dale at the party; there, at the far end of the room, were two middle-aged Italian women, friends of her mother, the brims of their huge straw hats almost scraping each other as one whispered something into the other's ear; and there, by the door, where the waiter had deliberately put them, were five middle-aged English tourists, the two men in baggy khaki shorts and shirts with rolled-up sleeves, and the three women in cotton dresses, sandals and Jacqmar headscarves.

'I couldn't get in touch. First I had to make that ghastly journey on the Orient Express all the way back to ghastly London, in order to take a look at a ghastly Sodoma at Sotheby's for Pippa. And then I went down with some kind of tummy bug. And then Pippa cracked two ribs and wouldn't let me out of her sight until she had decided that the doctor was right and they hadn't been broken.'

'What a hard life you have!'

'Well, yes, I do, you know. You're lucky. You're independent.'

'Couldn't you be independent?'

'I will — one day. But it all takes time. Not for you, of course, because . . .' At that moment the kindly old waiter whom Iris had always liked came over to ask what the signore and the signorina wanted to drink.

They decided on gin fizzes. 'Make sure it's Beefeater, Alfredo, don't try to palm off that Italian muck on us,' Dale commanded, bringing a look of startled hurt to the old man's face.

The drinks before them, Dale leaned across the table. 'Cheers! Or bottoms up! Or – as they say here – *salute!*' Gently he tapped his glass against hers.

'Cheers.'

He looked around him. 'What a hole!'

'If it's a hole, why did you decide to invite me here?' Iris sounded combative; but once again she was succumbing, against all her instincts of self-preservation, to the attraction of that vibrant, bass voice which seemed somehow to assume a physical form to touch something deep within her.

'Why? Because I get a certain kick out of walking in here, like a spy walking, bold as brass, into the camp of the enemy, and finding that I am accepted as one of *them*.' He waved a hand at the people around him. 'Perhaps you'd get the same kind of kick out of walking into an East End pub and being accepted there.'

'I doubt it.'

'Doubt what? Getting the kick, or being accepted?'

'Both.'

'Soon – all this will be gone. Like that.' He raised his right hand and clicked the fingers. 'Swept into the rubbish bin of history. All these *conti* and *contesse*, *principi* and *principesse*, beasts of prey and parasites. Do you ever have the kind of night in which, over and over again, you go on having the same dreary dream? The only way in which to escape from the cycle is to shake yourself awake and tell yourself: "Now stop it, stop it! Dream of something else!" It's the same with our clapped-out liberal democracies. They'll go on dreaming the same dreary dream until they shake themselves – or someone else shakes them – into one more interesting.' Again he raised his glass to her. 'Long live the revolution!'

'Aren't you sometimes afraid that the revolution might also sweep you into the rubbish bin of history?'

He laughed. 'Possible. Perfectly possible. But I suspect I'm too clever. Or cunning, if you prefer. There are people who know how to survive. I'm one of them. I *think*,' he added, suddenly pensive as he looked out over her shoulder.

'Is working for Pippa Lavery a way of surviving?'

'Of course. If it weren't for Pippa, I'd still be slaving in that third-rate little gallery in the Village. Or I might even be back home in Tulsa, Oklahoma. Neither an attractive prospect! Pippa's my lifebuoy. For the moment, at any rate.' He extended a forefinger to the side of her glass. 'Another?'

She shook her head. After a single fizz, she could not be intoxicated; but that was how she felt.

'I'm going to have another.' She had already noticed how greedily he had gulped at his drink, head thrown back and eyes half closed. 'So you're not a secret agent?' he said.

'A secret agent?'

'Like me. A worm in the already rotting bud of capitalism.'

She shook her head. 'No, I've never really seen myself in that role. Perhaps I have too little social conscience. Or perhaps ... I'm just too conventional and lazy.'

'You make me feel I'd like to give *you* a shake to wake you up.'

She turned her head away from him, without an answer.

It was as the two of them now sat silent, each momentarily lost to the other, that Jack walked past the bar. He had heard of Doney, of course – who in Florence had not heard of Doney? – but he had never been in. He halted at the doorway, knowing, yes truly knowing, although he still had to see her, that Iris was somewhere in there with someone or other. He peered. Yes, yes! He was right. He felt a panicky excitement.

On an impulse he entered.

'*Signore?*' There was something insulting in this waiter's upward inflection, as though with that single word he were really asking: 'What the hell is someone like you doing in a place as smart and expensive as this?' Old Alfredo would have been gentler.

A cry from Iris rescued him. 'Jack!'

He smiled across, uncertain what to say or do.

'Come and join us.'

'Okay. I was really on my way to ...' But he had really been on his way to nowhere. On a Saturday as cruelly long as every other Saturday since he had arrived, he had been merely wandering purposelessly down one street after another.

'You know Dale Somers, don't you?'

'No, I don't think I do.'

'Dale – this is Jack Prentice.'

61

Dale did not rise. He looked Jack up and down and then briefly lifted a hand, to let it flop back on the table: 'Hi!'

'Hi!' It was a greeting that Jack had never before used.

'*Il signore desidera qualchecòsa*?' It was the same waiter, loftily supercilious, who had greeted him at the door.

Jack hesitated.

'Have a gin fizz like us,' Iris suggested, sensing his embarrassment.

'Okay.' He looked up at the waiter: '*Un* gin fizz *per piacere.*' He turned to Iris. 'Did I say that all right? I wish I had your gift for languages.'

'"*Un* gin fizz *per piacere*" is hardly a test of proficiency in Italian,' Dale said. He had wanted to have Iris to herself. What on earth had possessed her to ask this dreary creature to join them? Then, as though a north wind had abruptly shifted to a southern one, his mood changed. He put out a hand and opened the book, its brown calf worn and shabby, which Jack had set down on the table beside him. He squinted down at the fly-leaf. 'Coventry Patmore.'

'Who's he when he's at home?' Iris enquired.

'A Victorian poet. Until I found that book — costing, oh, the equivalent of sixpence — on a barrow outside the house where the Brownings used to live, I'd never read him, just heard of him.'

'I wonder if he and the Brownings were pals,' Dale said, turning the pages.

'Probably. At least they must have met. Oh, yes, I remember now! I looked up the entry on him in the *Oxford Companion to English Literature* and it said that Browning wrote a poem to Patmore's first wife. Patmore married three times,' he added.

'Was divorce so easy then?'

'No. But early death was common.'

'Listen to this!' Dale was enthusiastic. 'Just listen!' He began to read, the deep voice investing the lines with an even more plangent sonority and an even darker pathos.

> 'I, singularly moved
> To love the lovely that are not beloved,
> Of all the Seasons, most
> Love Winter, and to trace
> The sense of the Trophonian pallor on her face.'

'Marvellous!'

'What does "Trophonian" mean?' Iris asked.

'Does it matter? It sounds even more splendid if one doesn't know.' Dale was once again eagerly turning the pages. 'Now listen to this! "With all my will, but much against my heart, We two now part . . ." This guy's got something, he's really got something.'

'Yes, you are right. He has not only got something, he has much, very much.'

The Italian voice came from behind Iris and Jack. They swivelled round in their chairs, Dale looked up. Entering, Jack had noticed the tiny, hunchbacked figure perched, like some disconcerting cross between bird and small child, on a stool at the bar. His suit, of black velvet with black silk piping, fitted his misshapen body so well that it was clearly a tailor's masterwork. The top edges of a bow-tie, huge enough to do duty at the front of a woman's blouse or the back of a woman's skirt, all but brushed against his small, pointed chin. His eyes, with their amazingly long, spiky lashes, glittered above high cheek-bones. 'Forgive me. It is very rude of me to burst in on you, with no introduction. But I heard you read – so eloquently, so beautifully. I could not resist . . . I am a poet myself,' he added, a hand resting on his narrow chest. 'Perhaps not so good a poet, but a poet.'

On an impulse, Jack said: 'Why don't you join us?' Then he was abashed by his own temerity. It was, after all, for one of the other two to issue the invitation; the table was theirs.

But Iris, always eager to make new friends, and Dale, always no less eager, were equally welcoming. 'Yes, join us, join us!' Iris cried out, as Dale reached out for another chair from the still empty next-door table.

'You do not mind? You wish me?'

'We wish you,' Dale said.

Knuckles resting on the table-top, the Italian lowered his body into the chair, as though it were painful to do so. He gave a little groan when finally he was seated. Then he looked around, to smile at each of them in turn. 'My name,' he said. He pulled a wallet out of the breast-pocket of the black velvet suit and carefully extracted three cards. 'Giuseppe Valeriano. Please.' He handed out the cards, bowing from the waist each time as he did so.

'I'm afraid I don't possess a card,' Iris said. 'In England few people do nowadays – unless they have them for business.'

'I'm in the same situation,' Dale said. 'I only had cards when I

63

was a high-class sort of salesman back in New York.'

In turn they told the Italian first their names and then, in answer to his questions, what they were doing in Florence. On hearing that Jack and Iris were employed at the Institute, Giuseppe cried out: 'Then you work for Mr Le Clerq! He has promised to give me *una serata* – an evening. There will be music, by a young Englishman studying composition with Dallapiccola, and I shall be reading from my new work *La Profanazione di Leonardo*. You will come?'

As Giuseppe went on talking – chiefly about his own work but sometimes also about the poetry of Italian contemporaries, of whom Iris, Jack and Dale had never even heard – Jack found himself hypnotized by the huge, shimmering bow-tie, in a pattern of wine-red arabesques embroidered on to a stiff black background, which rested above his narrow pigeon-chest. Unlike Iris, Jack had never been interested in clothes, whether worn by others or by himself. He possessed only three ties: a woollen one, a knitted dark-blue silk one, and that of his Oxford college, so frayed that, unless he took care with the tying, the lining could be glimpsed shining through the outer material of the knot.

Giuseppe became aware of his scrutiny. 'You like my tie?'

'Very much.'

'Maybe I give it to you!'

Jack laughed. 'I can't see myself wearing a tie like that.'

'Why not?'

'It's too – grand. Not my sort of thing.' He turned to Dale. 'You might be able to carry off a tie like that. Not me.'

Dale now also laughed. 'Thanks! People gossip enough about me already in Florence . . . Now Iris could wear a bow like that in her hair.'

The Italian was glancing in turn at them, with the nervous wariness of someone unsure of whether he is being made fun of or not. Then he said: 'I have many ties. I am not sure how many but maybe one for each day of the year. Tomorrow I will wear another tie. The day after tomorrow another tie. *Sempre differente*.'

'It must have been expensive to buy so many,' Jack commented.

Giuseppe gave a shrug of his twisted shoulders, which seemed to say: What does it matter if something is expensive or not?

'Have you published many collections of poems?' Iris asked.

Giuseppe pulled a face. 'I have published only in a magazine edited by a friend. *Decreti*. You have heard of *Decreti*?'

'Sorry. I'm terribly ignorant.'

'I will give you a copy.'

'That'll be a good test of my Italian.'

'Iris has a real gift for languages,' Jack said. 'We've been here little more than five weeks and already she can carry on a conversation.'

'I did take a few lessons back in England.' She looked at her watch. 'Gosh! I'm going to be late!'

'You don't have another appointment, do you?' Dale asked.

'I'm afraid so. At eight. In Bellosguardo.'

'But I was planning to take you out to dinner. I've even booked a table at the Nandina.'

'Sorry.'

'Couldn't you put your other engagement off?'

Could she? She hesitated. She wanted to put it off. 'No. I couldn't really do that. He's — he's an old man. A friend not so much of my mother as of my grandmother.'

'Who is this old man?'

By now Giuseppe and Jack were engaged in a conversation.

'He's called Henry — Harry Archer. A painter. Not very good, I gather.'

'Oh, that old bore!'

'Do you know him?'

'Oh, he once came to one of Pippa's parties. One of those English people who managed to survive very happily under Mussolini. Like Isabella Lambeni.'

Giuseppe, hearing no more than the name, tilted his misshapen body across the table. 'You know the Contessa Lambeni?'

'Who in Florence doesn't?'

'Most of its inhabitants, I should have thought,' Iris put in.

'The Contessa is a very dear friend of mine. Maybe she will come here now. At any moment. She knows that every day I am here from six to eight o'clock. Also from twelve to one.'

'Don't you have to work?' Jack asked.

Giuseppe laughed. 'I told you! I write poetry.'

When Iris and Dale got up, Jack got up too.

'You must also go?' Giuseppe twisted his body round and his head upwards to ask the question of Jack. There was a beseeching look in his eyes.

65

"'Fraid so. I've things to do.' But he had nothing to do. What he wanted was to accompany Iris on the jolting tram journey up to Bellosguardo.

'I will see you again?'

'I hope so. Florence is such a small world. But I don't suppose I'll ever come here again. It's not really, well, my sort of place.'

'Yes, yes! You *must* come here again! I will' – Giuseppe gave a radiant smile and then held out both his arms – 'treat you. All of you,' he added as an afterthought, now extending his arms to Iris and Dale as well.

'Funny little creature,' Dale muttered to Iris as they walked away.

'Rather sweet,' Iris said.

'I bet his poetry is awful,' Jack said, and then wished that he had not done so.

As they emerged into the street, noisy with honking cars and screeching and spluttering Vespas, a tall, graceful woman walked, head held erect, down the pavement towards them. Click, click, click went the immensely high heels of court shoes which at once made Iris think 'Ferragamo'. It was impossible to guess her age. Forty, fifty, even sixty? A hand encrusted with rings – there was even a large oval diamond on her forefinger – was holding together the top of a generously flared, pale-blue cashmere coat.

'Mr Somers!'

'Contessa!' Dale took the woman's hand and, bowing, raised it to his lips. But his manner was so stiff and cold that both Iris and Jack at once knew that, despite the elaborate greeting, he had no liking for her.

'Why didn't you come to my party?' She smiled, her head on one side.

'I was in London, on an errand for Mrs Lavery. Didn't she tell you?'

'She didn't come either. And not a word of excuse or apology from either of you!'

Dale was not in the least discomforted. He shrugged. 'Well, I thought she'd . . .' He gave another shrug. 'She told me she was going. So I assumed . . .'

'I think with Mrs Lavery it's probably better not to assume anything. I hardly know her, but I imagine she's rather – capricious?' She pushed open the door, then turned. 'Anyway –

do give me a ring. Or I'll give you one. Yes?' She was gone.

'That was Isabella Lambeni,' Dale said to Iris, ignoring Jack. 'Sorry, I didn't introduce you, but she's such a dreadful woman . . .'

'Dreadful? She seemed charming.'

'You probably know her story?'

'Not really. Just remarks here and there.'

'Well, she was damned lucky not to go to gaol like her husband. He was one of Mussolini's henchmen. Dead now. It's extraordinary how she's managed to survive – still in possession of the family vineyards, still in possession of the Palazzo Lambeni, most of it now divided into offices and apartments and bringing in a fortune in rents. There's gossip that what saved her – when less privileged collaborators found themselves in court – was her friendship, in inverted commas of course, with our own General Van Schmidt. Anyway' – he slipped an arm through Iris's – 'I'm going to give you a lift up to Bellosguardo.'

'I thought you lived near the Piazza San Lorenzo.'

'I do live near the Piazza San Lorenzo.'

'Then that's in the opposite direction!'

'Yes, it's in the opposite direction. But I'm going to give you a lift.'

'Well, that's mighty nice of you!' Iris replied with an exaggerated imitation of his American accent.

Arm in arm, totally ignoring Jack, the two of them began to walk away. Jack stood hesitating: should he follow them or walk in the opposite direction? Then Iris glanced round. She felt a pang of pity, he looked so forlorn.

'Goodbye, Jack! See you on Monday morning!'

'Goodbye.' He raised a hand in tentative farewell.

But she had turned away too quickly to see it.

9

Peering down through the wire-framed, half-moon glasses which rested on the end of his crooked, beaky nose, Harry Archer gave a small flick with the brush at the corner of Daphne's fluttering robe. He marvelled, as he often marvelled, that he could hold both the brush and the wooden cigarette box so absolutely steady, when a constant tremor would make the tea splash out of an over-full tea-cup as he raised it to his mouth. 'The Rape of Daphne'. Years ago he had painted the same subject as a fiftieth birthday present for Audrey Heaton; but then it had been on a canvas so huge that Johnny, always ungracious, had grumbled, 'God knows where we're going to hang it!' Sometimes the transition from those paintings which would cover most of a wall to those on small cigarette boxes or even smaller pin boxes and stamp boxes seemed to him somehow to represent a diminution in his own life: funds, ambitions, energies and friendships all narrowing and dwindling, just as his own once ample figure had narrowed and dwindled, so that, when he had shown Franco that bold self-portrait stored away under the bed in what had once been long-dead Renée's room, the boy had burst into cruel, incredulous laughter. '*È lei, signore? Ma è impossibile!*'

But of course it wasn't really him, the boy was right. That robust young man, pupil of Sargent and friend of Vernon Lee, Natalie Barney and the rest of them, was not this frail, feather-light octogenarian now dying not by inches but by millimetres.

He held the box up to the light. Then he gave another flick of the brush and another. Finished. Tomorrow Franco would take it down to that old scoundrel Moroni on the Ponte Vecchio and with any luck would screw out of him enough to pay off some at least of the outstanding bills.

Suddenly alert, he looked up, the box still in his hand. Up the precipitous drive, the grass high and yellowing on either side of it, he could hear a car growling and grinding. He rose, went to the window, peered out. Oh gosh, oh golly! He'd completely forgotten that he'd invited that grand-daughter of – of . . . He couldn't even remember the woman's name now. Someone who'd sat for him. He could see her, in a corner of the then tidy garden, with the sunlight on a bare arm and a parasol, pink and pale-blue, open above her, while her little Pomeranian – Lily? Lucy? – lay curled up at her elegantly shod feet. But the name, the name . . .?

There were two of them in the car, a girl and a boy. Through the windscreen he could see their faces turned to each other, as first the boy and then the girl burst into laughter. He hadn't invited two of them, had he? No, he was sure not. He'd invited just the girl. To dinner! Well, he'd have to take her down to the trattoria and hope that Anna would give him more tick. Embarrassing if she didn't. Deuced embarrassing.

Handsome boy. But the hair was too long. Hair like that gave him a sissy look. Well, at least he had had the good manners to get out of the car when she had got out. So few young people had any manners now. They were talking in the drive. Then, as the girl turned away, the boy grabbed her hand, raised it to his mouth and kissed it. She laughed and the boy also began to laugh. Then, beautiful and vigorous, the girl made her way to the front door.

'You're – you're – ?'

She smiled. 'Iris Crediton. Susan Lacey's grand-daughter. You were expecting me, weren't you? I haven't got it wrong?'

'Of course I was expecting you. And of course you haven't got it wrong. Do come in.' He stood aside to let her pass into a cavernous hall, the iron candelabra at its centre now holding a single flickering bulb. She both felt and smelled dampness, even rot.

'Thank you.' She looked around her, suppressing an impulse to shiver even on that warm autumn evening. 'Are these all your pictures?'

'Yes. Mine. Not all that good, I'm afraid.'

Again she peered round. 'Oh, I think they're very good!'

'No.' Sadly he shook his head. 'I thought them good when I

painted them. But the other day I was looking at a book I have of Sargent reproductions and I realized that I'd been mistaken. Now he *could* paint. My teacher, you know.' He began to shuffle ahead of her down the stone-paved vestibule and into the small study, lined with a faded mauve silk and with books piled here and there on its precariously uneven floor. It was here that he had been painting. He held out the box in a trembling hand. 'This is what I paint now. For the tourists. Better suited to my talents, I think.'

Iris screwed up her eyes. 'Beautiful! Such detail in such a small space!'

'Apollo raping Daphne. A recurrent theme in my work.' He gave a little laugh. 'Don't ask me why! You know the story of Daphne and Apollo?'

'Vaguely.'

'Years ago — when I was still a comparatively young man — B.B. authenticated for Duveen a "Tintoretto" of "The Rape of Daphne". But, believe me, it was nothing of the kind!' He gave another little laugh; the previously dull eyes, red-rimmed in hollow sockets, glinted with brief malice. 'Please do sit down.'

Iris sank down on to the low *chaise-longue* which he had indicated with a trembling hand. Its damask hanging in shreds, it had been covered with what might once have been a motoring rug in a faded plaid.

'Comfy?'

Was he being ironical? 'Thank you. Very.'

He put the trembling hand to his forehead. 'Now let me see. What can I offer you to drink? My Franco isn't here this evening, I'm afraid. He works for me, as his father and mother did before him. The father died, oh, quite young, and the mother, er, killed herself. So Franco is an orphan now, poor little chap. Don't really know what I'd do without him. Only sixteen, you know. . . . Well, now. A drink. A drink.' Hand still to forehead, he rotated slowly. 'How about some Marsala? I have some Marsala. Audrey Heaton brought me some when last she came to see me. Nice woman, Audrey. Impossible but nice. You've met her, of course?'

Iris shook her head.

'Well, you will, you will! One of the *characters* of Florence. As I suppose I am too,' he added, again with that little laugh. 'Yes, I must be one by now.'

'Can I help you?' He was wandering around the study, opening one cupboard door and then another, as though unsure where to find either the bottle of Marsala or the glasses.

'No, my dear, you just stay where you are.' He wandered out.

While he was gone, Iris once more reached out for the box. Perhaps she should buy it – provided it wasn't too expensive? It would make a good present for her grandmother, whose portrait by the same artist now hung above the chimneypiece in her drawing-room in Brighton.

'There we are!' One of the glasses was rattling against the bottle as he shuffled in with a tray of tarnished silver. 'Couldn't find any titbits, I'm afraid – not even some *grissini*. Drat that boy! Expect he's eaten them. You wouldn't believe his appetite! It's the age, of course.'

Despite the discomfort of the *chaise-longue* – there seemed to be something hard and unyielding, a book or perhaps just a broken spring, under the rug – Iris felt surprisingly at ease with the old man, as they sipped at the Marsala in the dim light from the lamp by which he had been working, talked and sometimes merely smiled at each other in silence. 'Oh, yes, yes, I've known almost everyone who has ever lived here for the past fifty years,' Harry would murmur from time to time, after telling her some story of some English, American, French, German, Russian or Italian character ('Once almost every soul you met in Florence *was* a character,') long since dead.

Eventually he spoke of her grandmother. 'Now there was a beauty for you. And such fun. I shall never forget that spring which she spent here with those two sisters of hers and that aunt.' The red-rimmed, sunken eyes gazed out of the window into the gathering dusk. His tongue moved over his lower lip. Then he threw back his head and laughed. 'I was in love with her, you know! But don't tell her. Don't ever tell her! And Audrey's Johnny was in love with her, too. But don't ever tell her – or Audrey – that either! On no account! No, no!'

Eventually, his arm in hers for support, they made their slow way down to the trattoria at the bottom of the hill. Only two tables were occupied, one by a solitary, sorrowful-looking man, scarcely younger than Harry, and one by a rowdy family, father, mother and three young children. Anna, seated at the cash-desk, looked resignedly doleful as they stepped across the threshold. Was she going to say something, Harry wondered. Deuced embarrassing if she did. But, good soul that she was, she didn't.

'*Come sta, Anna*?' Relief gave an unaccustomed strength to his voice.

'*Bene, grazie, signore. E lei*?' She even managed a warm smile. Oh, he did hope that that little rascal Franco would come back with some cash from Moroni!

The food was simple but good; the wine thin and raw. Of the latter, having sipped at his glass, he remarked: 'Not quite the sort of wine that comes from the Lambeni vineyards, I'm afraid. From time to time Isabella Lambeni sends me a dozen bottles. People are kind to a decrepit old gent like me, you know. Very kind. No complaints.' He eyed Iris, marvelling at the clearness of her skin, the brightness of her eyes and the sense of well-being which exuded from her. Yes, she took after the grandmother.

For a while, since the trattoria remained so empty, Anna came to sit with them. She spoke of her son, who had been with the Partisans and who now worked in a travel agency; of a daughter in America; of another daughter who had become a nun. When Iris herself ventured on a few words, Anna complimented her enthusiastically on the excellence of her Italian. Later, Anna gone, Iris told Harry: 'It's so much easier to learn a language if people keep telling you how good you are. I was in France for three weeks last year and it was so discouraging when people frowned or looked pained whenever I made some simple slip.'

'It's the same with making love. If your partner tells you how good you are at it, you at once do it so much better.' He gave his little laugh and then began to blush, wondering if he should have said anything so *risqué* to a girl so young.

Once more it was arm in arm, he now leaning heavily on her and pausing from time to time to gasp for breath, that they made their way up the hill. As they began the even steeper ascent of the drive, he pointed to a dim light in the windows to the side of the house. 'He must be back. Franco. The little rascal.'

As soon as they had entered the house, he began to call: 'Franco! Franco! Franco!'

Barefoot, in singlet and shorts, Franco appeared. He looked not sixteen but twelve. He had an attractively simian face and a sturdy little body. Harry asked him rapidly in Italian if he had had any success with the boxes and the boy nodded, yes, yes, *una buona riuscita*. He fumbled in a pocket of his shorts. Hurriedly Harry told him, 'Later, later.' Then he could not resist asking '*Quanto, quanto*?' When the boy told him the sum, he clapped bony hands together in delight, and then threw an arm round his shoulders and hugged him to him.

Soon after that Iris said that she must be going.

'I'd better get Franco to walk you down the hill.'

'No, no, please! I feel perfectly safe in Florence.'

'How will you go?'

'Oh, I'll take the tram. I've taken it before.'

'I sold my motor years ago. When Franco's father died and I had no one to drive me.'

He accompanied her out into the darkness. 'It was so good of you to visit me, my dear. I hope that it wasn't all too boring for you.'

'Far from it! I think it was the nicest evening I've had since I came to Florence.'

'Now you're just being kind.' Suddenly a thought came to him. 'Wait a moment. One moment.'

She waited, the darkness and silence crowding around her.

'Here you are.' He pressed something, wrapped in newspaper, into her hand.

'What is it?'

'Just that box. Or, rather, a finished replica. "The Rape of Daphne". Would you like it?' Suddenly he seemed doubtful.

'Of course I'd like it. What a marvellous present! But I'd like to have bought it from you.'

'Bought it! The idea!'

On an impulse she leaned forward, put her arms round him, and kissed him on his right cheek.

When she released him, he gave his little laugh. 'Now you *have* paid for it!' he cried out. 'More than I've ever received for any of my little boxes in the past!'

10

In the library of the Institute Ivor Luce, dressed in one of the dark pin-stripe suits which, despite their Savile Row tailoring, always looked too tight for his plump figure, stood desultorily turning over the pages of the same book of Sargent reproductions of which Harry Archer had spoken to Iris. The book had only recently appeared. Wretched paper, Ivor thought, feeling the grey roughness of the text between middle finger and thumb. Why should victory and austerity have to go together in England? An Italian publisher would be ashamed to produce such a book.

When he was a small boy, living out beyond Scandicci in the Renaissance villa in which he still lived, Sargent, then the guest of Vernon Lee, had painted him in the Indian costume which he had worn to a children's fancy-dress party given by another, equally rich Anglo-Italian family, that of Miss Sweeney, in a villa even more sumptuous. Some boys had set on him in a corner of the garden, where he had gone, a precocious aesthete, to inspect a little sixteenth-century theatre in which the former owners of the property, ancestors of a family long since ruined by profligacy, and their guests had mounted a performance – some scholars had claimed the first – of Machiavelli's *La Mandragola*. The boys had pulled off his turban and then played ball with it, throwing it high over his head, from one to another, as he rushed between them in an attempt to retrieve it. 'Be careful! Be careful! That brooch belongs to my mother!' The brooch, pinned to the front of the turban, dripped two pearls with a heart-shaped emerald between them. 'Be careful! The brooch! The brooch!' they mimicked his shrill voice.

Ivor closed the book and replaced it on its shelf. He had arrived too early for a drink with Mervyn and was therefore killing time.

What was it that Norman Douglas had once said to him? 'One should never kill time. In the last resort, time is one's only ally and friend.'

It was as he was pulling out another book, the first of the two volumes of *The Notebooks of Leonardo*, that he suddenly noticed the young man. His sturdy body propped against a bookshelf and one foot, in a scuffed brown shoe, resting over the other, he was absorbed in the book which he was holding in large, capable hands. In that Harris tweed jacket and those shapeless grey flannels, and with that atrocious pudding-basin hair-cut (where on earth had he found an Italian barber with sufficient lack of self-respect to cut his hair like that?), he could only be English. Ivor surveyed him over the now open volume of the *Notebooks*. He approved of what he saw. A butch piece. With possibilities. Definitely.

Having replaced the *Notebooks*, Ivor sidled round the table and crossed to the bookcase against which the boy was leaning. Victorian poetry. There was an awful lot of Victorian poetry in the Institute library — far too much in the view of the British Council representative, himself a poet, none of whose works could be located on the shelves when he had come to discuss a possible subsidy to the Institute. Not surprisingly, the subsidy had not been granted.

Ivor took down a volume of Sidney Dobell. He opened it at random and read:

I had a little bird,
I took it from the nest;
I prest it, and blest it,
And nurst it in my breast.

What absolute twaddle! One couldn't imagine Milton, Pope, Dryden or Byron — the poets whom he most admired — producing anything like that. He slammed the volume shut and pushed it back on to the shelf. Then he glanced over the young man's shoulder.

'I can't help noticing what you're reading. Landor.'

The young man looked up. Slowly and uncertainly he smiled. He had large, white teeth, and Ivor had always liked large, white teeth. 'There are two absolutely wonderful lines here,' he said.

'Read them to me.'

The boy hesitated. Then in a low, slightly tremulous voice he read:

'And the long moon-beam on the hard wet sand
Lay like a jasper column half uprear'd.'

Having finished, he looked up enquiringly, as though for approbation. Well, the boy certainly had taste in spotting those lines. Ivor had expected 'Rose Aylmer' or 'Dirce'. '"The Shepherd and the Nymph",' he said. 'Last two lines. Correct?'

'Absolutely.' The boy laughed.

'Landor lived a stone's throw from the villa in which a great-aunt of mine used to live. He was a man who liked to throw stones, both real and metaphorical. He also liked to throw tantrums and servants. Did you know that? Furious with a cook who had ruined a dinner, he hurled him from a first-floor window – only to stammer out, aghast, "Good God, I forgot the violets," as the wretched man landed among them. If you share my taste for Landor, you must come out to visit me. I could give you lunch or tea or dinner.'

'Thank you.' Jack slowly closed the Landor and put it under his arm.

'Why don't we have a drink? I've something else I ought to be doing, but I can forget all about it. Tomorrow I'll ring up and tell my host and hostess that I had one of my migraines. My migraines are as famous in Florence as the *tramontana* – that north wind which puts every self-respecting Florentine into a state of acute depression or wild fury whenever it blows down from the mountains.'

Jack hesitated. Then he thought: Well, why not? Giles and Margot were going out to a dinner-party; and when they did so, Maria, unknown to them – the children were fiercely loyal to her in their discretion – would be entertaining her woodcutter boyfriend. 'Thank you. I'd like that.'

As they emerged into the street, Ivor said: 'We'd better introduce ourselves. I'm Ivor Luce.'

'Oh.'

'Don't say "Oh" in that disconcerted tone of voice. Have you heard of me?'

'Well, actually, I have.'

'I hope that what you heard was favourable.' He put a hand to

Jack's arm. 'No, you don't have to answer that. I've always preferred having things said about me behind my back than to my face. And now tell me — who are you?'

'Prentice. Jack Prentice.'

'Oh, I've heard about you, too! From that attractive Crediton girl. You arrived together. You're teaching at the Institute. Are you teaching Landor to all those upper-class Italian virgins?'

Jack laughed. 'No. Most of the time I'm teaching business English to middle-class Italian men.'

'None of whom are virgins, I'll be bound!'

Eventually, after they had drunk for more than an hour at a table at the far end of a long, narrow bar crowded with middle-aged men in dark suits, Ivor took Jack out to dinner in a restaurant beside the Arno. 'Too cold?' he asked, pointing at the terrace built over the river. Jack shook his head. 'You look tough,' Ivor said, adding: 'I'm tough. But, unlike you, I don't look it.'

Jack liked Ivor; he had never met anyone like him. Ivor liked Jack; he had met many people like him. When Ivor was not retailing the gossip of Florence, they discussed literature, music and art. Oh, dear, the boy was so ignorant about some things — fancy never having heard of Winckelmann, or Leopardi, or Josquin! — and yet so knowledgeable about others.

Near the end of the evening, Ivor lent across the table. 'Would you be awfully offended if I gave you some paternal — or, at least, avuncular — advice?'

Jack felt himself blushing. What was coming now? 'No.'

'You must do something about your appearance, dear boy.'

'My appearance?'

'Clothes like that are all very well in England. But the Italians, even the poorest Italians, have a sense of style. You must have noticed? I'll tell you what, I'm going to take you to the family tailor and order a suit for you. I believe that everyone should start adult life with a really good suit, just as everyone should start the day with a really good breakfast.'

'Oh, but I couldn't possibly afford —'

'You don't have to afford. I said that I'd order the suit.'

'But I couldn't let you do something like that. We — we hardly know each other.'

'Don't we? I feel that I already know you well, Jack.' He sighed. 'Well, if you have that kind of pride, you can *earn* your suit.'

'Earn it?'

'I've set about rearranging the library at the villa. You can give me a hand from time to time. Now how about that?'

'I don't know much about cataloguing and things of that kind . . .'

'You don't have to *know*. Not now. All you have to do is *learn*.' Ivor smiled. 'Don't make life difficult for yourself. Life can be so easy for someone of your youth and intelligence — and looks.'

A stocky boy, seemingly no more than twelve or thirteen years old, was lounging against the parapet of the Lung' Arno, under a lamp post beside the entrance to the restaurant. Suddenly Jack noticed him.

'I've seen that boy before.'

'Which one?'

'Over there.' Jack pointed. 'Immediately after I got here, I was walking along the river and there were these two boys and a girl. I took a snap of them. That boy asked me —'

'Franco.'

'Sorry?'

'His name is Franco. He works for old Harry Archer. You know Harry?'

'I've heard of him. From Iris — Iris Crediton. She often goes up to see him.'

'It's a small world,' Ivor mused. His eyes were fixed on the boy. 'He's a real little ruffian, that one. But Harry has no idea. Thinks him an angel. God knows what Franco has stolen from the old chap! He's as poor as a church mouse but he still possesses some lovely pieces.'

Two middle-aged American men had emerged from the restuarant. Franco straightened himself and pattered after them in his soiled gym-shoes. He put out a hand and touched one of them on the arm. The American turned. The three of them began what appeared to be an argument. Then the taller and older of the two Americans threw back his head and laughed, pulled Franco briefly to him in an embrace, and finally gave him a playful slap across the back of the head. The three of them went off together.

'Well, that seems to have turned out satisfactorily,' Ivor said. Jack was puzzled.

When Ivor had been presented with the bill, Jack squinted down at the notes on the plate. 'That's an awful lot of money. Can't I pay my share?'

'Certainly not! I shouldn't dream of it. You're my guest. My honoured guest.' Ivor pulled some more notes out of his wallet and added them to the pile on the plate before him. 'People who undertip always maintain that waiters, taxi-drivers and porters despise those who overtip. Don't believe them. It's a fallacy.'

'*Grazie mille, signore!*' The delight of the waiter seemed to confirm this observation.

11

Mervyn was conducting Iris round the Palazzo Davanzati.

'You realize that this *palazzo* is in precisely the same condition in which Pope Eugenius IV found it when he lodged here in 1434? In 1904 it passed into the hands of a Professor called Elia Volpi, and he then set about restoring it, before presenting it to the city. Life here for the Davizza family must have been even more uncomfortable than for Hamlet, Gertrude and Claudius at Elsinore.'

He had then gone on vividly to evoke an aristocratic world in which no furniture was upholstered; rooms were too vast to be adequately warmed in winter by a single smoky fire; and all water was obtained by dipping down into the same dank, unhygienic shaft.

When they had left the Palazzo, he stood in the street, hands gesticulating and pointing in Italian fashion, while he continued to lecture: 'If the lives of the *grandi* have changed greatly since the prime of the Davizza family, those of all these ordinary people around us have remained remarkably the same.' He pointed at a middle-aged woman, dressed all in black, who was hurrying past them with two laden shopping-baskets. 'Probably that woman there and her brood have no running water. One of them goes to a communal tap with buckets. Look over there!' He now pointed upwards. 'That old granny is lowering a basket on a rope so that that urchin can put those vegetables into it. There's an extraordinary continuity of life in this city. Century after century people have gone to the same shops to get their shoes mended, to buy their groceries, to clothe their children; to the same tap-rooms to drink and to the same *trattorie* to eat; to the same churches to be married and to have their far too many offspring baptized and their parents buried.'

Iris, listening with all the avidity of youth for knowledge, thought how odd it was that she should find Mervyn so interesting and yet like him so little.

'Well, I think that's enough for one day!' Mervyn eventually announced after a prolonged visit to Orsanmichele, where he had lectured to her in a loud voice, to the amazement of a group of American tourists, on the wonders wrought by the church's Madonna in exorcizing demons, healing the sick and giving sight to the blind. 'In Italy it is always as important to see that one does not suffer from aesthetic as from physical indigestion. Too much art, too much olive oil . . . The one can induce as much discomfort as the other. At all events I hope I've given you some idea of what old Dante meant when he wrote, "*Cosi bello viver di cittadini . . . a cosi dolce ostello* – So fine a life for citizens . . . in so sweet a dwelling-place."'

'It was a wonderful tour.' Iris was not being insincere.

'Now how about coming back to the flat for a cup of tea? I know that Karen would love to see you.' Karen would, in fact – as Mervyn well knew – love nothing of the sort.

'It's very kind of you. But I ought really to trek out to the Conquests to pick up a book from Jack. A text-book. I need to look at it this evening for a class tomorrow.'

'Doesn't the super-efficient Miss Pryce have a copy? If she did, you wouldn't have to do the trekking, would you?' Mervyn hated having to say goodbye. These days, his desire to be near Iris had become an unappeasable hunger.

Iris was dubious. 'She might have a copy. Yes, I think she uses that text-book, as a matter of fact. But the difficulty is . . .' Should she attempt to explain the difficulty of asking any favour, however small, from someone so unfriendly? She decided not to.

'Yes, I can see that there might be many difficulties with Miss Pryce. She is not, I'm afraid, the most *agevole* of people, is she? Whereas that rather farouche young man . . . he seems to be essentially a decent and helpful sort.'

As they said goodbye, Iris once again expressed her gratitude: 'That was marvellous! Really marvellous!'

'My pleasure, my dear, my pleasure. As our American cousins say. I rather like the phrase. I remember that, after I had been given a lift in Paris by Edith Wharton in what Henry James called her "fiery chariot", I thanked her, only to receive a lofty, "My pleasure, Mr Le Clerq, my pleasure." It had all too clearly *not* been her pleasure, since she was in one of those dyspeptic moods of hers and had not cared to have her chauffeur make a detour up the crowded and noisy Champs-Elysées. I was very young then — as young as you are now. But, alas, I wasn't as attractive as you. Had I been, perhaps Mrs Wharton would have been a little more . . . Ah, well!'

As Iris was walking off, she heard him call her name. She turned.

'I forgot to ask you. How are you getting on with Caravaggio?

'Caravaggio?'

'My book. The book I gave you.'

Oh, Lord! She had completely forgotten about the book, which was lying somewhere buried under text-books and exercise books in her small, crowded room in the *pensione*. 'I've read about a third,' she lied. Then, from his expression, at once cross and hurt, she realized that he knew that she was lying. 'I'm so busy always,' she added feebly. 'Unlike Jack, who knows so much, I'm constantly having to mug up things ahead of teaching them.'

'Well, mug up on Caravaggio. It will do you far more permanent good than mugging up on the subjunctive or the use of "should" and "would".' At that, with a wave, he hurried off.

Margot, looking harassed and tired in dressing-gown and bare feet, opened the door to Iris. 'Oh, hello!' She sounded unwelcoming. 'Did you want Giles? He's away, I'm afraid. At Certaldo, representing the Institute at yet another Boccaccio celebration. He knows nothing about Boccaccio. You'd have thought Merv would have gone. On a Sunday too! But no doubt Merv was entertaining one of his Florentine young ladies!' Iris was disconcerted by the accuracy of this supposition. 'It all falls on Giles. It's too bad. Perhaps he should have sent Maria in his place, since her boyfriend lives there. No one would have noticed the difference, I imagine.'

'Actually, I wanted to see Jack.'

'Oh, Jack! I don't think he's in. But I'm not sure. Come in and I'll give him a shout. Come in, come in!' she repeated irritably, as Iris hesitated. Iris entered, and Margot hurried off to the far end of the narrow corridor, edging, with a muttered 'Fuck!', round a child's bicycle abandoned on its side in the middle. 'Jack! Jack!' she called. Then even louder: 'Jack!' She turned, shrugging her shoulders. 'Out. Sorry. Can I give him a message?'

'I wanted to borrow a book off him. I may come back later. I thought I'd have a walk up to the Piazza Michelangelo. It's such a lovely day.'

Margot was not listening. Her back turned to Iris, she was now shouting: 'Children, will you please, *please* remove this bicycle to the garage? Piers, Piers! Prunella! Maria! Maria!' She turned: 'Where *is* that girl? She's never around when one wants her. I suppose she's taken the children out to one of her assignations,' she added darkly. Then, suddenly, her mood changed. 'Why don't you come and have a cup of coffee with me? Perhaps, by the time you've had that, Jack will have returned. Yes?'

Iris hesitated. Then she said: 'It's awfully kind of you. But I think I'll have that walk. I want to take another look at the David.'

'I hate that statue.' Margot was vehement. 'It's so out of proportion.' She laughed. 'But then I don't really *go* for beefy men. Few women do in my experience. It's queers who do. What about you?'

Iris laughed, embarrassed. The image of Dale, lanky and fragile, had come into her mind. 'I must think about it.'

As so often in Florence, Iris was fascinated by the beauty of a wall. She stopped, examined the saxifrage dangling from between the dark-red, almost black stones (the colour of raw liver, she thought) and then pressed fingers against some emerald moss, which yielded like damp plush. Beautiful! The wall was high and, at its top, two cats, one a miniature tiger and the other a huge, tousled black ball, eyed each other balefully.

As she turned away, an elderly woman, straw basket in one hand and large straw hat pulled down over her eyes, walked energetically towards her. Her legs were lithe and strong, as she set down her feet, shod in green espadrilles, firmly on the greasy, uneven cobbles. Her small head was erect on an unusually long neck. Dark glasses covered at least half of her face.

'Do you usually look at other people's walls?' The voice was loud and sharp.

Iris turned. Was this Englishwoman joking? 'Sorry. It's so beautiful. I've never seen a saxifrage of quite that purple colour.'

'Then either you've not been in Florence very long or you're extremely unobservant. That particular *sassifraga* is as common as the average English tourist.'

Iris pressed fingers again to the moss. 'I love the feel of this moss.'

'Well, then, come and feel it on the other side.'

Iris was nonplussed.

'Come in. I'm Audrey Heaton,' she added. 'Heard of me?'

'Yes, as a matter of fact I have. Mervyn Le Clerq told me only this afternoon that I ought to meet you.'

'Oh, Mervyn! If he thinks that, then why does he never invite me to one of those grand parties of his? I bet he invites you,' she added shrewdly. 'He has such a weakness for pretty young girls.' She held out her basket. 'Be an angel and carry this. I'm not supposed to carry anything heavy. But since I now have the misfortune to live on my own, who's going to carry anything for me? Those Conquests next door are a decent enough couple, but neither is ever at home. And I don't like to ask that girl of theirs to do anything, since she clearly has her work cut out with those two ill-behaved brats.' They had been walking up the lane. They now turned off it through an archway, from which a wooden gate, rotten with age, hung askew from a single rusty hinge.

'Who are you?'

'Me? My name's Iris. Iris Crediton.'

'Iris Crediton!' Audrey was delighted, halting, turning round and putting both hands on Iris's left shoulder, to lean there as though for support. 'But I knew your mother! And your grandmother! I thought there was something about you . . . when I saw you standing there, gazing at my wall . . . something about the set of the eyes . . . and the tilt of the body . . . Oh, what a small world! How lovely! I *adored* your grandmother, absolutely adored her. She's still alive, isn't she? But we long since lost touch. Harry — Harry Archer — did this marvellous portrait of her. In my view the best thing of his. I wonder what became of it.'

'It hangs over the chimneypiece in my grandmother's flat in Brighton.'

'You don't say! Oh, I'd love to see it again. But I never go to England. I hated the War years there, just as my dear friend Norman — Norman Douglas — hated them. Couldn't wait to get back here.'

By now they were entering the *villino* through a half-open door into an old-fashioned kitchen, with two primuses resting on top of its vast, unlit range and a substantial, heavily scored kitchen table in its middle. Who had scrubbed both floor and table so scrupulously, Iris wondered. Later, she was to discover that it was Audrey who did the scrubbing.

Audrey pulled off her hat, chucked it across on to a bent-wood rocking chair, and then raised a hand to fluff out the thin, close-cropped hair, red peppered with grey, which stuck up around her still pretty face.

'Let's have some Punt e Més. To celebrate our meeting.' She stooped to a cupboard and brought out a bottle and two coarse tumblers. Having almost filled the tumblers despite Iris's protest of 'No, no! Please! That's far too much for me! I've got the feeblest of heads,' she sat down on an upright chair, legs wide apart, leaned forward, and began to interrogate Iris. What was she doing in Florence? Where was she staying? Was she enjoying herself? Her pale-blue eyes, the amazingly soft skin slightly puckered around them, expressed a hungry interest. The inquisition over, she splashed more Punt e Mes into their glasses, reseated herself in the same boyishly ungainly way, and then asked: 'Now what have you heard about me?'

'Oh . . .' What had she heard? Iris hesitated. 'Well . . . that you write.' She hesitated again. It would hardly be tactful to add: 'That, along with Harry Archer, you're the oldest member of the British community in Florence.' So she went on: 'That you've known everyone in Florence.'

'Everyone who is – or was – anyone,' Audrey corrected. 'Yes, that's true.' She nodded. 'While my Johnny was still alive and I still had some money, we entertained a lot. Our Sunday afternoons were famous, you know. Even D.H. Lawrence and that awful Frieda of his turned up at one of them. He spent the whole time sulking in a corner of the garden, one of the cats on his knees, because Aldous – always so brilliant – was monopolizing everyone's attention. Happy times, happy times,' she mused aloud. Then she looked up, the pale-blue eyes challenging Iris: 'And what have you heard about my private life?'

'Nothing,' Iris answered truthfully.

Audrey laughed gaily. 'You will, you will! No one has a private life in Florence. Here all private lives are public ones. And if your private life isn't interesting enough or exciting enough, then your enemies – and even your friends – create another for you. In such cases "living a lie" takes on a rather different meaning. The lie is not one's own but the lie created for one by others. Not that I've ever lived a lie,' she went on proudly. 'Johnny and I never concealed anything from anyone. I'm proud of that.'

There was a silence. Then Iris asked, for something to say and not because she really wished to know the answer: 'What are you writing at present?'

'That's the trouble. That's why I'm so strapped for cash. From time to time I get these creative blocks. I had this wonderful idea for a literary guide to Florence and I managed to screw an advance for it out of Nathan and Walsh. But that was just after the War had ended. With inflation that advance is worth *nothing* now. I've told them that they'll bloody well have to up the sum. Their answer to that — totally unreasonable — is that according to the contract they should have had the book two years ago. I ask you! Writing a book isn't like — like making a pair of shoes or building a house. Now is it?' Suddenly aggressive, she seemed to be challenging Iris in place of Nathan and Walsh.

'I suppose not.'

'It's clear you've never written — or tried to write — a book, my dear. The wind bloweth where it listeth, you know. You can't force the wind — with a dose of creative bismuth or bicarbonate of soda, as it were. Or a literary fart,' she added. She laughed, then grew pensive. 'Mind you, Johnny was far more self-disciplined and productive than I am. A novel a year, regular as clockwork. Plus all the journalism. I admired that. I'm just not that kind of writer. I suppose I'm more — more a Flaubert to Johnny's Dickens. Yes, that's how I think of it. That's the distinction I want to make.'

When, finally, Iris got up to leave — the Punt e Mes, constantly poured into her tumbler, had made her feel tipsy — Audrey asked her: 'Would you like to see Johnny's room?'

'Oh — er — yes.'

Audrey led the way down a passage the flagstones of which had been as scrupulously scrubbed as the kitchen table and floor. She spoke over her shoulder: 'I've changed nothing. People come back to us more easily that way.' Momentarily Iris puzzled over the last sentence; then she forgot it.

The large, square, high-ceilinged room looked out over the well-kept garden. There was an Art Nouveau bedstead, covered in a damask counterpane embroidered with white lilies on a dark-green ground. There was a mahogany partner's desk, on which papers and books were laid out in neat piles. There was a round table, covered with a lace-fringed cloth, on which innumerable photographs, most of them in silver frames, had been set out in serried ranks.

Audrey opened a cupboard, to reveal suits, flannel trousers and sports jackets hanging there. 'I brush them every so often. Wonderful materials, excellent cut. Johnny was so – fastidious.'

Iris was peering at one of the photographs. Faded and sepia in tone, it showed what she at first thought to be a stout, elderly man, dressed in riding-breeches, boots and open-necked checked shirt, and cradling a large Persian cat in his arms. Then, with a shock, she realized that this was a woman.

'Yes, that's my Johnny shortly before she died. I particularly like that one,' Audrey said.

Later, Ivor was to tell Jack a story about Audrey and Johnny, which Jack was in turn to tell to Iris.

The two women had gone into the Church of Santo Domenico in Siena, as an act of homage to St Catherine. It was there that the Saint (who the two friends were convinced had been, as they put it, 'one of us') had performed many of her miracles and had had many of her visions. Audrey was dressed in a chiffon dress, high-heeled shoes and one of those wide-brimmed straw-hats which had ensured that she had kept her smooth, pink-and-white complexion into middle and even old age. Johnny was in breeches, boots, silk shirt, cravat, hacking-jacket and a trilby.

Suddenly a furious priest had rushed out of a confessional box. '*Signore! Signore!* Have you no respect for the Saint, her religion, and her church? Take off that hat of yours at once!'

Audrey had been embarrassed and enraged. Johnny had been delighted.

Although Jack himself needed the text-book the following morning, he at once went off to fetch it for Iris. He would borrow a copy off Miss Sweeney, Mr Greville or even one of his students in the class, he decided.

'Are you sure you don't need it tomorrow?'

'Sure.'

'It's awful having constantly to keep one step ahead of one's students. I'm such a fraud!'

'I'd like to ask you in. But Giles has just returned from somewhere or other in a thoroughly bad mood and has now settled down to some writing in the sitting-room. My own room is in an utter mess. Maria's supposed to do it out, but she never has the time, and I'm just too lazy. But perhaps I could treat you to a coffee at the little bar on the corner? It's not all that bad. One sees all the locals.'

'It's awfully kind of you. But I've been invited out to dinner and I must first rush back to change.'

'Do you have to do that? You look fine as you are.'

She laughed at his unworldliness. 'Of course I have to. I could hardly go to a smart Florentine dinner-party dressed like *this*.'

'Oh, well . . . Then let me walk you to the tram.'

As they walked towards the tram-stop, Jack was tongue-tied, as so often with Iris. He wanted to entertain and amuse her, he wanted to impress her with his knowledge; but somehow no words would come.

Then suddenly he said: 'I came on a wonderful line of poetry yesterday evening. I was just flicking through a volume of Swinburne and I came on it.' Self-conscious now − why·on earth was he mentioning this to her? − he quoted: '"And in the dark shall no man gather fruit."'

Iris considered the line; then shook her head. 'I'm afraid it doesn't do an awful lot for me.'

'Oh.' His face began to redden. Then he rushed on: 'I think that fruit there means, er, sexual pleasure. And dark means death. That's the most terrible thing about death, you see, the loss of sexual pleasure − or so Swinburne thought.'

'His idea of sexual pleasure was pretty bizarre, wasn't it?'

'Yes, I suppose it was. Ivor − Ivor Luce − tells me that I must read a book by someone called Mario Praz: *The Romantic Agony*. He's promised to lend it to me.'

'I've never thought there was anything romantic about agony.'

'Well, neither have I. *Atalanta in Calydon*,' he added, suddenly remembering.

'Sorry?'

'The play from which that line comes. The Swinburne play.'

For a while they walked on in silence. What a twit she must

think him! Then Iris asked: 'What have you been doing today?'

'Just — wandering. Miss Sweeney asked me to tea but somehow I couldn't face it. . . . I ought to have gone. I feel sorry for her. Once they had pots of money. You know, it was her father who built the railways in Tuscany.'

'Grandfather, surely! She can't be *that* ancient.'

'Perhaps.'

The tram was clattering towards the stop ahead.

'I must run. See you! And thanks a lot!'

'Enjoy your dinner-party.'

But she did not hear him. On the step of the tram she turned and waved. He waved back.

Then he stood motionless, watching the tram until it had lurched from sight round the corner.

12

'I've never travelled in a Rolls-Royce before.'

'Not even to a funeral?' Ivor asked.

Jack shook his head. 'Only in a Daimler.'

'That's hardly the same thing.'

'Is this the only Rolls-Royce in Florence?'

'It used to be. But then, a year or two ago, Adrian Lowry arrived in one.'

'Who exactly is Adrian Lowry? I keep hearing his name.'

'Adrian? He's a vulgarian who was shrewd enough to buy up property in London when it was dirt cheap because of the bombs. How he got all his money out of England is something which no doubt is still being investigated. I doubt if he'll ever be able to get himself into England again, without going to gaol. He bought himself the Acireale villa out near Antella. When, last spring, it was announced that the Princess Royal was coming on a visit, he wrote to the Ambassador and offered to put villa, servants and Rolls-Royce at her disposal. He got back a letter from some Second or Third Secretary who coolly acknowledged the offer but said that H.E. would not be availing himself of it.' He paused. 'The Princess in fact stayed with us.'

'With you?'

Ivor nodded. 'She's a nice old bag. Although not exactly the most entertaining guest in the world.' The car had coughed and jolted to a halt, although there was no apparent reason for it to have done so. Ivor leaned forward, drew back the glass between himself and the driver, and asked, '*Che succede, Marco?*' Marco once more attempted to start the car, peered at the petrol gauge, and then, long-lashed eyes blinking and youthful cheeks scarlet, gabbled something.

'Oh, this is unbelievable. We've run out of petrol!' Ivor once again leaned forward and there was a further exchange in Italian. 'And he doesn't even have a can of the stuff in the back! This is a lesson to me. One should never employ people merely because they're good-looking. He's new,' he added. 'My father told me to interview the applicants and this was the one I chose.' He laughed. 'Oh, well, never mind! Why don't we take the bus? It's years, literally, since I travelled in a bus. The last time I did so was in London, and then it was so long since the previous occasion that I amazed the conductor by handing twopence to him. You don't mind taking a bus, do you?'

'I do it all the time. When I'm not walking.'

There were no seats vacant on the bus; but seeing Ivor, an elderly man, looking at least twice his age, arose to offer his. '*Non, non, Giorgio! Grazie! Grazie!*' Ivor waved his hand back and forth in refusal. Then he turned to Jack: 'He's one of our *contadini* – one of our peasants. He must be seventy if he's a day. He came out of hospital only a week or two ago. Italy is still a very feudal country. Thank God.'

Beside Jack, dressed all in black and with a black cloth bound round her head, stood a woman as elderly as the man, a huge basket crammed with groceries and vegetables placed between her sturdy legs, so that it should not fall over. From time to time she muttered and crossed herself as, winding up the precipitous route, they passed some church or shrine. At a sharp turning, faced with an oncoming bus, the driver braked violently, making the woman first crash against Jack and then ricochet off him to the floor. Her basket lay beside her, the vegetables scattered for other passengers to retrieve. At her impact with Jack, the woman let out a scream; she let out an even louder one at her impact with the floor. Now she lay on her side, moaning. The man who had offered Ivor his seat and a teenage boy attempted to lift her. But whenever either of them exerted any force, she would screw up her eyes, pull her mouth out of shape, and emit either a groan or a squeak. The driver, paying no attention, drove on.

'Poor old dear,' Ivor said. Then, amazing Jack with his concern, he knelt beside the woman, the knees of his elegant beige trousers collecting dust and dirt. He, too, now attempted to coax her up, with more success than the other two. '*Ah, signore! Signore! Ah!*' she kept wailing. But eventually she was upright. Ivor retrieved the last of the potatoes from under a seat and dropped it into the by now righted basket. '*Grazie, signore! Grazie!*'she whimpered, as she rubbed now at an elbow and now at a knee.

'This is where we get off,' Ivor eventually announced.

It was where the woman got off too. Ivor held out a hand to help her down. 'Oops-a-daisy!' Then he took her basket from her. '*Non, non, signore!*' she cried out. But he insisted. 'We'd better walk her back to her home. You take this basket and I'll help her along.'

It was amply clear to Jack that the woman, no more than slightly bruised, was putting on a performance. Yet here was Ivor, apparently so cynical, egotistical and spiky, showing her all this solicitude. He himself would have left her to her own devices.

At the door of her little house, the woman took an apple out of her basket and, now smiling and totally recovered, handed it to Jack. It seemed unjust that she should be rewarding him and not Ivor.

'You ought to have this.'

'Yes, I suppose I should.' Laughing, Ivor took the apple and put it in the pocket of his jacket, making it bulge inelegantly.

They passed under a high arch and began to walk up a long drive, flanked by cypresses, towards the Renaissance villa.

'It's amazing!'

Ivor glanced quizzically at Jack.

'You approve?'

'I find it almost impossible to believe that people can actually *live* in a place like that.'

'During the worst of the winter, I myself find it hard to believe that we can live in it. But we do. Mind you, we should be much more comfortable in an apartment in the centre of Florence. But then where should we put all the furniture and pictures and books?'

A manservant greeted them. He eyed Jack with the same kind of lofty contempt with which Mervyn's manservant had eyed him at the party, and then, since Jack was visibly sweating from first the journey in the ill-ventilated bus and then the hike up to the villa, asked if *il signore* wished to remove his jacket. Jack almost did so; then he thought of the damp-stains that there would certainly be under the arms of his shirt and shook his head. '*Va bene. Grazie.*'

'I'm glad you're making *some* progress with your Italian.'

'I've absolutely no talent for languages.'

'What you really mean is that you have absolutely no talent for letting yourself go.'

'I don't get you.'

'You *will* hang on to your Englishness − a North Country Englishness at that. Let it drop from you. Abandon it. Think like an Italian, behave like an Italian. Then you'll soon be speaking like an Italian.'

Jack could not imagine himself doing any of these three things.

'Tea!' Ivor announced. 'I brought back tins and tins of Earl Grey from my London visit. You like Earl Grey?'

'Well . . . yes. Thank you.'

'You don't! I thought you wouldn't.'

'Let me give it another try.'

'That's the spirit!' Ivor put an arm round Jack's shoulders, propelling him forward. Jack could smell his lemony perfume. He was not accustomed to perfume on men.

They sat in a drawing-room, the shimmering eau-de-Nil damask of extravagantly looped curtains and chair-covers and the dark-green of carpet creating the impression that they were imprisoned under water. Leaning far back in his armchair, Ivor stretched his long legs out ahead of him, hands in pockets. His sparse red hair fell in a cow-lick over his freckled forehead; the hands, clasped in his lap, were also freckled. He turned the ring, an intaglio in a heavy gold setting, around his little finger. 'This was my mother's favourite room,' he said. 'She used to play *that*.' He pointed at a shut Steinway grand. 'She was not a musician of the standard of Iris's mother − she was too lazy and disorganized for that. But I once heard them playing duets and − and it was unforgettable.' He closed his eyes. 'I can hear them playing now. You're not musical, I take it?'

Jack shook his head. 'Well, not what you'd call musical.' He almost told Ivor of the amateur jazz band in which he had played at Oxford. Then he decided not to. He craved Ivor's good opinion and thought, mistakenly, that with such an admission he might forfeit it. 'Is your mother dead?'

Ivor sighed. 'Yes, I'm afraid she is. She was altogether too bold in her opposition to the Fascisti. Unlike my father. Unlike many of the other English here. When one of the servants reported her to the police for concealing two escaped Australian prisoners of war, she was put in gaol. Her health − which was always poor − suffered. She died of tuberculosis.' He jumped up and pulled at a bell-rope. 'Where the hell is that tea?' Then he pointed to a portrait above the chimneypiece. 'That's her,' he said.

There was an oppressive sense of invalidism about the pale, thin woman outstretched on a settee, a vase of small white roses beside her and a shuttered window behind. There was also a subdued voluptuousness.

'Did that painter — that painter whom Iris knows — Harry . . .?'

Ivor laughed. 'Good God, no! Harry Archer could never paint a portrait as well as that. That's by Sargent.'

'Oh.'

'Do you know who Sargent was?' Ivor asked, suddenly cruel. 'Have you ever heard of him?'

'Of course.'

'Truly?'

'Of course.' Jack felt angry that Ivor should doubt him.

A young manservant, tall and muscular, with huge hands, came in carrying a silver tray. He set it down on the table between Jack and Ivor, having deftly balanced it on one hand as he used the other to clear away copies of the *Illustrated London News*, the *Burlington* and *Country Life*. Jack watched him. His hair was red; there were freckles on the hands, as there were on his forehead.

'*Grazie, Aldo.*'

'*Prego, signore.*'

In all innocence, Jack said: 'It's unusual to see an Italian with red hair and freckles. He looks more like a Scotsman.'

'Perhaps that's because my grandfather came from Scotland.' Ivor stared at Jack, his eyes — which, Jack suddenly realized, were precisely the same green as the manservant's — flickering with amusement. Jack looked back, bewildered and vaguely uneasy. 'There are a lot of people with red hair and freckles working on our estates.'

Jack gave a nervous smile. Was he correct in inferring what he did?

'My father has always been very philoprogenitive,' Ivor continued. 'Unlike his only son. Perhaps one day he'll meet the same fate as Don Giovanni, and the statue of some wronged husband will turn up to drag him down to hell. But somehow I doubt it. He has a rare knack of getting away with things.' He reached for the silver teapot. 'As it comes?'

'Please.'

'Oh, don't look so shocked! Far more miscegenation has gone on in Florence during the last hundred years than many people realize. I even know of an English duke whose father was a Florentine waiter. It's been a good thing. Good for the English, good for the Italians. . . . Here! Have a sandwich!'

Tea finished, Ivor asked Jack if he would like to see over the house. As they mounted the grandiose staircase, he pointed down a corridor: 'All those rooms are shut now.' Later he pointed down another corridor. 'I won't take you down there. Otherwise we'll rouse my father, and I'd rather that didn't happen.' He opened a door, allowed Jack a quick glimpse of a room full of late autumn sunlight, and then pulled the door shut again. 'That was my mother's room. Then, for a brief while, Mrs Malcolm-Watts used to occupy it whenever she came to stay. Have you ever heard of Mrs Malcolm-Watts? No, of course you haven't.' With a sudden bitterness, he went on: 'She was the mistress of King George of the Hellenes for a time. Then, when that was over, she became . . .' He broke off with a shrug.

Now they had only the attics above them. Ivor pointed up the by now narrow staircase. 'Believe it or not, before the War eight servants slept up there. Now there are only two. The rest have their houses on the estate. Without those houses they'd take themselves off to work in the hotels instead of for us. More money, more eventful.' He opened another door. 'This room may interest you.'

The room, a damp patch in one corner, its floorboards bare and stained, and thick, black curtains trailing in tatters from its single window, was full of antiquated photographic equipment: wooden cameras on tripods, vats for developing, machines for printing and enlarging, rusty lamps, screens. 'Not used for years,' Ivor said. 'My father's studio. Once.' He made a grimace, a hand resting on one of the cameras. 'In his time, he was a really keen and really talented photographer.'

'Why did he give it up?'

'Now there's a question! Would it be disloyal of me to give you the answer?' He crossed to the window and jerked one of the heavy black curtains first one way, casting the room into semi-darkness, and then back again. A cloud of dust arose. 'Well, why shouldn't I? Many years ago, before the First World War, my father and an Italian friend of his — a highly respectable citizen of this city, in fact once its mayor — used to use this studio for photographing from, well, life. Studies of womanhood. In the raw. Mostly peasant womanhood. Although from time to time . . . Yes, there were even guests who got a kick out of being photographed up here in the buff. I've never really been sure what precisely *is* the *buff*. Do you know? No, of course, you don't. No one does.' Suddenly he slumped down on a simple upright chair. 'Once one of the models was a girl of — what? — nine, ten? My father's always been rather stingy — most of the money was my mother's, you see — and so he paid the girl's mother rather less than she'd expected. Perhaps even rather less than he'd promised. She became demanding. He was not prepared to give in to her demands. So she threatened to go to the police. My father shrugged his shoulders at that — he's always had a knack of shrugging his shoulders at things when they've gone wrong. The result was a nasty scandal — for him, for his friend. He had to use up a lot of my mother's money and the former mayor had to use up a lot of goodwill to ensure that neither of them went to prison. After that, my father gave up his hobby. Perhaps my mother told him he must do so. Perhaps he just decided to be prudent.' He jumped up from the chair. 'Now come over here and look at this. It'll tell you more about the life of the expatriate community of Florence in the first quarter of this century than any book.' He crossed over to a brass viewer for stereoscopic photographs, set on a marble stand which seemed to have been specially made for it. Jack edged forward to stand beside him. From a pile, Ivor picked up a double photograph, mounted on stiff board. He inserted it.

'Recognize who that is?'

Jack looked through the twin apertures, stooping slightly to do so. The scene was clearly the Piazza Signoria with the Loggia in the background — he could make out what Giles, conducting him round the city, had told him was Cellini's masterpiece, the 'Ajax with the Body of Patroclus'. In the foreground stood a tall girl in a long skirt and straw boater, the crook of a folded parasol over one arm and a bead-fringed handbag dangling from the other. Her face looked both serious and vulnerable.

'No idea.'

'That's the then Princess May of Teck, who became our present Queen Mother. Queen Mary. She looks so touching there, I always feel. The family came to live in Florence — in the Pitti Palace — for the same reason that many English families did:

shortage of money. It would be folly to come to live here for that reason now, wouldn't it?' He inserted another card, peered through the twin apertures himself, and then signalled to Jack to do the same. Jack was both astonished and shocked. There were some rocks and the sea beyond. Before them, gawky and self-conscious, were two figures, totally nude, a teenage boy and a girl, facing the invisible cameraman with a gaze of nervous defiance. Ivor laughed, his body close to Jack's and a hand on his shoulder. 'Rather a contrast to the Queen Mum, wouldn't you say?'

Suddenly a voice rasped behind them. 'Ivor — what are you doing up here?' The question might have been addressed to a delinquent child.

'Oh, father . . .' Ivor's whole manner changed. He became uncertain, ingratiating. 'This is Jack Prentice, who's come out here to teach at the Institute. Mervyn thought it would be an essential part of his artistic education to be shown round the villa.' The idea that Mervyn had taken an interest in Jack's artistic education was preposterous. Iris's artistic education was a wholly different matter.

'How d'you do, Mr Prentice.'

Felix Luce had the same red hair, the same freckled complexion and the same beaky nose, striated with broken blood-vessels, as his son; but he was so diminutive that he came up only to Jack's shoulder. The cut of his suit, the jacket wide-lapelled, buttoned high and with turn-ups to the sleeves, the trousers narrow and lacking creases, was as old-fashioned as his elastic-sided brown boots and the way in which his hair was parted in the middle. Jack had put out his hand but Felix did not take it. 'Prentice, did you say?'

'Jack Prentice, father.'

'One of the Shropshire Prentices?'

Jack shook his head.

'One of the Yorkshire Prentices,' Ivor volunteered mischievously.

'Anyway, what are you both doing up here?'

'I was showing him . . .' Ivor pointed towards the viewer.

'Far better to show him the garden before the light goes. Show him the garden!' Felix's voice, previously faint and husky, had acquired a sudden strength and edge. 'This room is meant to be kept locked. Who unlocked it? Sophia? Aldo?'

Ivor did not answer. It was he who had unlocked the room when he had decided to bring Jack to the villa, and his father knew that he had. 'Would you like to see the garden?'

'Yes. Thank you.'

'I don't want you to bring your young visitors up here. I've told you that before.'

'Yes, father.'

They left the room ahead of the old man, who walked a few steps down the corridor with them and then, as though he had forgotten something, abruptly turned back.

Ivor was silent until they had reached the ground floor. Then he whispered: 'As you can see, even at seventy-seven my father remains a domestic tyrant. Unfortunately I can't rebel. My mother made one major mistake in her life when she married him instead of one of the Corsini — who was so mad about her that, when she turned him down, he took himself off to Africa, to die there, in the best traditions of Victorian fiction, of a sudden fever. She made another major mistake when she drew up her will, and left her money in trust, with all but a fraction of the income to go to my father. When he dies, then of course . . .' They were now walking through the garden, which descended in a series of fan-like terraces down the steep hill. At the bottom of the hill, Florence spread out, smokily blurred. 'A good motive for murder, really.' Ivor laughed. 'If only I had the courage to commit it and the ingenuity to get away with it. Perhaps you could commit it for me!'

'I don't think I'd be much good at a murder. I'm so bad at lying. I always begin to blush when I've lied.'

'I must watch out for that. Oh, I'm a wonderful liar! . . . Yes, you could murder my father for me. Why not? No one would suspect you, because there'd be no motive. You could regard it as an *acte gratuit*, like the murder which that young man commits in Gide's *Les Faux-Monnayeurs*. Now have you heard of Gide?'

'Heard of him. Not read him. He came to Oxford as a guest. They had him to dinner at Magdalen — Oscar Wilde's old college. He asked to see Wilde's room, so, after dinner, they took him there. In total silence, the frail old boy tottered round the room, constantly stroking the panelling. It must have been rather moving.'

'He's an awful character.'

'Oh, do you know him?

'Met him in Morocco. Long after Wilde met him there.'

'You seem to have known everyone.'

'Far too many people.'

They had now come to the last of the terraces, a geometric garden, with topiary representing birds and animals, huge urns trailing flowers, and statues from many of which time had eroded the features. In one corner stood a classical pavilion, modelled on the Erechtheum. Ivor walked towards it. 'Come in here. Let me show you something amusing.'

Jack followed him inside. 'Now look out through there —' he pointed to a window — 'at the garden.' Jack looked out. 'All right?' Ivor extended a hand.

Suddenly, rainbow-hued in the late autumn sunlight, innumerable jets of water rose up into the air from between the interstices of the flagstones.

Jack gasped. 'Beautiful!'

'It was built as a practical joke by one of the Cremoni — the first owners of the villa. That particular count clearly had an odd sense of humour. His invited guests would be strolling in all their finery through the garden and then, with a turn of this tap, hey presto! they were drenched.'

Jack laughed. He liked the idea, cruel though it was.

'Now there's a sequel to that. When I was about ten or twelve, some aristocratic Italian friends of my father — like him, and unlike my mother, admirers of the bull-frog — came to a party to celebrate Mussolini's famous March on Rome. I hid myself in here, and then, as they were all chattering over there' — again he indicated the garden — 'I put a hand to the tap.' He laughed joyfully at the recollection. 'Although I at once ran away, before the victims of my little joke had had a chance to notice me, my father at once knew that it was I who'd been the culprit. I was whipped, yes, really whipped, as one might be whipped in some Soho brothel — despite the protests and pleadings of my mother. But I never regretted what I did. Never, never. It remains one of my most pleasurable childhood memories.'

When they had quitted the temple-pavilion and had begun to make their way back up to the house, Ivor suddenly stooped and picked a carnation. He caught Jack by an arm, swivelled him round to face him, and then put the carnation in his button-hole. Rubbing the palm of his right hand over the lapel of the jacket to smooth it, he said: 'That makes you look a little more elegant.'

'Oh, I'll never be elegant, I'm afraid!'

'Why not? You can learn. It's like learning to ride a bicycle or drive a car.'

When they were once more back at the house, Ivor asked: 'Would you like to come to a concert this evening? You say you're not musical but that may only be because you've never tried. The Lener Quartet. A programme of Beethoven.'

'Sorry. I have to see Audrey Heaton.'

'Are you lying to me?'

'Of course not.'

'No, you're not blushing! But why on earth should you have to see Audrey Heaton?'

'Because Giles has got me a job with her. To make a little extra money.'

'You're certainly not going to make any extra money by doing a job for Audrey. Anyway, what is this job?'

'She's started on a new book − a literary guide to Florence. And she wants someone to help her with her research.'

'Oh, my dear boy! She's been working on that guide for *donkey's years* − as Miss Sweeney would put it. Before the War Audrey persuaded both old Jonathan Cape and Geoffrey Faber to give her advances. Since the War . . . You'll never get paid!'

'Do you mean that?' Jack was crestfallen.

'Of course I mean it. Poor dear Audrey, like poor dear Harry, never has any money. She and Johnny lived on Johnny's income from some family trust. Then, when Johnny died . . . Like everyone else in the colony, I've lent Audrey money and I've given Audrey money. In her case, the two things are the same.' He sat down on a stone bench beside the front door and patted it, to indicate that Jack should sit down beside him.

'Now I'll tell you a rather sad and also a rather amusing little story. I heard that Audrey was once again so broke that she could no longer even get credit to buy food. By then, like many other people, I'd grown weary of handing over money to her, so I went to her local grocer and instead handed over some money to him. Would he please deliver a food parcel to her, saying that it was a gift from someone who wished to remain anonymous? A few days later, I called on the embattled old dear. There, in a corner of her kitchen − one always enters her villa by the kitchen these days − stood a large carton. After a while she pointed at it. "Look at that!" she said. "Just look at that!"' Ivor gave a creditable imitation of Audrey. '"Some bloody fool ordered that to be sent to me from the local *spezieria*. No imagination, no taste! Does he – or she – think that I'm the sort of person who eats dried beans, tinned peaches and the kind of cheap salami I wouldn't even feed to the cats?"' Ivor laughed. 'There's something magnificent about her! I always think of that description of Mrs Patrick Campbell: "a sinking battleship firing on its rescuers" – something along those lines.'

When reluctantly Jack said that really he must be going, Ivor at once volunteered to send him back to Florence in the Rolls-Royce – provided that it had returned. Jack was appalled. Someone would certainly see him, and no less certainly that someone would talk. Everyone was always saying that Florence was such a small world.

Ivor was insistent. 'No, no! You can't stand in that horrible bus again. I won't have it. In any case, I want to punish Marco for stranding us like that.'

Marco was clearly furious at being punished in this fashion. He slammed the door on Jack with the full force of a muscular arm and then, scowling and muttering under his breath, clambered into the front seat.

Ivor stooped to wave to Jack through the open window. Jack waved back; and, as he did so, he had a sudden, piercing recollection of waving to Iris and of her waving back to him as she had boarded the tram after borrowing the text-book from him.

At the moment when, with a deliberate clashing of gears, the stately old car began to move off, something hard landed in Jack's lap. It was the apple given to him by the old woman. Ivor had thrown it there.

Holding the apple in one hand, Jack touched the carnation with the other. It felt stiff and alien. Even its smell seemed somehow wrong.

When the car had passed out under the high archway and turned into the road, Jack pulled the carnation out of his button-hole and stared down at it. Then, with a sweep of his arm, he flung it out through the window open beside him.

He raised the apple; hesitated; bit into it. Its juice fizzed against the large, white teeth which so much attracted Ivor.

13

Mervyn had told Iris to meet him at the entrance to the Institute. That way, he told her, it would be more convenient for her as she came out of her class; but the truth was that he did not want Karen, in bed with influenza, to know that in her place he was taking the girl to Isabella Lambeni's.

'I feel badly about missing my next class.'

'Miss Pryce won't feel badly about earning some more money.'

'Giles was distinctly chilly when I ran into him just now.'

'He's always distinctly chilly over any extra expenditure. Don't give it a thought.'

They had now descended the steps of the Institute and were walking towards the taxi which Mervyn, not himself a driver, had on constant call. 'One would think that the Institute would provide a chauffeur-driven car for its Director,' he grumbled, as they walked towards it. 'One can't imagine the French being so stingy. How can one be expected to be "representational" when one is representing one's country in a beat-up, pre-war Fiat? I ask you!'

'Does Contessa Lambeni really want me?'

'Why shouldn't she really want you?'

'Well, she hardly knows me. And she's expecting your wife.'

'She'll be delighted that Karen isn't coming. Dear Karen suffers from some of the smugness of her country of origin. No one can say that the Swedes behaved conspicuously well in the War, but none the less she can't resist making it clear to Isabella that she thinks that she and her kind behaved conspicuously badly.'

'Isabella collaborated?'

'An ugly word.'

'For an ugly thing?'

Mervyn waited for Iris to clamber into the back of the taxi and then clambered in beside her. Having instructed the driver where to take them, he turned to her: 'Oh, the moral certainties of the young! Try to put yourself in Isabella's position. When she was seventeen, she married this brilliant and handsome Italian aristocrat, a widower several years older than herself. The widower's mother was a Russian, a Romanov – and we all know what happened to most of *them*. The widower had political ambitions. When Mussolini came to power, what were his choices? Exile? Banishment to the Lipari Islands? A withdrawal from the only vocation of interest to him? Remember, he had children by both his first wife and by Isabella. And what were Isabella's choices when the War broke out? She adored her husband, she adored her children and her step-children. Was she to demand to return to England on her own? Was she to oppose everything of importance in her husband's life? Was she to ruin his career for him?'

'She could have just sat things out on the sidelines.'

'Yes. True. But the sidelines are not for people like Isabella. She has to occupy the centre.' Suddenly his hand covered the hand which Iris had rested in her lap. 'Oh, the moral certainties of the young!' he repeated with a sigh. 'When you reach my age, you're much more tolerant. I can't claim to have done anything heroic in the War – although I think that I did do some useful things with ciphers at Bletchley. For the matter of that, I can't claim to have done anything heroic in the whole of my life. I think that only those who have done heroic things themselves – Ivor Luce's mother, for example, who hid two escaped prisoners of war and went to gaol for it – have the right to criticize others for not having been heroic. Have you ever done anything heroic?'

Iris laughed, withdrawing her hand from under the hand resting, sponge-like, on top of it. 'Not really, no. I've never had the chance.'

'Would you have taken the chance if it had come along?'

'Who can say? I was at school with a girl who seemed to live in a constant state of fear about everything in life – from a visit to the dentist to a game of lacrosse. She eventually won a George Cross posthumously, when she was killed nursing at Anzio.'

'People say that Ethel Pryce was heroic in the War. She also got some kind of decoration, I think. Unfortunately, heroes and heroines are not always likeable, are they?'

'Ethel's all right.'

'All right? Would you like to be described by others as "all right"?'

'Well, that's better than being described as all wrong — which is how a lot of people describe Isabella.'

'I don't think Isabella's all wrong.' Suddenly he gave way to asperity, as he often did when people disagreed with him. 'Wait till you know her properly.'

Iris had been correct in her surmise: Isabella had not cared for it when Mervyn had suggested that he should bring her along to luncheon in the place of his ailing wife. 'How nice of you to join us — and at the last minute too! I'd been meaning to ask you over but somehow, as so often in my disorganized life, never actually got round to doing so.' Isabella's life, on the *piano nobile* of the Lambeni *palazzo*, was in fact so far from being disorganized that it was organized with a ferocious energy and efficiency. Iris could see this at once, as one servant showed her in and another servant then hurried over with a tray laden with drinks. '*Che cosa desidera la signorina?*' What the *signorina* really desired was to leave immediately.

'Iris! Come over here, Iris!' Having been abandoned by Isabella, who had gone over to greet some other guests, Iris was now rescued by Mervyn. 'Contessa, I want you to meet this delightful English friend of mine, if you haven't already done so. I know she'll want you to show her your Fabergé collection. She's a great lover of art.'

Having placed on her nose the glasses which were dangling around her neck, the Contessa looked Iris up and down. She knew these delightful English and sometimes Italian friends of Mervyn's only too well; but this time she approved. This girl was clearly *di razza*. She was dressed elegantly, she held herself well, and she had an air of ease and self-possession. 'Yes, you must visit me out at my villa. Perhaps dear Mervyn could bring you?'

'Of course! I'd love to do that,' Mervyn said. 'Then I can also pop into your chapel and have another look at that Ghisolfi.'

'If it is a Ghisolfi.'

'Of course it is. I assure you it is.'

'B.B. seems to have doubts.'

'It's odd that B.B. has so many more doubts about ascriptions now that he is rich than he had when he was poor.'

'Naughty, naughty!'

Iris was looking around to see if the room contained anyone she knew. At its far end, a wide, high arch was filled with cut-velvet curtains draped in elaborate swags. One of the curtains twitched; a hand appeared around it. Then she glimpsed the head, no more, of Giuseppe Valeriano. He was peering out at the gathering with what seemed to be an expression of agonized impatience. Was he a guest? Did he work in some capacity for Isabella? He reminded Iris of one of those Velasquez dwarfs in jealous attendance on royalty. The curtain fell, the head disappeared.

Again Iris looked around the room. Then, to her relief, she glimpsed Harry Archer and Audrey Heaton, seated in obvious discomfort on two spindly, straight-backed chairs facing each other. Audrey saw her and beckoned vigorously.

'My dear, how lovely to see you! I didn't know that you knew Isabella.'

'I don't. Well, hardly. But Mrs Le Clerq's ill and so Mervyn . . .'

Harry laughed, his narrow, bowed shoulders shaking and his glass shaking with them. 'Mervyn is so clever at finding attractive understudies for Karen.'

'That young colleague of yours is helping me with my book,' Audrey announced.

'Who do you mean?' Jack had not told Iris of the job.

'Jack. Jack Prentice. A rather gauche young man. Needs the kind of polishing that Florence – and ever so avuncular Ivor – will certainly provide. But I like him. He's not unintelligent. Kind, too.' Part of Jack's kindness had consisted in telling Audrey not to bother about settling with him at once, when she had explained that she was awaiting a long-overdue payment for a review from the TLS.

Harry was staring at Iris. Then he said: 'I want to paint you.'

'On the top of a cigarette box?' Audrey asked unkindly. She and he had been sparring partners for almost half a century.

'Of course not! She's pretty enough to go on a chocolate box, but I shouldn't dream of putting her on a cigarette box. What an idea! Though I suppose that, if I did, Moroni would have absolutely no difficulty in selling it at once. No, what I have in mind is a portrait in oils as a companion piece to the one I painted of her grandmother.'

'You haven't the strength for anything large,' Audrey said firmly. 'You know you haven't.'

Harry shrugged and sighed. 'Anno domini, anno domini!'

'Now you mustn't spend all your time with people you already know!' It was Isabella, in a pleated Fortuny dress, the grey-green of which struck Iris as perfectly complementing the grey-pink of her hair. 'That's not the object of the exercise. You must come and talk to Adrian Lowry and Adriana Salsomaggiore. It's much easier to remember who goes with whom when the Christian names are almost the same.'

Tall, wiry, silvery-haired and dark-skinned, Adrian looked like one of those maharajahs who achieved distinction as cricketers in the years before the War. He was drawing on a cigarette in an amber holder as Isabella approached with Iris in tow. Beside him was a squat, cheerful-looking woman, in flat-heeled shoes and a black velvet tricorne hat. Having made the introductions, Isabella left them to it.

Adrian's tone was languid: 'I've heard so much about you. I've been looking forward to meeting you. Correction. *We've* been looking forward to meeting you. Haven't we, Adriana?' It was an adroit way of making the relationship between the two of them clear.

Adriana nodded energetically. 'Mervyn seems to be bespotted with you,' she said with a strong Italian accent.

'Be*sotted*, dear, be*sotted*! Adriana is our Florentine Madama Malapropa. She is also — in case you don't know it already — one of Italy's leading dress-designers.' Not for the first time, Iris wondered why it was that dress-designers so often seemed incapable of designing even half-way attractive dresses for themselves.

'And what do you do?'

'Nothing. Absolutely nothing. Has no one told you? I'm stinking rich. I own the only Rolls-Royce in Tuscany apart from Ivor Luce's. And Ivor's is about as old as he is. Which is saying very old.' Since Adriana gave a braying laugh, Iris assumed that all this was said in joke.

It came as a relief when, soon after, they were summoned to lunch.

As they walked down the passage to the dining-room, Mervyn was at her elbow. 'I saw you with Adrian and his cover-girl,' he hissed.

'His cover-girl? I thought she was a dress-designer.'

'Oh, my dear Iris, I love your *naïveté*. Cover-girl means that she's the girl he uses as his cover. When he's out in Florentine society. He could hardly bring his manservant to a party like this, now could he?'

Adrian and Adriana were only a short distance behind them. Iris hoped that they had not heard.

It was a long and tedious lunch, with course succeeding course and wine succeeding wine. Isabella had deliberately placed Iris between the two most boring of her male guests. One was an extremely fat, loudly wheezing and heavily perspiring French businessman, who was so busy scoffing food and gulping wine that he had little time for conversation. When he did converse, it was on the subject of notable meals which he had eaten during his visit to Italy. Did Iris know Al Cantunzein in Bologna? The pasta was a dream! Dal Bolognese in Rome? That, of course, was frequented by everyone who was anyone in the arts. The Danieli Terrace in Venice? The food was not always consistently good, but the view made it all worthwhile . . .

On the other side of Iris was a pale, studious-looking young man. He smiled a lot but spoke little. When he did speak it was with a stammer and about the farming of his estates. It was a relief to get up from the table.

As she stood drinking her coffee in a corner, Mervyn approached. 'What a bitch Isabella is! My object in bringing you here was to have you sitting next to me. Instead, I had Audrey on one hand and that dreary American woman — the one you met at my party — on the other. I could see either any day of the week, if I was crazy enough to want to do so.'

'Now come along, Mervyn!' It was Isabella. 'You must have plenty of time at the Institute to talk to your charming friend; I'm sure. I want you to come and meet the wife of the Portuguese ambassador. She's a great lover of Italian art and has just bought — at my persuasion — your book on Pinturicchio before her visit to Siena.'

Finally the party broke up.

After Iris had said her goodbyes, Isabella suddenly called after her, as she was about to descend the staircase, with Mervyn beside her: 'Oh, by the way, Miss Crediton . . .'

Iris turned back. 'Yes?'

'You don't know what's happened to that friend of yours, do you?'

'Which friend?'

'The Somers boy. The one who works' — she gave the word an

odd, upward inflection — 'for Pippa Lavery. Has he gone from Florence?'

'I don't think so. I saw him two or three days ago.'

'How strange. I wanted to ask him to this luncheon, so I twice left a message, once with Pippa — who sounded, poor darling, as if she had once again been hitting the bottle — and once with her major-domo, asking him to ring back. But not a word. A little off-hand, even rude — *if* he got the messages, that is. Anyway, if you see him, do tell him.'

'Yes, I'll tell him.'

Iris rejoined Mervyn, who was impatiently waiting for her at the bottom of the marble steps. 'How things went on and on! That taxi's been here for more than half an hour. God knows what it will cost. Dear old Giles will be complaining once again.'

'Do you charge up your taxi-journeys?'

'Certainly. If they're taken on behalf of the Institute. I was there in my role of Director. Certainly.' Mervyn was flustered.

They sat in silence in the taxi. Mervyn turned his face to her, shifted uneasily and then once again put out a hand to place it over hers. More quickly this time, she withdrew her hand from under his. He drew a deep sigh, compressed his lips and then looked at himself in the driving mirror, tilting his head to do so. He did not like what he saw. How grey and tired he looked, how thin his hair! No wonder she was being so unresponsive.

Where the road took a bend and then lurched over a narrow bridge spanning a stream, Iris suddenly saw Jack, sitting on the farther bank under a yellowing willow, his back propped against it. He was always going off on solitary hikes on the hills around the city. She waved but he did not see her. He looked forlorn, with the Harris tweed jacket draped over his shoulders and a book — no doubt the collected works of some obscure Victorian poet — lying on the grass beside him.

'Who were you waving at?'

'I thought it was Mr Greville. But it wasn't,' she lied, without knowing why she did so.

At the gates to the Boboli Gardens, she saw the back of Dale — yes, yes, it must be he! — disappearing inside. Only in Florence, she later thought, could two such sightings of friends have occurred in such quick succession. Excitedly, hand to door-handle, she demanded: 'May I get out here? Would you mind?'

'Oh! oh, dear! Well, yes, if you wish . . .' Mervyn tapped the driver on the shoulder and asked him to stop. 'I'd thought we might make *una piccola girata* of the eastern end of the city. There's a lot more of interest there than many people realize. But if you must . . .'

'It's just that I'm supposed to meet someone in the Boboli tea-room at four.' Iris was already beginning to get out of the taxi.

'The tea-room? I didn't think that the tea-room was open at this time of year.'

She laughed. 'Well, I hope it is. Because that's where we're meeting.'

'Who *is* this someone?'

But she had already begun to race away towards the entrance to the gardens.

Fortunately Dale was strolling so slowly that, breathless, she soon caught up with him. 'Dale! Dale!' she gasped. 'It was wonderful . . . There was this awful luncheon party given by Isabella Lambeni, with the most boring, bitchy people – and then I was in a taxi with Mervyn and – and then – then – I saw you!'

Unsmiling, Dale put up a hand and caught her by the hair. Then he pulled her face sideways and towards him. Their lips met.

They sat side by side on a stone bench, gazing across the Arno. Below them, two young priests were squatting on the grass, talking earnestly. One of them was sucking greedily on a cigarette pinched between forefinger and thumb, while the other held a newspaper half-open before him. Were they discussing the news?

'Isabella Lambeni asked about you.'

'Asked about me? What did she ask?'

'Whether you were in Florence. She'd left messages for you first with Pippa and then with her major-domo.'

'I got the messages.' He turned to her and smiled.

'But you didn't ring back?'

'I didn't ring back.'

'Why not? She was going to invite you to the party.'

'I don't want to have anything – anything at all – to do with that woman.'

'Why do you dislike her so much?'

'You know why I dislike her so much. I've told you.'

Remembering what Mervyn had said to her in the car, Iris parroted: 'Unless one has been a hero or heroine oneself, does one have the right to demand that other people should behave heroically?'

'One has the right to demand that other people should behave well. She didn't behave well. She behaved conspicuously badly.' He hunched his body forward, hand to chin. 'Let me tell you a story which an Italian friend – no, not one of the Florentine smart set, a trades union leader – told me the other day. Isabella had this close woman friend, an Italian aristocrat, who had a student son. The student son got involved in some preposterous scheme to assassinate Mussolini, was caught, and was eventually condemned to death. Knowing that Lambeni was so close to the bull-frog, the mother visited Isabella to ask her to intercede for the wretched boy's life. Had Isabella seen the woman and then said that there was nothing she could do or was prepared to do, it wouldn't have been so bad. But Isabella absolutely refused to see her. In fact, when the woman said she wouldn't budge from the *palazzo* unless Isabella saw her, Isabella then ordered her to be ejected. By force.'

'That sounds like typical Florentine gossip to me.'

'No, Iris, it's *not* gossip. And I'll tell you why it's not just gossip. My friend was one of the people involved in the plot. He was the dead boy's closest friend. He managed to survive, because the working-class community from which he came concealed him for many months until the Allies arrived.'

Iris stared down at the two priests, who, no longer serious, had suddenly begun to hand-wrestle with each other. Then she gave herself a small shake and rose to her feet. She extended a hand: 'Home?' She was tired of Isabella. She did not wish to see her or hear from her or hear about her for some time, perhaps even forever.

Dale did not take the hand. He still looked angry – it almost seemed to Iris, as much with her as with Isabella. 'Yes, home. Your home. Let me see that *pensione* of yours.'

'I saw you yesterday. Just for a moment,' Iris told Giuseppe.

Tired of talking shop in the common room, she had left the Institute between classes for a coffee in Doney. There, she had found him perched on his usual high stool at the bar, in yet another of his showy ties and yet another suit expertly tailored to his twisted little body.

'Yesterday?' He frowned.

'At Isabella Lambeni's. At her lunch-party.'

'Isabella Lambeni's?'

'Yes, you were standing behind a curtain.' Had she imagined it? Mistaken someone else? He was still frowning.

'But I was here at lunch-time. And why should I hide behind a curtain?'

'How odd! Then I must have . . . It must have been someone else.'

He shrugged. 'Maybe.' Then he turned away and picked up his glass.

'Well — ciao!'

'Ciao, signorina!'

He turned abruptly away from her to say something to the barman.

14

That Sunday Jack hiked, rucksack on back, the four miles out to the Certosa del Galluzzo. There was a chill in the air, and the paths which he took, often little more than gulleys with steep walls as their banks, were choked with autumn leaves. Ivor had suggested a meeting, but for the moment Jack had felt that he had seen enough of Ivor. Giles had said that he would have to put in a day of work at the office. In the absence of Maria, who had gone off to her village in her Sunday best, Margot had decided to take the children for a walk in the Cascine. Would Jack like to accompany them? He had hesitated; then, as though impelled to luxuriate in a solitude which none the less irked him, he had shaken his head and said: 'Thank you. But I've got other plans.' He knew, from the expression on Margot's face, that that had sounded abrupt and even rude. But if he had told her that his 'other plans' consisted merely of a walk by himself to the Certosa, would that not have sounded even ruder?

As he was leaving the house, she had asked: 'Why do you always carry that rucksack?'

'Books.'

'Why not just carry one book? Under your arm.' Her tone had been sharp. She was not relishing a morning alone with the children.

As he wandered from one to another of the tidy, well-swept subterranean chapels under the Certosa, he felt a cobwebby dankness on the back of his neck and on the arms from which he had rolled back his shirt-sleeves during his walk. There was a guided tour ahead of him, which he had deliberately avoided joining. It was led by a bossy Carthusian monk, who, when anyone seemed to be in danger of escaping, would clap his hands together, as though shooing away an invisible flock of pigeons, and cry out: 'Please-a! Please-a!' At one point two English girls detached themselves from this party and wandered over to where Jack stood examining a tomb. One of them, high-coloured, high-busted and high-spirited, came and stood close beside him. Then she asked: 'What would be the date of that?' She pointed.

He looked in his guide-book: 'Fifteenth century.'

'I really only asked because my sister and I were arguing about whether you were English or not. I said you must be.'

'And what did she think I was?'

'Australian.'

'Australian! Why on earth should she think that?'

'Search me! Perhaps because you look such an open-air type.'

'Oh, Pat!' the other girl protested. She began to giggle, tugging at the strap of the Kodak camera around her neck.

At that moment the monk, having noticed their absence, once more clapped his hands together and began to call out: 'Please-a! Please-a! *Signorine*! We move-a! We move-a!'

'We move-a,' the girl called Pat said, with a sigh. Again her sister giggled. Then the two of them hurried off.

Later, Jack saw them outside the convent. 'Excuse me!' the girl with the camera called to him. 'Would you awfully mind . . .?' She held out the camera.

Jack snapped the girls twice and then, on an impulse, took his Box Brownie out of his rucksack. 'Let me photograph you with this.'

The girls posed stiffly, eyes screwed up against the autumn sun and arms held rigid to their sides. As he lowered his head and peered into the view-finder, Jack thought how attractive they looked, in their simple cotton dresses, their legs and arms bare and their thick blond hair dishevelled.

The girls then took more photographs, making Jack pose first with one of them and then with the other.

'Give us your address. When we've had the snaps developed and printed, we can send you copies.'

Jack tore a page out of the notebook which he always carried in his rucksack, jotting down in it notes on what he had seen or, more often, had read. He wrote down his address, in the handwriting – strong, large, clear – which Ivor had flatteringly told him was so expressive of his character. 'D'you live in Florence?' he asked as he handed the paper over.

'I do,' Pat said. 'I'm here as a nannie. To the Michelozzi

children.' She assumed, wrongly, that Jack had heard of the family — who had entertained Iris on more than one occasion. 'I've always had a thing about Italy, and becoming a nannie seemed to be the only way of getting there. Flora is my sister. She's just come out to stay for two weeks between jobs.'

Flora squealed: 'Look! Look! The bus is leaving! It's leaving!'

'Are you taking the bus?' Pat asked.

He shook his head. 'Walking.' Then, as the girls scampered off, waving to him, he thought: Why the hell did I say that?

Disconsolately he wandered into a building with 'Farmacia' emblazoned on its front in elaborate gold curlicues. It was not, as he had imagined, a shop for herbal remedies but for the Florentine version of Chartreuse, distilled by the monks and packaged as though it were scent. The party of tourists to which the two girls had belonged was crowded round the counter. One of them, a German, was trying to bargain with the monk in charge, holding up the fingers of his right hand as he reiterated 'Fünf, fünf, fünf'. In his left hand he clutched a bottle by its neck.

On an impulse, Jack picked up a far smaller bottle, with a label depicting a jolly, tonsured and sandalled monk peering into what appeared to be an outsize saucepan. He would buy it for Iris. Why not? He had asked her what she would be doing today and she had lied: 'Oh, I have all kinds of chores — darning stockings, washing my hair, writing letters.' The truth was that she was waiting to hear from Dale whether he would be free of Pippa or not. If he was, they planned to go to *Don Carlos* at the Teatro Verdi. Throughout the hike to the Certosa, Jack had been wishing that she were with him.

Having bought the bottle — he would now have to be extremely careful about what he spent until the end of the month — Jack put it in his rucksack and wandered out into the autumn sunlight. He would try to find another route back, he decided after consulting the map lent to him by Giles — 'You might as well keep it,' Giles had said. 'Fat chance I ever have of getting out of Florence!'

Soon Jack was lost. But he did not really care. It was such a beautiful autumn day, and it stretched ahead of him wholly ⸻ of any engagements or duties. Perched on the parapet of a ⸻king down and seeing the viscous slime which sealed ⸻er, he wondered if anyone still used it — he rummaged ⸻ck and got out the bottle of cheap Chianti, the stub of cheap salami ('I wouldn't even feed the cats on that,' he could hear Audrey say) and the loaf of coarse bread which he had bought at the local *spezieria*. Suddenly, as he now munched his extemporized sandwich and now gulped from the bottle, his spirits lifted. He felt happy. He felt glad to have left his family and friends and to have come to this alien place.

When he finally got up — for a long time, he had just sat on the parapet with the sun warm on his face and the wine warm within him — he reached down for his rucksack and then, slightly tipsy, swung it up on to his shoulder with more than usual violence. Its side hit the side of the parapet. There was an ominous crack. At first he thought that he had smashed the empty Chianti flask; but when he looked inside, he saw that what he had smashed was the bottle of 'Chartreuse'. Oh, hell, hell! The liquid had begun to soak both into the pullover and into the copy of the *Collected Poems* of Tennyson which he was carrying. He tipped out all the contents. Then, furious both at himself and at the inanimate malice of parapet and rucksack, he knelt to gather up the jagged fragments of the bottle and throw them, one by one, over his shoulder into the well. That contentment which he had experienced as he had sat, eyes shut, feeling the sun warm on his face and hearing the birds twittering around him, had been smashed as the bottle had been smashed.

He picked up the rucksack again, put his arms through its straps and trudged off up the hill ahead of him.

He was passing through an impoverished square on the outskirts of Florence — tall, grey houses shut in its flagstoned rectangle from all but a patch of sunlight — when suddenly, with amazement, he saw Giles and Violetta. Hadn't Giles said that he had to put in a day of work at the Institute? Why was he here, sitting out on a lichen-covered stone bench in front of a disused fountain? Why was Violetta beside him? And why was his arm around her shoulders? They were talking together; then Violetta's laugh rang out, over the empty basin in which the fountain, a stone boy holding a stone dolphin, stood. Jack had never heard her laugh like that. In fact, come to think of it, he had rarely heard her laugh at all. The laugh was full of youth and joy.

Jack knew that they must not see him; and he also knew that he must pretend that he had not seen them. He changed course, walked up an alley at the corner of the square, passed under an arch (even here he could still hear Violetta laughing), passed under another arch, and so effected a detour.

It was only a few days later that he knew that Margot had made the same discovery as himself.

He had returned from work with a message from Miss Sweeney for Giles: her older sister was ill, tomorrow she would not be able to take her classes. Having deposited the rucksack containing text-books and exercise books — 'You know, dear boy, you really should buy yourself a brief-case,' Mervyn had told him reprovingly on one occasion, when they had run into each other — he walked down the corridor towards the sitting-room. Its door was half open. He heard the raised voices.

'Why the hell should she *invent* a story like that? What would be the point?'

'Malice.'

'Oh, come off it! She *saw* you! God knows there are enough malicious people in Florence, but she's not one of them.'

'Isn't she? That shows how little you know her.'

Jack retreated. He had no wish to be involved. But who was this 'she'? Miss Sweeney? Ethel? Or could it be Iris? No, certainly not her.

That evening, as the three of them sat eating their dinner, Jack was oppressed by the misery and anger which Giles and Margot both exuded. A black ligature seemed to have been wound, tighter and tighter, around Margot, making of her a hard ball of resentment. Contrariwise, in the case of Giles everything that had once held him together seemed to have been loosened, so that there was something disconcertingly amorphous and nerveless about him. From time to time they spoke to Jack, or to Maria as she entered and left the room; but they rarely spoke to each other and then only in clipped sentences, never meeting each other's gaze.

Later, there was a knock on Jack's door and Margot was there. Her eyes were red, clearly from weeping. Oh, God, had she come to ask him if he knew anything about Giles's infidelity? But she merely said: 'I meant to ask you to try to be sure to turn off lights. You left the light on in the bathroom yesterday evening and in this room this morning.'

'Oh, I'm sorry.'

It was as though the burden of her desire to complain about something, anything, about wasted electricity if not about her wasted love for this husband who – in a situation classically banal – was having an affair with his secretary, had proved too much for her.

'I hope you don't mind my mentioning it. But things do run up.'

'No. Not at all.'

She edged further into the room, as though she wished to question him or confide in him. Then she backed out.

Two mornings later Jack's attention was caught by the children, Piers and Prunella, in the garden. It was yet another saint's day, and they had a holiday from school. Margot and Giles had both left for work, and Jack, who had no first period on Tuesdays, would soon himself be leaving. Maria, who was childlike in the enthusiasm with which she would take up some activity and then, bored, would abandon it, was making pasta in the kitchen, rolling it out on a marble slab, and then, her thick, black hair screening her face as she stooped above it, cutting it into strips with a long, sharp knife.

What drew Jack's attention to the children was the tinkling of a bell. He got up from his bed, on the edge of which he had been sitting, reading 'Maud', and walked over to the window. What were they doing?

Prunella and Piers were both wearing black dresses belonging to their mother, hitched up at the waists so that they would not trip over them. Piers was carrying a brass vase, around the neck of which he had tied a length of string. He was swinging it back and forth. Prunella was holding the brass bell which her mother used in the dining-room to summon Maria. From time to time she gave it an energetic shake. Both of them were chanting in unnaturally deep voices, frequently splintering into reediness. At the far end of the garden, where it abutted on to Audrey's, they seemed to have dug a shallow trench. Beside it was the box in which Piers's xylophone had been packed on that occasion when it had tumbled, with so much else, out of the high cupboard in Jack's room. Suddenly it came to Jack: they were miming a Roman mass, such as they must have witnessed with their parents, with the brass bowl doing service for thurifer and the dinner-bell for the bell in the hand of the acolyte.

Suddenly Maria, who must also have been watching them, erupted through the door from the kitchen to the garden. *'Non, non! Cattivi! Basta!'* Her voice was shrill in its anger. She grabbed Prunella by an arm and jerked her towards her, as though she were a doll. Piers ran off around the house, laughing hysterically. Maria pulled Prunella into the house. Presumably the Italian girl had been outraged by this parody of a rite sacred to her.

Silence and stillness followed. Maria went on absorbedly making her pasta; the children must be playing some other game in their own room. Jack walked out into the garden.

The box lay beside the newly dug trench, in which a single worm was wriggling among some crushed blades of grass. Jack stared down at the box. On its lid either Piers or Prunella had written in a childish hand 'DADDY' and then, under that, 'R.I.P.'

Had some murderous impulse in their mother – die, die, die for your treachery – transmitted itself to them? Or was this funeral no more than a macabre game? Jack kicked at the box. Then he was stamping on it, until it was flattened under his shoe. But, as he prepared to turn away, he could still read that ominous 'DADDY, R.I.P.'

Jack was returning from a long walk in the Cascine, where he had found, at its far end, the memorial to the young maharajah who, in the early years of the century, had died of the tuberculosis which he had hoped against all hope that the air of Italy would cure. The thought of this youth, facing his doom – in resignation? despair? terror? – in a land wholly alien to him, had depressed Jack. Now he must return to the Institute, to take one of the late evening classes designed for office workers and shop assistants, which he found so unrewarding.

As he was walking down a long avenue of trees, now almost wholly bare, he heard a female voice calling: 'Hey! Hey there! Mr Prentice!'

He stopped; turned; looked to see who it was. Then he saw the two girls whom he had met at the Certosa. They were at either end of a rectangle of grass, each holding a tennis-racket. He walked over.

'We found some courts, but we weren't allowed to play there because it's a club,' Pat told him.

'You're not a member are you?' Flora asked.

'Heavens, no!'

'But you play tennis?'

'I *can* play. A bit.'

Flora proffered her racket. 'Then play for a little with Pat. I'm worn out.' Her wide forehead was glistening with sweat. 'Autumn in Florence is as hot as midsummer in England.'

'Have you really had enough?'

'Really and truly.'

He took off his jacket and draped it over the arm of a tree. 'Keep an eye on that for me,' he told Flora. 'It has a wallet in it, and the wallet contains all my worldly wealth.'

Flora leaned against the tree, her arm along the coat. 'I'll guard it with my life. Unless I decide to make a bunk with the wallet myself.'

Energetically, Jack and Pat raced back and forth, slamming or lobbing at each other. Since the grass stuck up in tufts, the bounce of the ball was often erratic; and since there was no enclosure, one or other of them would often have to go off in search of it in the surrounding bushes or undergrowth. At some particularly successful shot, Flora would clap and shout out: 'Well played! Well played!'

Suddenly, prompted by the sun now shining in his face, Jack looked at his watch. Gosh! He would be late. 'Sorry! I must get back to a class.' For a moment, he was tempted merely to give the class a miss. But if he did so he would be in disgrace, as Tim had been the previous week, arriving back in Florence a day late with an inadequate excuse after 'a weekend of shagging' (as he had confided in Jack) in Naples. He might even be sacked — a fate which Tim had only narrowly avoided.

'A class! At this hour?'

"Fraid so. You see how hard they work me."

He handed the racket to Flora and pulled on his jacket. Then he took a handkerchief out of his trouser pocket and mopped at his face.

'Let's have a real game some time,' Pat said.

'Yes, let's. There must be some courts we can hire. You've still got my address?'

'Of course,' Pat said.

'You never sent me those snaps.'

'They're still waiting to be developed. We haven't finished the roll.'

'Well, hurry up and finish it. I want to see them. Anyway – I must fly!'

Waving, he ran off from them, down the long avenue of trees.

Bare arms raised to shield their eyes from the setting sun, they watched him until he had vanished from sight.

That evening, between classes, Mr Greville sniffed, took out a handkerchief and blew his nose, and then sniffed again. He turned to Tim: 'Do you smell something peculiar in here?'

'Nothing more peculiar than usual. There's always a musty smell. And often a smell of garlic,' he added, since Mr Greville believed in eating large quantities of garlic not for its taste but for his health.

Mr Greville sniffed again. Then he looked at Jack, who had been too much absorbed in mugging up his next lesson in Business English to have heard him.

What Mr Greville was sniffing was the healthy smell of sweat.

15

'Is everything all right, *babbo*?' Franco asked in Italian. In a knitted woollen cardigan, jettisoned by Harry when he had discovered that moth had fretted the sleeve, a striped red-and-blue scarf, one end thrown over a shoulder so that it dangled down his back, and a full checked cap, he was about to go down into Florence on his Vespa.

'Oh, I think so, I think so. Yes, I think that, by and large, one could that, um, everything's all right.' So weak now that there were many days when he got out of bed only to stagger, supported by Franco or, if alone, hand groping wall, down the stone corridor to the lavatory, Harry forced a smile. He wished the boy would not call him *babbo* — Daddy. It was so unsuitable and, well, silly. They were not related, not in the least. What might people think? Someone might jump to the conclusion that his relationship with the boy was similar to that of Felix Luce to so many of the people employed in his villa or on his estate.

The boy put a rough hand to Harry's forehead, to see if he still had a fever. Frowning, he shook his head. The forehead felt hot. Then, smiling at the old man, he ran the back of the hand down his grey, shrunken cheek. 'Get well, *babbo*,' he said, though he knew that the injunction was pointless. Only two days ago Signorina Heaton had told him: 'I'm afraid we've just got to prepare ourselves for the worst.'

Harry wished that the boy wouldn't touch him like that. He'd never liked being touched, and the way in which Italians constantly squeezed one's arm or one's knee, threw an arm round one or grabbed one's hand was the thing about them which, above all, got on his wick.

'Have you got some money?'

'Don't worry, *babbo*.'

'But it's a long, long time since I gave you any.'

'I sold that box. Remember? To an American tourist outside the Bargello. It was a picture of the Bargello, so that's why I took it there.'

'Clever boy!' The old man smiled up at the boy and quickly, mischievously the boy grinned down at him, exposing the gap where, in some fight — why was he always fighting? — he had lost a front tooth. 'Soon I'll have finished this one for you.' Harry put out a trembling hand to point to the half-painted box on the bedside table. 'Just as soon as I feel a little stronger.'

Harry listened to the din, first strengthening and then diminishing in volume, as the boy took off on his Vespa. Vespa meant wasp. It was — he smiled to himself at the recollection — his nickname for Renée because she could be so, well, waspish on occasions, frightening away so many of their friends during those last dissatisfied and finally despairing years when arthritis had prevented her from working in her beloved garden or even walking more than a few steps. Vespa was an appropriate name for that beastly machine. Its noise suggested the buzz, a thousand times amplified, of some persistent wasp trapped against a window-pane. Italian men loved that noise, as they loved all noise. Audrey said that Franco, in common with almost every other owner of a Vespa, had deliberately removed the silencer from his as soon as he had bought it. That way, he could, in effect, proudly announce to every pedestrian and motorist: 'Here I am! I'm coming! Can't you hear me?' He would be baffled by Ivor's pride in the almost total silence of the engine of his Rolls.

Harry leaned across the bed and picked up the box. Then he put it down again. Tomorrow. He felt too tired today. He really only wanted to slide back into that confused state, half awake and half sleeping, in which it was as if suddenly some helicopter were dizzily carrying him back over the long, slow, serpentine river of his life, to gaze down with a mixture of pleasure, bewilderment and awe. There was Willie, Willie Maugham, by the pool of the Villa Mauresque, pointing down at Cyril Connolly (how could he have done such a thing in the presence of poor Renée?) and stammering: 'You know — you m-m-might have m-m-more sexual success if you c-c-consented to have that t-t-tiny appendage c-c-cut off.' There was that boorish Lawrence man, coughing into a handkerchief at a café table in the Piazza Repubblica and then surreptitiously peering into it to see if he had brought up any blood. There was dear Janet Ross, in one of her towering headdresses, all feathers and flowers and trailing ribbons, recounting gleefully how she and Ouida had had a public slanging match from their carriages in the Via Tornabuoni over the Italian nobleman whom each of them had loved, until Reginald Turner had interrupted her: 'Why not challenge her to a duel with hatpins?'But everything was so confused, people, times, places, so that perhaps it might have been Raymond Mortimer and not Cyril Connolly to whom Willie had made that remark; and perhaps it was in the Piazza della Signoria that that Lawrence creature had examined his blood-streaked sputum; and perhaps that slanging match had really occurred between Violet Trefusis and . . . It was as though that helicopter were now whirling him round and round in a glittering cloud of dust, so that only occasionally, here and there, he could make out who it was and where it was and when it was.

At that Harry fully dropped off, his sharp chin transfixing his narrow chest, an arm dangling over the bedside, and his mouth half open.

'Mr Archer! Mr Archer!'

He stirred; opened his eyes; raised a hand to wipe off the thread of saliva that he felt, a sticky cobweb, on one of his burning cheeks. It was that girl, that Crediton girl, whose grandmother, so many years ago now, had inspired him to paint the only really decent painting (yes, one had to face it) he had ever painted.

'Hello, my dear. Hello!' He sat up, tugging at his rumpled sheet.

She stooped over him, so that he could smell her scent and could feel a tendril of her hair brushing his forehead. She righted the sheet with a competent hand. He found himself wishing that, like Franco, she would put that hand first to his forehead and then, turning it over, run its back up his cheek in a caress.

'I met Franco in the lane. On that awful Vespa of his. He was going so fast, he all but ran me over. He told me not to ring but just to walk in. Was that all right?'

'Of course, my dear. Of course. You're always welcome here. Always.'

'This is one of those afternoons when I don't have a class until five. I thought perhaps I could do something for you. Some shopping?'

'Franco's gone off to do that. I'm sure he always charges me more than he spends – that's why he insists on going down to the market where everything is so much cheaper. His mother used to do that too. Brought me back wilted lettuces and butter that was rancid.' He laughed, and the laugh then became a cough. 'That's the Italian way. Somehow you lose your self-respect unless you manage to cheat anyone who employs you. With us, it's the other way around.'

'Oh, I don't think Franco . . . He seems so devoted to you.' But Iris did not really believe that. The boy, with that impudent smile of his, had always struck her as a hardened little crook, exploiting the dying old man who had done so much for him after the death of both his parents.

'Cupboard devotion, my dear. The devotion of those cats of Audrey's, all the time clamouring to be fed and then, when they *have* been fed, stealing what they can off the table. Franco's an alley cat, let's face it.'

Iris found a terrible sadness in his cynicism, even though, in this case at least, she shared it.

'Would you like me to make you some tea? I gather that the doctor told you to take as much liquid as you could.'

'It's too late now to do what the doctor tells me. But make yourself a cup by all means.'

'I've just had some tea. I was at the Conquests, talking to Margot.'

Over the cups of tea in the kitchen, Margot had spoken of Giles and Violetta. ('Oh, I know it's disloyal to speak of all this to you. But how could he, how *could* he? What does he see in her? That's what I ask myself. She's not in the least attractive or even sexy. She's not all that intelligent. All she is is a good secretary. Surely that's not enough.') Her eyes had filled with tears, which she had angrily wiped away with the back of a hand. ('Maria and the children will be back at any moment now. I mustn't let them see me like this. That's the most awful part – pretending to the children that nothing is wrong.') Then she had reached out and taken another slice of chocolate cake. ('Food becomes a drug. Look how I'm putting on weight.')

'But let me make you a cup,' Iris now offered. 'Please.'

'Oh, all right.' He was grudging, ungracious.

The kitchen was in a hideous mess, with unwashed plates piled in the cold-water sink and even on the floor, a washing-up cloth draped over a coal-scuttle, and the butter-dish left out on the table, with a cockroach scuttling away from under it as she approached. Should she attempt to put things in order? Would that annoy him? Would that annoy Franco? Half-heartedly, as she waited for the kettle to boil on the primus stove, she set about putting the butter away in the larder, sweeping up breadcrumbs from the table, even washing one or two of the plates.

'There we are!'

Harry peered at the tray. 'Oh, my dear! Those are breakfast cups!'

'Sorry. It doesn't matter, does it?'

'It doesn't matter to *me*. I was thinking of you.'

'It doesn't matter to me either.'

'Well, that's all right then.'

'As it comes?'

'As it comes. I've reached an age when one has to take everything as it comes.' His resigned bitterness was like an unpleasant taste in Iris's mouth.

Then, suddenly, as he now sat propped up on the pillows which she had laboriously stacked behind him, he was the Harry who had charmed her grandmother and her mother. He asked her about the Institute; he teased her about what he called Mervyn's 'crush' on her; he paid her some delicate compliments and then peered up at her, from under wrinkled, hooded lids, to see how she took them. She was glad that she had forced herself to come, instead of going for a walk in the late autumn sunlight as she had been tempted to do.

'Anyone at home? Anyone at home?'

How could Audrey suppose that there would not be anyone at home? She knew that he now never ventured out.

Iris went to the door of the bedroom. Behind Audrey, at the far end of the passage, was a tall, robust woman in a shako-like hat and a long, heavily frogged navy-blue coat reaching almost to her ankles. But for the dainty feet and the absence of trousers, one might have mistaken her for a guardsman.

'Oh, Iris, *you're* here!' Audrey was taken aback to find that she had been forestalled in her errand of mercy. 'Eva and I were on our way back from San Miniato – she particularly wanted to view the Michelozzo Tabernacle – and so I thought I'd just drop in to see how Harry was faring. You know Eva, don't you? Eva Seebohm. . . . Eva, this is Iris Crediton – a recent and highly valued addition to our sadly diminishing colony.' As the woman in the military-style greatcoat extended a hand to give Iris's an emphatic shake, something said by someone at some time – was it Margot or Mervyn or Ivor? – returned to her: '*Sufficient unto the day is the Eva thereof.*' But this Eva, with her open smile and her direct gaze, seemed in no way to deserve such a comment.

Eva stooped over to greet Harry. Clearly they had met before.

'Do get two more cups, my dear. But not, dear, not breakfast ones this time.'

'Oh, but we don't need any tea. And if we did, breakfast cups wouldn't upset us. Would they, Eva?'

'Goodness, no!' Eva's accent was New York.

Iris hurried off to the kitchen, where eventually, having rummaged in a number of cupboards, she found two delicate porcelain teacups full of dust. Having washed and dried them, she carried them in.

'Oh, look what the dear girl's brought. The Crown Derby! Oh, well, never mind. Why not? It *is* an occasion to have you and Eva here – even if it's only for some stewed Indian tea.'

'Did I make it too strong?' Iris asked.

He smiled roguishly up at her. 'Well, let's say you have a generous nature.'

Soon Audrey was talking, in a proudly proprietorial way, about what Eva was doing in Florence. Originally she had planned to write a biography of the painter Romaine Brooks; but then she had extended that idea to the writing of a book about what Audrey called 'our whole little circle'. It was a pity that Hardy had already used the title *A Group of Noble Dames*. That would have been just perfect for the book. (Was she joking or in earnest, Iris wondered.) Johnny had been the presiding spirit of the little circle, Audrey went on to explain – 'It was she who held us all together.' Back in the villa, there were piles and piles of letters and diaries and photographs, a real treasure-trove. Eva was now working through them. 'Of course I give her all the help I can. I'm glad to do that. As a memorial to Johnny. But that does mean that I'm not getting on with my own little book. I have that nice boy to help me, the one from the Institute, but without direction he tends to get lost. How could it be otherwise? It's a world totally strange to him. Now if I were writing a book about Landor or Clough or the Brownings, it would be another matter!'

'I like that boy,' Eva said.

'We all like him,' Audrey confirmed. 'Particularly Ivor,' she added.

Eva gave a throaty laugh. 'I'm not in Ivor's good books at present,' she said. 'I'm not quite sure why. Perhaps I should have been more attentive to him when he visited New York last winter.'

'Ivor likes attention. He needs it,' Harry croaked. He held out his cup, his hand trembling so much that there was a rattle of china on china. 'A drop more, my dear. But please — a lot of hot water with it.'

'Oh, don't go on bullying the poor girl for having made the tea stronger than you would have liked. I *like* strong tea.' Eva flashed Iris a smile.

Eventually Franco's Vespa could be heard buzzing up the drive. Audrey put hands to her ears. 'Oh, that noise! How can you bear it? In fact, how can you bear that boy?'

'Oh, he's all right,' Harry said. 'He's not a bad soul.'

'Where did he get the money to buy a Vespa? That's what I ask myself. They're far from cheap.'

Harry shrugged.

'I expect that, without knowing it, *you* paid for it.'

There was a knock at the door.

'*Avanti!*' Harry called.

Franco entered; saw the three women; bowed to them in mock deference before asking Harry: '*Tutto va bene, babbo?*'

'*Grazie, Franco. Tutto va bene.*' That '*babbo*' again! It was embarrassing even in front of a friend as old as Audrey.

'What does "*babbo*" mean?' Eva asked, when Franco had quit the room.

'It means "Daddy",' Audrey said. 'Isn't it ridiculous?'

'I think it's rather sweet. It shows that he must be fond of you.'

'Cupboard fondness,' Harry said.

'No, I think he's genuinely fond of you,' Iris said. Something about Franco's expression, gentle and pensive, as he had looked across at Harry, had suddenly convinced her.

'It's easy to see that you're a newcomer to Florence,' Audrey said. 'And young.' She leaned forward across the bed. 'Eva's been such an angel, Harry. You wouldn't believe. When she heard about all the money owed to me — by the *TLS*, by *Time and Tide*, by those rogue publishers — she at once insisted on advancing me some.'

Eva, who did not share Audrey's robust attitude to the discussion of money, turned her head away in embarrassment. Then she muttered, as though excusing herself for some misconduct: 'Well, I had this little windfall. I played the market and, for once, it turned out well.'

'You're lucky to have something to play with,' Harry said. 'Money! Money! Money! When one was young, one never thought about it. Now one thinks of little else.'

Was he short of money, Iris wondered. Should she – could she – offer him a loan or even make him a gift out of her lavish allowance?

'Franco's young, and he certainly thinks of money,' Audrey said. 'How you love to generalize, Harry!'

'Always did,' Harry agreed.

When Harry's eyelids first fluttered and then closed with weariness, the three women decided to leave him. Outside, Eva offered Iris a lift in the sports car lent to her by the son of the American consul.

'I think I'd like a walk.'

'But you said you were going to the Institute. That's a long way from here, isn't it?'

'Not all that far.' She looked at her watch. 'I have more than half an hour until my next class.'

'Well, as you wish.' Suddenly Eva sounded huffy.

As Iris hurried down the drive – perhaps, after all, she ought to have accepted that lift – she heard a crunch of gravel behind her. It was Franco. '*Signorina! Signorina!*' he called. In one hand he was holding a bunch of chrysanthemums, wrapped in some yellowing pages of *The Times*. He drew abreast of her, panting. Then he held out the bunch. '*Per lei.*'

She hesitated. Perhaps, unknown to Harry, he had picked them from the garden. Perhaps some other visitor had brought them for the invalid. It would be a nuisance to carry them all the way to the Institute and then to transport them on to the *pensione* after her class was over.

'*Grazie,*' she said. '*Grazie mille. Sone belle.*'

He gave an impudent, knowing smile. '*La signorina è bella.*' Then he scampered back up to the house.

It was a single cry, shrill and prolonged.

It aroused Iris, half-asleep over an out-of-date copy of *Vogue*

128

given to her by Isabella Lambeni. ('How can you bother with anything so trivial?' Dale had demanded. 'For God's sake, Iris, you have a *brain*.') Suddenly alert, she sat up in her chair, mouth open and brows knit.

The cry appeared to have come from Ethel's room to the left of her. Was Ethel all right? When they had returned together from the Institute, too uneasy with each other and too tired, as so often, to have much conversation, Ethel had sighed: 'Now I have three private lessons before dinner,' and Iris had reacted: 'Oh, Ethel, how you do work! I feel so lazy. I haven't a single private pupil.' Ethel had given a grim smile: 'I shouldn't have a single private pupil either, unless I needed the money.'

Iris got up and crossed to the intervening wall. She pressed her ear to it. She could just hear two voices, one of them Ethel's and the other a man's. They were talking in Italian, but what it was that they were saying it was impossible to distinguish.

Iris decided that that cry, expressive of hunger and satiety, pain and pleasure, defeat and conquest, must have come from somewhere out in the street. Unless, of course, half-awake and half-asleep, she had dreamed it.

The cry was of a kind that she had never before heard in her life.

She returned to her copy of *Vogue*.

~∞~

'Well, now, my dear, I'm going to leave you.'

Like a dry leaf twitched by a capricious wind, Ivor would often abandon Jack in this fashion. There would be no forewarning; there would be no excuse. It was as if suddenly he had decided that he had had enough either of Jack's company or of any company at all. Once, as the taxi in which they were travelling had stopped in a traffic jam (Felix had gone off in the Rolls on a visit to Percy Lubbock in Lerici), Ivor had pushed at Jack a bundle of notes, far too many for the fare, had muttered 'I'll have to get out here, I'm afraid,' and with surprising agility had leapt out and, without a backward glance, had hurried off down an alley so slummy that it was unlikely that that was his true destination.

Now, outside Doney, Ivor had once more precipitately vanished: this time into a haberdasher's. Jack stared through the window at a display, old-fashioned in its dusty symmetry, of buttons, buckles, elastics and ribbons. What on earth could Ivor be buying in such a shop? He was almost tempted to go in and see. Then he heard a voice behind him: 'Signore Jack! Good evening. Hello.'

It was little Giuseppe Valeriano, who had presumably just concluded the second of his two daily visits to Doney. Although it was not raining, he was carrying, hooked over one arm, a black silk umbrella, perfectly rolled. It looked far too large for someone of his stature.

'Oh, hello, Signore Valeriano.' Although Giuseppe had more than once urged Jack to call him by his Christian name, Jack had never been able to bring himself to do so. He was too conscious both of a social and of an age difference, even though he knew nothing of Giuseppe's background and even though there were few more than a dozen years between them.

'You will come and have a drink with me? My Contessa does not come this evening, so I am a little *giu*. Sometimes she comes, sometimes she does not come. Always I wait.' He smiled. '*Sempre fedele*.' When Giuseppe talked of 'his' Contessa, there was no need to enquire which Contessa he meant.

Was it possible, Jack had once wondered aloud, that Giuseppe and Isabella Lambeni were lovers? Iris had laughed in scorn. 'Lovers! Don't be silly. You've only got to look at that sad little misshapen body.' Dale had been less dismissive of the notion: 'She's so generally perverse that she might also be perverse about that.' 'But if they were lovers, they'd hardly keep meeting publicly in the smartest café in Florence. Now would they?' Iris had countered. Dale had shrugged: 'Probably not.' Such arguments about the precise nature of the relationship between the ill-assorted couple were already common at the time. They were to become even more common in the future.

Jack hated it that Giuseppe invariably insisted on treating him, charging anything which either of them consumed to his account. Not even Ivor had an account at Doney. Could it be that it was eventually Isabella who settled this account? Or was Giuseppe's inability or unwillingness ever to produce cash, even for a simple espresso or a grappa, a sign of wealth even greater than hers?

'Oh, do let me pay this time!'

'No, no. You are a guest in Italy!'

'Well, don't imagine that, when you're a guest in England, people will pay for you there!'

'English people are very *ospitale* and generous.'

'English people in Florence, perhaps.'

'You are too cynical for someone so young.' But Giuseppe did not really think that. What he most liked about Jack was what most people liked about him: his simplicity, eagerness and innocence.

Jack was carrying with him Laurence Binyon's translation of *Il Purgatorio*. Borrowed from the Institute Library, it had in it the bookplate of its original owner.

Opening it, Giuseppe exclaimed: 'This book once belonged to Reggie Turner!'

Unable to understand his excitement, Jack asked: 'And who was he?'

'You don't know who was Reggie Turner? He was one of the

great *personaggi* of Florence. An *intimo* of Oscar Wilde. So kind, so amusing. Unsuccessful as novelist, totally unsuccessful. But successful, always successful, as a friend.' Giuseppe went on to tell a story of Reginald Turner and 'dear Willie Maugham'. Maugham had been boasting about the sums which first editions of his books were fetching. Turner had then retorted: 'My most valuable editions are my second ones. They just cannot be found.'

From there he had gone on to speak, in his voluble, faulty English, first about Dante and then about the Black Death. Did Jack know that it was estimated that from half to two thirds of the population of Florence had died in the Black Death? It was not fanciful, he went on, to attribute to it, so universal in its horror, even more than to such figures as Dante or Petrarca, the dawning of the Renaissance. People subjected to so much suffering could not believe that God was exacting punishment for their transgressions. If that were the case, why should the just and unjust die in equal agony? And why was it that God's anointed servants, whether saintly monks or mighty prelates, should not be immune?

So far from fretting at such lectures, Jack was enthralled. It was above all for this rapt attention that Giuseppe, a compulsive talker, valued Jack so much.

Eventually they wandered out into the street. Jack realized that if he did not hurry he would miss dinner. Should he telephone? Margot had more than once ticked him off for not notifying her in advance when he would be out to a meal – 'You really can't expect us to hang around waiting for you, when you've no intention of turning up. In any case, it's wicked to waste food in a world when so many people are starving.' Yes, he'd better telephone. But as, undammed, Giuseppe's eloquence flooded over him, he kept postponing the call.

Giuseppe was now comparing St Francis and St Dominic, founders of the great religious orders of the Franciscans and the Dominicans. To Dante, the Spanish Dominic was *l'amoroso druido della fede cristiana* – 'the passionate lover of the faith of Christ'. He was dedicated to holding Christians by force and even torture, if need be, to the strictest orthodoxy. Francis, on the other hand, regarded belief as the consequence of a personal search for God, preached love towards all creatures, and abjured all worldly pomp and power.

They were now passing the Ospedale degli Innocenti, with Giuseppe still pouring out information and comments. He gestured at the della Robbia medallions, turned and began to say something about Brunelleschi, and then, looking over his shoulder, plunged off the pavement to point out a detail of the stone-work with the ferrule of his umbrella. As though he had suddenly taken flight, like one of those saints who, at totally unexpected moments, soared off the ground to circle their earthbound brethren, Jack saw him rise up in the air, umbrella in hand; and at what seemed precisely the same moment, he heard a screech of brakes and a thunderclap of impact, and smelled burning rubber. As he rushed forward to the misshapen little body of Giuseppe, lying sprawled in the gutter, the now broken umbrella equally misshapen beside him, two people jumped out of a Rolls-Royce. One was Adrian, whom Jack had never met but whom Iris had once pointed out to him in the street; the other was Adrian's manservant and lover Luigi, a handsome young Italian, with sleek black hair and thick eyebrows meeting in the middle of his forehead.

'Oh, hell!' Adrian said, stooping over Giuseppe. 'It was his fault, his fault.'

Jack, kneeling now, put out a hand to touch the sleeve nearest to him. 'Giuseppe! Giuseppe!' It was the first time that he had ever called him that; now it came quite naturally. 'Are you all right?'

Giuseppe opened his eyes. He tried to sit up. '*La mia colpa,*' he gasped. He pulled a face, a hand clutching at a shoulder.

'Well, of course it was his *colpa*. I'm glad he realizes that,' Adrian said. 'You saw that it was his fault, didn't you?'

Jack did not answer. 'Are you all right, Giuseppe?'

'*Penso di si.* Yes. Yes.' Again he clutched his shoulder and again he pulled a face. 'Pain,' he said.

'I wasn't driving,' Adrian said, as though not merely to Jack and Giuseppe but also to the crowd, simultaneously horrified and exalted by its horror, which had gathered around them. 'But anyway it wasn't my driver's fault. This chap just walked out into the road, just walked out like that. Crazy!'

Jack helped Giuseppe to get to his feet. The Italian shifted his weight on to one leg, grimaced and then shifted it on to the other. Jack put an arm round him, feeling the crooked body like that of some wounded bird against his own.

Adrian turned to the young Italian. 'You'd better take him to the hospital, Luigi,' he said. 'Make sure that all's well. Get them to X-ray him, if they think it's necessary.' He pulled out his wallet, extracted some notes, and then, having carefully counted them, handed them over. 'Use this. Let me have receipts for anything you have to spend.' He turned to Jack. 'I'm sorry I can't come with you, but a friend of mind is waiting for me. I have to take her to the opera. She'd kill me if I made her miss Stignani.'

Back at the wheel of the Rolls, Luigi looked sulky. He had been planning to drop off Adrian and Adriana at the Teatro Verdi and then to visit an American student girlfriend, a newcomer at the Pensione Dante, of whose existence Adrian knew nothing. Tapping on the steering-wheel whenever they were stuck in a jam or at traffic lights, he hummed 'Voi che sapete . . .' A love of opera was what had first brought him and Adrian together. There had been a scene between them that morning when he had learned that it was Adriana and not he who was to have the second ticket for Stignani in *Aida*.

Giuseppe closed his eyes, so that for a panicky moment Jack thought he had fainted. Then he began to wheeze with laughter. '*Mamma mia*! I could have died! I am lucky, Jack, I am lucky! I have – what do you say? – the luck of the devil.'

He did indeed have the luck of the devil. There were bruises and abrasions, but that was the sum of his injuries.

'Now we'll see you home,' Jack said.

'No, no, I will take a taxi! Please!'

There was a long argument; then, at last, Giuseppe consented to get back into the Rolls and to give his address to Luigi. Luigi scowled and, with obvious disgust, repeated the address. Then, when Giuseppe had confirmed it, he shrugged his shoulders.

As the Rolls moved off, Giuseppe smiled wanly at Jack. 'Thank you, Jack. You are very kind. A good friend. Maybe' – now he laughed outright – 'I will write a poem about you, or for you. To express my *gratitudine*.' Again he closed his eyes. His frown of concentration suggested that he might, even at that moment, have embarked on the poem.

As they travelled eastward, the street-lighting grew dimmer and more sporadic, and the houses meaner. Jack leaned forward to say to Luigi: 'I'm sorry to take up your time like this.'

There was no answer. Perhaps he had not understood? But he had appeared to understand Adrian perfectly well when he had spoken to him in English.

Jack tried again: 'We're probably making you late for something else?'

'*Si.*' The monosyllable was chilling.

'I'm sorry.'

No answer again.

Eventually Luigi appeared to be lost. He drove to the corner of a square – could it be the square in which Giles and Violetta had been seated before the disused fountain? – peered up one street and then peered up another, and finally turned the car around. His voice conveyed a weary irritation as he asked Giuseppe for directions. Giuseppe leaned forward with a wince, pointed and pointed again.

Eventually they drew up before a tall, narrow house, its ochre-coloured stucco fissured with cracks. Luigi did not alight from the Rolls, merely watching with barely restrained impatience as Jack helped Giuseppe out.

'*Grazie,*' Giuseppe said to him, with a parody of a salute, hand to forehead.

'Thank you so much,' Jack said.

Luigi, eyes narrowed, did not answer. He engaged the gear-shift, the Rolls glided forward.

Giuseppe hobbled to the door and then pulled a key-ring out of the pocket of his overcoat. The coat, previously so elegant, was now both torn at a sleeve and streaked with dry mud. 'So,' he said. He smiled. 'I say you good-night.'

'No, no, I'm going to see you in.'

Once again, as when Giuseppe had resisted being driven home, an argument followed. Then Giuseppe shrugged: '*Va bene.*' He inserted the cumbrous key in the door. He groped for a light switch and pressed it. The walls of the narrow staircase were peeling, and here and there people had scrawled political slogans across them. In England, Jack thought, it would have been not political slogans but obscenities. Giuseppe put his hand to the newel post, and then shuffled on to the first step. He grimaced, gave a little groan.

Suddenly, on an impulse, Jack moved forward and swept him up in his arms, as though he were a child too tired to climb. 'No, no! Please!' Giuseppe protested. But Jack began racing up the staircase with him. 'Here?' he demanded at the first landing. 'Farther! Farther!' Giuseppe answered. Now both of them were laughing. Exhilarated, Jack raced up to the next landing, and again Giuseppe told him, 'Farther, farther!'

It was at the top of the house that Jack eventually put down his burden. Panting, he watched as Giuseppe took out another key and placed it in the keyhole. 'My kingdom,' Giuseppe said, turning the key and pushing the door open.

The kingdom was a narrow attic, its only illumination provided by a gigantic skylight. Giuseppe put his hand to the light switch. 'Cold,' he said. It was very cold.

The room contained a camp bed, two upright chairs, a table covered with papers, a cold-water sink, a small electric cooking stove, its wire snaking across the floor, and a wardrobe so large that it took up at least a quarter of the space.

Giuseppe fell across the bed. Jack stood, still panting, looking around him.

'You would like some coffee? No tea. Sorry.'

'What I'd really like is a drink. Have you got such a thing?'

'*Si, si!*' Giuseppe struggled up off the bed.

'Tell me where it is and I'll get it.'

Giuseppe pointed to a bottle of vermouth behind a pile of books. There were two glasses on the draining-board of the sink.

'You are the first visitor ever to come here.'

'I can't believe that.'

'I am telling you the truth.'

'But the Contessa — has she never been here?'

'The Contessa! How could I ask her here? Never, never!' Giuseppe was shocked. 'This is a bad house,' he added.

What did he mean? Did prostitutes live on the other floors? Jack was puzzled. 'How bad?'

Giuseppe shrugged.

As they were drinking the thick, bitter vermouth, Giuseppe suddenly staggered to his feet and pulled open first one and then the other door of the breakfront wardrobe. Inside were innumerable suits and shirts, marshalled on hangers. There was a tie-rack from which ties cascaded in a brilliant abundance. Jack rose to his feet and gazed at the exhibition. Then he put out a hand and felt between his fingers the softness and smoothness of one silk tie and then another. 'My wealth,' Giuseppe said gravely. 'All my wealth. Except for' — he indicated the table strewn with papers — 'except for my poetry.' He stepped forward, put out his hands, and gripped Jack by the forearms. 'I am happy,' he said. 'I am a happy man.'

Jack believed him.

The next morning breakfast was late. 'Maria overslept,' Margot said crossly, as she began to lay the table. She herself, as so often these mornings, was in her dressing-gown. At the Consulate there had been complaints about her habitual lateness. 'She's getting dressed.'

'She's certainly taking her time about it,' Giles grumbled. 'I *must* get to the Institute before eight-thirty. I have a class at nine-thirty and there's a report I must draft first.'

'Couldn't Violetta draft it for you? . . . Oh, Jack, instead of just standing there, perhaps you could put on the kettle.' Piers had wandered into the room. Margot now turned to shout at him: 'Do go back to your room. Go back at once! I told you to stay there until Maria fetched you.'

'But I'm hungry!'

'Do what I tell you.' She slammed down some plates. Then she said over her shoulder to Jack: 'You know, it was awfully inconsiderate of you yet again not to tell us that you wouldn't be home for dinner.'

'I was involved in an accident.'

'An accident? What kind of accident?'

Jack began to tell her. But she was not really interested, suddenly interrupting him to say: 'Would you get the milk from the larder?'

Maria eventually appeared. With a sorrowful languor she moved in and out of the dining-room, splashing the coffee out of its over-filled pot as she set it down, forgetting the butter, stretching across Jack with a toast-rack full of charred toast, so that he could smell that feral odour of hers which he always found so exciting.

'Poor girl,' Margot said, when she had dispatched Maria to see to the children. She now felt not irritation with her for her lateness but a solidarity with her in her misery. 'Apparently her wood-cutter has given her the brush-off. She was in tears last night.'

'Was that any reason to oversleep this morning?' Giles asked.

'Yes, I think it was.' Margot herself knew how each morning unhappiness could pinion one to one's bed, reluctant to face yet another day, and how each night sleep was wooed, often unsuccessfully, as the most efficacious of anodynes.

'And what made her woodcutter take this step?'

Margot shrugged. 'I suppose he got word . . . someone gossiped. No doubt just as the well-to-do gossip in Florence, so the poor gossip in her village.'

A half-eaten slice of toast still on his plate, Giles got up. He raised his coffee-cup and drained it. 'Well, I'll be on my way,' he said curtly. 'You'll follow later?' Sometimes he and Jack walked to the office together.

'Yes. I've nothing to do until nine-thirty.'

'Lucky man! How nice it would be to be young and heedless and without any responsibilities.'

After Giles had gone, Margot picked up her own coffee-cup and made for the door. 'Well, I suppose I'd better have my bath and get dressed. I'm going to be late.'

Maria entered and began to clear the table round Jack. He looked at her, but she would not return his gaze. There was a red crease down one side of her neck, where she must have twisted it in sleeping. Her unbrushed hair was thickly tangled. Her lower lip was caught between her teeth, as though to stop herself from crying.

He wanted to say something to her. He wanted to get up, go to her and comfort her. But he was frozen in his awkwardness and embarrassment, as she was frozen in her desolation.

17

～∞～

On that visit three things surprised Iris.

First, she had not expected that, situated in the palpitating heart of Florence, there would be this tranquil courtyard with its stiff, glossy evergreens in beige-coloured tubs, its central fountain and its stone benches. Secondly, she had not expected that the *palazzo* itself, once the home of a fourteenth-century banking family ruined when Edward III had defaulted on a loan, should have about it such an air of forlorn desuetude. Thirdly, she had not expected Pippa Lavery to appear as she did: small, squat, inelegant, her hair cut straight in a fringe, to provide a shiny, black frame — varnished, it looked — for a face masculine in the largeness of its features. Dale and others had so often spoken of her alcoholism, ascribing it now to an atrocious childhood, during which she was by turns bullied and indulged, neglected and pushed into prominence, by her widower father, a Greek millionaire from Smyrna, and now to a series of marriages and love-affairs which had invariably ended with her buying her freedom with a settlement grotesque in its generosity, that, as they entered the coolness of the courtyard from the unusual warmth of the street, Iris whispered: 'I feel nervous.'

'Nervous? What of?'

'Her.'

'She won't eat you. If you were alcohol, she might drink you. But you're not.'

'I don't understand why you want her to meet me.'

'I never said I did. *She* wants to meet you.'

'Why?'

'Why? Because she's heard so much about you.'

'From you?'

'Partly. But from other people too.'

At the far end of a terrace Pippa lay out full length on a rattan settee, cushions piled around her and strewn across the marble floor. A coil of wicker, like a broken spring, was attached to one of the legs of the settee, and she was winding another coil around a forefinger as they approached her. A long, misty glass stood on the floor beside her. She stretched down for it and gulped, then raised her eyes to submit Iris to a close, if abrupt, appraisal. Then she shook her head, the frame of thick hair swaying from side to side, as though she were vigorously denying something.

'Here she is at last,' Dale said. 'You wanted to meet her and now you are meeting her. Iris Crediton.'

'Hello.' Pippa smiled, revealing uneven, yellow teeth. Then, with a single, supple movement, she had jumped off the settee. She held out a hand which, slightly grubby with its nails bitten to the quick, might have been that of a schoolboy. 'I keep hearing about you. Everyone in Florence — with the exception of B.B. and myself — seems to have met you.'

'She was far more frightened of meeting you than she would be of meeting B.B.'

'Why should that be? I'm not at all frightening.' Pippa turned to Iris and flashed her a smile irresistible in its warmth and spontaneity. 'Am I?'

Iris shook her head.

'Actually it's I who ought to be frightened of you,' Pippa went on, raising her glass to her lips.

'Oh. Why?'

'Why? Well, it's obvious, isn't it? There's nothing more frightening than the rap-rap-rap of the younger generation knocking at the door.' She pointed to a chair with a peremptory gesture. 'Sit. Please,' she added, as though as an afterthought.

Iris sat.

'Is that chair very uncomfortable?'

'Not at all.'

'You look as if it were.'

'Let me get some drinks,' Dale said. He spoke as though he were as much host as Pippa was hostess. 'Pippa? Do you want that refreshed?'

Pippa held out a glass. 'The usual, darling.' She turned to Iris. 'The usual is ouzo. Have you ever had ouzo?' Iris shook her head. 'Greek,' Pippa explained. 'It looks just like water. So sometimes I pretend to people — and even to myself — that it's water I'm drinking. But then, without thinking, I put in an ice-cube and that at once gives the show away. Ouzo goes cloudy if you add any water to it. An interesting scientific fact. Why? I've no idea at all.'

After Dale had disappeared to get the drinks – 'Oh, do let Ettore get them!' Pippa had protested but he had paid her no attention – the two women sat in an uneasy silence, Pippa once again wrapping the coil of wicker round her forefinger and Iris staring out over the rooftops of Florence. Then Pippa said abruptly: 'You're good friends.'

Startled, Iris gazed at her in interrogation.

'I don't mean you and Mervyn,' Pippa said drily. 'You and my Dale.'

The possessive pronoun, at once accusatory and monitory, made it difficult to answer. Iris pointed at the view. 'He showed me a watercolour he painted of that.'

'He's got a small talent. Nothing much.'

Iris was embarrassed that Dale, approaching with a tray, might have heard this last comment.

'I was telling your friend' – Pippa hesitated, frowning, as though trying to recollect the name – 'I was telling Iris here that you have a small talent. For painting, that is.'

'Whereas you have a large talent for drinking.' He set down the tray, then smiled across at her, as though he had paid her a compliment.

Pippa burst into laughter: 'How right! And I also have a large talent – inherited from my dear, departed father – for making money. A talent which you, my pet, do *not*, most emphatically do *not*, possess.'

Iris felt that they were playing some familiar game, at once banal and dangerous, during which either of them might suddenly exclaim: 'Ouch ! Be careful! That hurt.'

Suddenly Pippa pointed to a row of windows. 'See those rods on the window-frames?' Iris looked and nodded. 'Those are the rods on which the materials of the Arte de Calimala – the Guild of Foreign Cloth – were hung out to dry. If nineteenth-century England was a nation of shopkeepers, then medieval Florence was a republic of merchants.' She looked over to Dale. 'I know a lot about Florence, don't I?'

'You know a lot about everything. I wish you'd write a book.' He turned to Iris: 'Pippa used to write once. Stories. Poems. Published in the *Criterion*, the *London Mercury*, the *Adelphi*.'

141

'Oh, don't remind me! Dreadful stuff.' She raised herself on the settee, extended a hand and placed it on Dale's knee. She squeezed. As when she had said 'my Dale', she seemed to be obliquely asserting an ownership. She looked at him, head on one side, smiling. Then she turned to Iris: 'He's a good-looking boy, isn't he? But there's a certain' — she hesitated — '*debolezza* about him. Do you know what *debolezza* means? No, of course, you don't.'

'Feebleness?'

'Yes, you do know.' Pippa clapped ironically. 'Bravo!'

'There's nothing feeble about me. Nothing at all. One day you'll realize that.'

'Well, then I look forward to that day.'

'I'll show you.' His face was taut with anger.

Pippa laughed. 'Yes, show me!' She stared contemptuously at him as she quoted: '"I will do such things — what they are yet I know not; but they shall be the terrors of the earth."' Again she laughed.

'Oh fuck off!'

He shouted at her with such violence that Iris feared that, at any moment, one would strike the other. Then simultaneously they both burst into laughter. Pippa held out her glass. 'More of the same. Lots more of the same. And see if your girlfriend needs a refill.'

'Thanks. This is fine.'

'Haven't you had enough for the moment?' Dale asked. 'It's barely six o'clock.'

'Oh, get moving, buster!'

With a shrug he took the glass from her.

Suddenly, leaning forward, her stubby hands dangling between her knees, Pippa changed. It was as though her one aim now was to charm Iris, as she asked her about the *pensione*, about her work and about her family. When, after an inexplicably long interval, Dale returned with her glass, she told him, as she took it from him: 'I like this girl. Definitely. Why don't we invite her to come to Zermatt with us? Wouldn't you like to come skiing with us?'

'I've never skied.'

'Now's the time to learn.'

'I have my job.'

'Leave it. Teachers at the Institute are constantly quitting.'

'I undertook to stay on for the year.'

'Do you have to keep the undertaking?'

'Of course she does!'

'Well, then we could go over Christmas. The snow won't be all that good, but never mind. You'll be my guest,' she added, with the insolent implication that Iris would not herself be able to afford the trip.

Iris was silent.

'You don't like the idea?'

'It all depends on working things out . . .'

Pippa looked at Dale. 'You'll persuade her.' She turned to Iris: 'He's very persuasive. Don't you find that?'

Soon, as she constantly sipped at her ouzo, Pippa began to sink into a morose depression. She said less and less, staring either across at the rooftops or down at the marble floor. From time to time she whistled under her breath. Then, as though she had suddenly remembered something, she jumped to her feet. 'Well, I'll leave you both to it. I must see to some papers sent to me by my broker.' She held out her hand. 'Goodbye, Iris. It *is* Iris, isn't it?' The palm against Iris's palm felt cold and clammy from the glass around which it had been folded.

Iris nodded. 'Goodbye, Pippa.'

'You will forgive me for leaving you. But I have to keep a close eye on all my investments. Otherwise I shouldn't be able to afford all the luxuries which I like to afford.' She looked across at Dale, as though to say: 'There's one of the most expensive of those luxuries.'

'See! There was no reason to feel nervous of meeting her, was there?' Dale said as soon as Pippa had disappeared.

'Yes, every reason. She — scares me.'

'Not nearly as much as you scare her.'

'Why should I scare her?'

'Simple. She told you why. The younger generation knocking on the door. You're at least twenty-five years younger than she is.' He jumped up. 'Let's have a stroll. Before the light goes completely. Yes?'

'All right.'

Out in the street, crowded with people hurrying home from work, he linked his arm in hers. Then he raised his other arm and pulled her around towards him. He kissed her, his tongue for the first time entering her mouth. He stood back, touched her hair twice, and then gave it a long, gentle stroke. 'Beautiful,' he said. 'Beautiful hair. So soft. So blond.' There came into Iris's mind a vision of that bell of coarse, shiny, black hair framing Pippa's face. She felt a triumph, and then a shame because of that triumph. She raised her hand to his cheek. 'Dear Dale.'

Arm in arm they wandered through the city. Dale began to talk of how in Renaissance Florence, as in eighteenth-century England, patronage had served as a manifestation of power. 'Just as a tour of eighteenth-century country houses becomes a lesson in the history of the period, so a tour of all these *palazzi* and private chapels serves the same purpose . . .' Then in the middle of his lecture, he broke off. 'You're not listening to me. Bad girl! You're not listening to me. If you don't listen to me, how am I to educate you?' She thought how odd it was that, whereas she enjoyed it when Dale talked away like this, when Mervyn did so it had now begun to get on her nerves.

'I don't know if I *want* to be educated. I don't have Jack's desire for knowledge and self-improvement.'

'Oh, Jack!' He said it with a contemptuous laugh. 'Perhaps we should bring Jack and Pippa together.'

He propelled her into Santa Maria Novella, seemingly empty. Through the dimness, his arm round her waist and his cheek to hers, they peered at Brunelleschi's wooden crucifix in the Gondi Chapel. Then, once again, as in the street, he pulled her round and towards him. This time his kiss was even more passionate, one hand going down to her buttocks, as he hugged her against him.

'*Infame!*' It was a furious little old woman, dressed all in black and shod in black boots, who had walked up behind them. She glared at them as they separated; then cowered as, grabbing Iris's hand, Dale laughed openly in her face.

'Poor woman!' Iris said, ashamed, as they hurried, hands still linked, up the aisle of the church.

'Why?'

'We shocked her.'

'Excited her. That's more like it.'

'Perhaps we did both.' She felt a dizzy exhilaration, as though she were leaping up the sheer side of a mountain, with the air growing thinner and thinner and the light brighter and brighter. She was no longer ashamed that the scandalized old woman had caught them in that embrace before the dying Christ. She was thinking only of his hardness against her, and of that hand pressing her buttocks. Suddenly, she began to run, dragging him behind her.

Once more out in the street, the door of the church creaking back and forth from the violence with which she had thrown it open, Dale said: 'May I take you somewhere?'

'Where?'

'Somewhere. Somewhere I know. Please.'

For a moment she was puzzled; then she understood. At once, without a qualm, she made up her mind. 'Why not?'

He raised an arm for a passing taxi; then pushed her into it and clambered in beside her. It was ancient and so small that their thighs and knees touched. He took her hand in his and ran the ball of his thumb up and down now one finger and now another. The constant stroking was extraordinarily erotic. He might have been caressing her nipples.

She did not ask where it was that he was taking her; but she knew that it could not be back to Pippa's. From streets of grandiose *palazzi* and churches, they passed into ones of tall, comfortable nineteenth-century houses, and then on to others in which the lamps shed a feeble light on cracked and peeling façades and the taxi kept bumping over pot-holes, to throw them, laughing, first towards its roof and then against each other.

On their arrival outside an elongated, ochre-coloured house, Dale leaned forward in his seat and, with an extravagant gesture, tossed a handful of coins on to the seat beside the driver.

'*Grazie, signore! Molto gentile!*' It was clear that the driver was amazed by this largesse.

'You must have given him far too much.'

'Yes, I did. For luck. A kind of casting of one's bread on the waters.'

He took her hand and led her up to the heavy wooden door. Having, with difficulty in that light, scanned the names against the bells – 'I never remember which bell it is,' – he eventually pressed one.

Far above a window opened and a woman's voice called down: '*Qui è?*'

'Dale.'

'*Ah! Il signore Dale! Momento!*' After that *momento* had passed, a key crashed down on to the steps below them.

Half-way up, the light, for which there had been a push-button switch in the hall, expired on them, and they climbed on in a

145

darkness relieved only by a glimmer from a window far above.

'Exciting,' Iris said.

'Yes, this climb always excites me.'

Always? So he had brought other women here. The thought of it both infuriated her and sharpened her excitement.

On one of the landings an ordinary-looking middle-aged woman, in a dark-blue skirt, light-blue cardigan and bedroom slippers trodden down at the heels, greeted them with a smile. *'Buonasera, signore Dale. Buonasera, signora.'* She was so natural that Iris felt no embarrassment. The woman stood aside for them to pass into the flat ahead of her. There was a smell of onions frying and, underlying it, a smell of damp and decay. From the far end of the long corridor, dimly lit by a single naked bulb, came the sound of children's voices and laughter.

The woman drew a key out of a pocket of her cardigan and inserted it in the lock of the door closest to them. *'Ecco! Tutto è pronto!'*

Everything is ready. Did that mean, Iris wondered, that Dale had known all along that he would be bringing her here and had told the woman so in advance?

Except that, with its crisp sheets and hard, fat bolster, the bed was a double and not a single one and that, beside the washbasin, there was also an enamel bidet, with a linen towel draped over its cracked rim, the room was not much different from her room in the *pensione*. But, unlike her room in the *pensione*, it was a room of which she would remember every smallest detail for the rest of her life: the candlewick bedspread with the orange outline of the iron which, in a moment of carelessness, someone had left on it; the worn red plush of the curtains, their pelmet tilted·askew; the cheap oleograph of a Madonna and child on one wall – the wallpaper was made up of seething clusters of roses, pink on dark-grey – and the photograph of a couple, the woman in a bridal dress, and the man in tails, on the other; the linoleum gleaming up as though it had been scrupulously polished only that day.

In her underwear, Iris shivered involuntarily.

'Cold?'

'No.' She shook her head. 'Only – a little frightened.'

He drew off his underpants; then, totally naked, came over to her. He put his arms around her; then removed them to lift up her petticoat and to pull it over her head. 'It's not the first time, is it?'

'Of course.'

'Oh, Christ! I always assumed that anyone who'd been in the ATS . . .' He laughed.

'Do you mind?'

'Do I mind? Of course not! It's that much more thrilling. Like being the first to tear the wrapper off a box of chocolates.'

'Is that all I am to you — a box of chocolates?'

'Silly! But I do love chocolates. Always make a pig of myself over them.'

Suddenly he was kneeling on the floor before her. He pulled down her knickers. Her hand went out — of its own accord, it seemed — and she clutched at his hair.

'I'll just see the signora.' He pulled some notes out of his wallet. 'Wait a moment.'

Iris waited by the half-open door. She could hear Dale and the Italian woman talking and laughing together and, beyond them, the children still also talking and laughing. Then he returned.

'I always give her too much.'

'How did you get to know her?'

He shrugged. Then he said: 'Well, as a matter of fact, through Giles. In a drunken moment, he confided in me that there was this widow who was prepared to let out a room by the hour. I suppose he himself brings some girl — or a series of girls — here.'

'Poor Margot!'

'What the eye doesn't see . . .'

As they began to descend the stone stairs, Iris, alerted by irregular footfalls, peered down over the banister. Someone was descending below them. Then on the wall of the landing two flights below she saw a misshapen shadow: a huge head, one shoulder higher than the other, a hump for the back. She leaned far over the banisters. Then she hissed: 'Wait!' She put a hand to Dale's arm.

'It's just one of the other inhabitants.'

'No. I'm sure it's Giuseppe Valeriano,' she whispered. 'The little poet.'

'Giuseppe! But what would Giuseppe be doing here?' he whispered back.

'Perhaps he lives here.'

'In a hole like this! Don't be silly. He'd live somewhere very posh.'

'I'm sure it's him.'

Downstairs, the front door slammed, making the house judder.

'Well, whoever it was, has gone. Come!'

Twice on the stairs he paused to embrace her.

'Oh God, I feel tempted to take you back again.'

She too longed to return with him to the room. But she laughed: 'No, no! I must get back. No!'

'Tomorrow,' he said. 'Tomorrow let's pretend that what happened today never happened. Let's pretend that it's all for the first time. Let's!' Then he added: 'I've already warned the signora that we'll be back for more tomorrow. Perhaps we could even rent the room just for ourselves and no one else. We could make it our secret nest!'

Two days later, Dale arrived in Doney carrying a parcel wrapped in brown paper. 'A present for you,' he told Iris, as he placed the parcel on the table between them and then pulled out a chair.

'For me? What is it?'

He drew the parcel towards him and, with his long fingers, began to unpick the string. The brown paper rustled as he let it flutter to the marble floor. He leaned forward, head on one side, the tip of his tongue protruding between his teeth, as he stared down, absorbed, at the square box now revealed.

'What is it?' She craned her neck to see.

'Marvellous,' he said, as though to himself. Then he looked up, to smile at her. 'An ant colony. An ant colony under glass. I'd never seen one before. I was passing this pet shop and there it was. Have you ever seen one?'

Iris shook her head. He had pushed the box towards her. She could feel herself grimacing, and tried not to do so. There was something horrific in that ferocious insect life sealed off by the clear pane of glass.

'A paradigm of human existence?' he said. Then he gave that little hiccough-like laugh of his. 'Anyway, it's yours.'

'Thank you. But don't you want to keep it yourself?'

'No. Certainly not. As soon as I saw it, I said to myself: "I'm going to buy that for Iris." And buy it I did.'

'Thank you,' she repeated, watching him as he stooped for the fallen paper and then began to rewrap the box.

For a few days she kept the ant colony in her room, even

148

though its presence there filled her with unease. Then, waking up in the middle of one night and unable to sleep again, she had switched on the bedside light, got out of bed and, taking it up off her desk, had examined it. Even at this hour, a few minutes after three, the ants were scurrying hither and thither about their frantic errands. It was then that she decided: she would have to get rid of it.

That evening, when she was having dinner with Giles and Margot, she gave the ant colony to Piers. But the child, too, was obviously repelled by it, staring down at the ants in their labyrinthine passages without a word.

'Isn't it wonderful?' Margot had prompted. 'Miraculous really. You can watch everything they do in the smallest detail.'

Iris never saw or heard anything more of the ant colony on her visits to the house. Nor did she ask about it. She presumed that Piers had either given or thrown it away.

18

Audrey faced Jack, one hand stroking the plump tortoiseshell cat in her lap and the other resting on the begrimed, unlit kitchen range.

'It's too bad,' she said. 'Australian friends have written to tell me that that *Spectator* article of mine on the disappearance of the head of the "Primavera" from the Ponte Santa Trinità has appeared in the *Sydney Morning Herald*. But have I received any extra payment? You bet your life I haven't! When I get on to the *Spectator* crowd they just say that the copyright rests with them. I ask you! Oh, I do wish I hadn't let my membership of the Society of Authors lapse. They might have done battle for me. But all those little sums — Royal Society of Literature, PEN, the Society of Authors — add up and add up. Oh, you're so lucky not to have to worry about money.'

He laughed. 'I don't have any money!'

'Not having any money is different from having to worry about money. When one's young, money doesn't matter. One has it or — more often — one doesn't have it. But when one has become used to a certain standard of living, when one has inevitable outgoings on a house of this size . . . Johnny would be horrified if she could see how I now have to live.' She drew a deep sigh in yet again invoking her dead lover's shade. Then she screwed up her eyes, as she stared down at the cat. 'Well, actually, of course, she *does* see, I'm convinced of that. *She* sees me — and *I* from time to time see *her*. Oh, I don't mean as I see you or Tabitha here. But with a sixth sense — or, if you like, with a third eye. Anyway' — she gave herself a shake and, with a violence which shocked Jack, shoved the cat off her lap — 'we'd better talk business.'

Jack nodded. He wished that talking business meant talking money. He had still not been paid.

'You found that Dante passage?'

'Yep.'

'I do wish you'd say "Yes" and not "Yep". "Yep" — if you'll forgive me for remarking on it — sounds just a teeny-weeny bit common.'

Having foraged in his rucksack, Jack produced the library copy of Laurence Binyon's translation of *Il Purgatorio*, and held it out.

Audrey glanced at the spine. Then she burst out: 'Oh, no! Not, *not* Binyon, *please*, I beg of you!'

'Don't you like Binyon's translation?'

'Of course I like it. I gave him loads of advice on it. But *it's still in copyright!* I've explained this to you,' she went on, although in fact she had done nothing of the kind. 'Why can't you take things in? What's the matter with you? You seem bright enough when we talk to each other.' She pursed her lips, making an attempt at patience. 'If something is in copyright,' she went on, speaking so slowly that it might have been either to a foreigner or to a child, 'it means that one has to pay a reproduction fee. "One" in this case is little me. That's what's stipulated in the small print of my contract — loon that I am, I failed to read it right through. So — nothing in copyright is going in my book. So — no *Aaron's Rod* and no *A Room with a View*. Got it?'

'Got it.'

She went on telling him about the state of her finances: Adrian had given her some advice about the buying of shares but out of sheer obstinacy she had neglected to take it; she had quarrelled with old Lady Petrie, so that when the old girl had finally kicked the bucket there was no mention of yours truly in the will; since the War bank loan charges had become absolutely iniquitous . . . Suddenly she broke off. 'Are you listening to me, my dear?'

'Yes, of course.' Jack blushed at the lie. In fact, he had been daydreaming about an incident of that morning. The door of the lavatory shared by male and female members of the Institute staff had a loose bolt which the porter was constantly called on to fix. Having given the door a shove to open it, Jack had found himself looking down at Iris, who was seated in front of him, the displaced bolt between her feet. 'Oh, sorry! Sorry!' Retreating in horrified embarrassment, he had frantically pulled the door shut. Iris herself had seemed totally unperturbed by his intrusion. Now the recollection of her, looking up at him as he, for a horrified second, had looked down at her, excited him so much that he felt the beginning of an erection in his crumpled grey flannels.

Audrey was peering at him. 'Your complexion used to be so fresh.' She peered even closer. 'Clear. Clean. Why have you got those spots?'

Jack put a hand to his face. Ivor had also remarked on the spots in a teasing, joky way — *boutons de jeunesse* he had called them. 'I've no idea.'

'Diet. Are you eating enough fruit and vegetables?'

'Oh, yes, I think so.'

'I wonder if that Conquest woman feeds you properly.'

'She feeds me very well.'

'Well, then you've been luckier than I've been on those occasions when she's had me over for a meal. Perhaps you eat too many sweets.'

'I'm not a sweet-eater.'

'That's what Johnny used to say. And then, on the sly, she would polish off a whole box of chocs. So naughty. Like a child.' She drew a deep sigh. 'Oh, this money business. Far worse than *spots*. Spots are a mere bagatelle in comparison. What *am* I to do?' Suddenly an idea came to her. 'You see quite a bit of Ivor, I gather?'

He nodded. 'He's been very kind to me.'

'I bet! . . . Well, when next you see him, do somehow let slip — naturally, in the course of conversation — that I'm *sbandata*. Do you know what that means? It's used of a ship on its beam ends. But it doesn't have the same idiomatic meaning as in English, so don't, don't say that Audrey is *sbandata*, or otherwise he'll imagine that I'm a ship. Just say that Audrey is *broke*. Got it? Totally and utterly broke. He's a good, generous soul is Ivor, and he might, he might just come up with a temporary sub. Disraeli's "two nations" describes our little colony here. Half of us have no money and half of us are rolling in it.'

'I wish I had some money to lend you.' Jack meant it. He was fond of Audrey and admired her courage.

'So do I. But you haven't. Anyway — you're a good chap.' She got up and patted him on the shoulder. 'A good companion, as that ghastly Jack Priestley might say . . . Well, that's enough on the book for today. But, please, *please* do remember — I want nothing, nothing whatever that's in copyright! Now, do you want to come with me to see Harry?'

'Oh, all right.'

'You don't *have* to come.'

'No, I'd like to come.'

'He's obviously on the way out. And that little crook Franco is robbing him blind. Tragic! All that "*babbo, babbo*" stuff . . . It makes me want to puke.'

Harry's attitude to Jack, unlike his attitude to Iris, was uncertain. Yes, there was an innate decency about the boy; and yes, he was certainly intelligent. But, well (as he put it to Audrey, who had first brought Jack to see him) he was not quite out of the handkerchief drawer, now was he? Or even out of the sock drawer, for the matter of that, he had added with an asthmatic laugh. 'I must confess that I find that "ee-bah-goom" accent of his just a little – er – rebarbative. And couldn't you tell him that "I don't mind if I do" is not really an appropriate response to the offer of a cup of coffee?'

'Oh, you really are an awful old snob!'

'Well, if I had a diamond to give you – which I haven't – I'm sure you'd rather it was polished than unpolished.'

'At least you admit that he's a diamond.'

Now Jack sat beside Harry's bedside, reading to him the letters which had arrived that morning. Like all his other faculties, the old man's sight was failing. 'If you come on anything likely to embarrass either you or me, just omit it, won't you?' Would the letter from Cox and King's drawing attention to the size of Harry's overdraft, a complaint from his niece that he had had no business to sell some silver which 'belonged as much to Mummy as to you', and an enquiry from the Italian Inland Revenue about a delayed income-tax return, embarrass him? Jack hesitated before each and then read it out. Harry's response on each occasion was to close his eyes and emit a fragile whimper.

Meanwhile, in the kitchen, Audrey was attempting to prepare him a cup of Benger's. There were three milk bottles in the larder, but as she held each up to her nose, she realized that its milk had turned. So far from the ice-box having any milk in it, it did not even have any ice. The butter was uncovered on a cracked saucer. Some potatoes in a brown-paper bag were green and sprouting shoots. There was a misty glass – Georgian, it looked, fancy treating it like that! – on the kitchen table, with a sediment of red wine clotted at its base. Poor Harry had always been so fastidious, Renée even more so – 'One could eat off that kitchen floor,' Johnny used to say (not that the old dear could ever have got down to any kitchen floor in her rheumaticky and obese old age). Audrey ran cold water into the wine-glass, and then, inserting forefinger and middle finger – no sign of a mop or a drying-up cloth of course – attempted to remove the wine sediment from within it. But why the hell should she be undertaking such a task?' 'Franco!' she yelled. Then, making her way down the passage to the room which she knew to be his, she yelled even more loudly: 'Franco! *Franco!*'

The boy eventually appeared, barefoot, in long, wrinkled khaki underpants reaching almost to his knees and a grey cashmere sweater which she knew at once to be Harry's, not his. He yawned, mouth wide open, and then rubbed at an eye. Clearly, he had been sleeping.

'That kitchen is disgusting,' she told him in Italian.

He shrugged. 'Too much to do.'

'Too much sleeping,' she countered. 'Does the siesta hour now extend until' – she looked at her watch – 'six-twenty?'

He laughed, as though she had made a joke. 'I got to bed very late last night, *signorina*. And then the master called me twice in the night. He can't even lift up the *orinale* for himself, let alone get to the *gabinetto*.'

'Well, come along with me and find me some fresh milk. I want to make him some Benger's. It's so easily digestible and also so nutritious.' During her last weeks, poor dear Johnny had virtually lived on the stuff, difficult and expensive though it had been to obtain at that period.

He shook his head. 'No Ben-ja.'

'What do you mean?'

'*Finito.*'

'Oh, it's too bad! If I'd known it was *finito* I could have got him some more. Or *you* could have got him some more.'

Franco explained, with what struck Audrey as a malicious glee, that Benger's could only be obtained either from the English chemist or from that expensive *drogheria* in the Via Tornabuoni, and neither was prepared to extend any further credit.

Oh, it was so humiliating, Audrey exclaimed inwardly, as much for herself as for Harry.

The boy gave another of his impudent grins. 'I'll be going

down into the city soon. Then' – he shrugged – 'I'll try to find this Ben-ja.'

'Well, make us some tea *now*!'

He shook his head. 'No tea! Coffee.' He pushed past her, without even a '*Scusi*' or '*Permesso*,' and pattered into the kitchen.

'Harry, I really do think that you should give that boy his *congé*,' Audrey said on her return to the bedroom. 'The squalor in that kitchen of yours! And he just gets cheekier and cheekier.'

Harry again closed his eyes to emit another fragile whimper – he sounded just like an ailing kitten, Audrey thought. 'Oh, Audrey, do leave things alone! He's not perfect, I know, far from perfect. But he's not a bad little blighter. Has a kind of affection for me.'

'Has a kind of affection for your property – that's more like it!'

'Who'd I find to replace him? It's not much fun doing all kinds of intimate things for an old codger like myself in the last stages of decay. And what do I pay him?'

'Well, what *do* you pay him?'

Harry's chest rose and fell with effortful laughter. 'Often nothing. Nothing at all.'

Jack felt not merely physically oppressed by the pent-up smells of the sick-room (he had glimpsed a half-full *orinale* under the high brass bedstead) but emotionally oppressed by the bleakness of once well-to-do lives reduced to a lonely and anxious penury. His maternal grandmother, dying in her tiny council house, had at least been surrounded by solicitous relatives. Her protracted going had been almost *happy*, for God's sake.

When they at last left the house, it was to find Franco tinkering with his Vespa outside the front door. Audrey at once halted to admonish him: Couldn't he find somewhere else to conduct these repairs? The wretched *macchina* was dripping oil on to the gravel and someone would then step in it and bring it into the house. Why, why, why couldn't he be more careful?

The boy, squatting beside the Vespa in those outsize, creased khaki underpants and Harry's cashmere sweater – the odds were that that would get covered in oil too – merely grinned up at her as though to say: 'What a silly old woman you are!'

Audrey made a tsk-tsk noise as they walked away. Then she turned and shouted over her shoulder: '*Sfrontataccio!*'

The boy did not even look up at the insult; he might never have heard.

'Oh, I shouldn't have said that to him. But really! He exemplifies all that's worst in the Italian character. Spurious charm. Dishonesty. Slackness. Deviousness.'

'I think he's all right.'

'*All right!* If that's what you think, my dear, then clearly you know very little about character in general and about the Italian character in particular!'

'If you could choose any city in the world, which would you most want to visit?' Ivor asked.

'Moscow,' Jack replied.

'Moscow! I could have guessed you'd say that. I suppose you're one of these Reds who are supposed to be under all of our beds – and sometimes are even *in* Adrian's bed, from all that one hears.'

Such was his innocence, that this last remark puzzled Jack. Was Adrian a Communist sympathizer, despite all his wealth? 'I'm not a Communist,' he said with the thoughtful solemnity which Ivor and many other people found so appealing. 'Not now. But I was – briefly – during my first year at Oxford. It's just that it would be exciting to see a society in a process of drastic change, instead of merely reverting to what it used to be, as here.'

'When you're my age, you'll have learned that almost all change is for the worse. Frankly, for you to want to visit Moscow is about as lunatic as it would be for me to want to visit Wigan. The place is quite unutterably dreary.'

'You've been there?'

'For my sins. Before the War. I had this friend – well, the less said about him the better . . . He looked extremely fetching, especially in a fur toque, but later I learned that he was not really a journalist, as he was pretending to be in London, but some kind of spy. God knows what he expected to learn from *me*. Anyway, I got a terrible allergy from the soap, and there were no green vegetables or fruit to be had even for dollars or pounds, and all that one could say about the staffs in the hotels and restaurants was that the government pretended to pay them and that, in return, they pretended to work . . . Well, why go on? The point of my original question was to ask you if you'd like to come to

Venice with me over the Christmas holidays.'

'To Venice?'

'From your astonishment one might infer either that you thought that Venice was situated at the eastern end of Siberia or that you had never heard of it. The idea is that you should come as my secretary companion – all expenses paid and some pocket money too.'

'But I can't take shorthand and I can only type with two fingers. Very slowly.'

'I don't imagine that I'll have anything to dictate to you. Or that I shall be engaged on some literary masterpiece or even writing letters. Your only tasks will be to see to the accommodation, run a few errands for me, and, well, keep me amused. I loathe being on my own,' he added. 'The trouble is that I have no inner life. A terrible admission, but there it is. So how about it?'

'Well ...' Jack stared out of the car window, deliberating on the offer.

'No great enthusiasm, I can see. I suppose you don't want to be away from Miss Crediton.'

Jack felt himself blushing. It had been acute of Ivor to have guessed at his obsession.

'No, it's nothing to do with Iris, nothing at all.' Why had Ivor referred to her as 'Miss Crediton' in that formal manner, when he always used her Christian name in addressing her?

'Well, if it *is* anything to do with Miss Crediton, I can tell you that she *won't* be in Florence over Christmas. I have it from the horse's mouth – a phrase particularly apt in the case of Pippa Lavery – that your Miss Crediton, that Somers boy and Pippa herself are all off to Zermatt to negotiate what I have no doubt will be some particularly slippery slopes. Pippa will be paying the piper but whether she will also be calling the tune ... She has a strange way of tormenting herself with these *ménages à trois* – which is lucky for Somers. He can, as it were, both have the cake which she provides and eat cake bought with the money which she gives him. . . Anyway, how about it? Do you come to Venice?'

'I think that perhaps Giles and Margot . . . They might be offended if I took myself off for Christmas.' Increasingly he had become aware how important his presence had become in the unhappy household: to the couple, who so often used him as an intermediary; and even more to the children, above all Piers, who had taken to haunting his room, distracting him from his work or his reading, as though their panicky bewilderment drove them to look to him for reassurance.

'Christmas is a family affair. You're not one of the family.'

Jack almost said: 'In an odd way, I am.' But Ivor would then have asked him to elaborate and he would have been obliged to betray Giles and Margot. Instead he replied dubiously: 'Well, I suppose you're right.'

'There's no supposing about it, Venice is so beautiful in the winter — whether in that clear, cold sunlight or wrapped, like some expensive gift, in layer upon layer of tissue-paper fog. You *must* see it. How can you pass up such an opportunity in order to eat indigestible turkey and even more indigestible Christmas pudding with that dreary crowd?'

Jack smiled. 'I think you've persuaded me.'

'I should jolly well hope so too!' Ivor patted him on the knee.

They had arrived at the Palazzo Lambeni.

'D'you think it's really all right for me to come too?'

'Of course it's all right. It's not a luncheon- or a dinner-party. Just a cocktail. Isabella constantly brings the most unsuitable people to my cocktail parties, so why shouldn't I bring a wholly suitable person to one of hers? In any case she loves new blood. She gulps it down as though she were a Transylvanian vampire.'

The long *salotto*, dominated by frescoes which Bernard Berenson had pronounced *not* to be by Tiepolo ('Sheer malice! He just can't forgive Isabella her wartime admiration for the bull-frog,' had been Ivor's comment to Jack), was already clamorous with voices. Jack felt stunned both by the noise and by his trepidation at having been reluctantly persuaded to arrive as an uninvited guest.

'So this is your protégé!' Isabella looked Jack up and down. 'Well! He's not exactly what I'd expected, but he looks charming, most charming.' She turned from Ivor to Jack. 'If you're attentive, you can learn a lot from Ivor. Many people now famous got their start in life from him. He's a downy old bird, aren't you, Ivor?'

'You make me sound like one of those boiling fowls that poor dear Audrey serves one up for dinner.'

The mention of Audrey reminded Jack that he had still not spoken to Ivor about her need for cash. It was hard to let such information casually drop, as she had suggested to him.

'Who do you know here?' Isabella demanded.

'Well . . .' Uncertainly, Jack looked around him. 'I can see my boss over there.'

'Oh, you don't want to talk to him! You must see enough of him at the Institute.'

'And there's Iris – Miss Crediton. I'll go over to chat to her.'

At that, Jack hurried off.

'I'd have thought he saw even more of the Crediton girl than of Mervyn at the Institute,' Isabella said.

'I'm afraid that he's besotted – or, as our dear Adriana would say, bespotted – with her.'

'And she's bespotted with the Somers boy,' Isabella said, 'who's far and away the better-looking and more entertaining of the two. He'd be *my* choice, no doubt about it.'

'There, my pet, I have to disagree with you. Prentice has what are called sterling qualities – although admittedly these days sterling has sharply fallen in value, as we all know to our cost.'

'Iris!'

'Jack!'

'You never told me you were going to be at this party.'

'*You* never told *me*.'

'That's because it was only quarter of an hour ago that I knew that I *was* going to be at it. I wasn't invited, I was brought.'

She smiled. 'I don't have to ask who it was who brought you.'

He nodded. 'Yes. Ivor.'

As so often with her, he found himself wishing that he could say something extraordinarily witty or perceptive. If only he could talk like Ivor! He made a clumsy shot at it: 'I really hate parties. I'm the sort of gate-crasher who wants to crash the gate not to get into a party but to get out of it.'

But she was no longer listening to him. 'Pippa's over there.'

'Pippa?'

'Pippa Lavery. You know.'

He nodded.

'But I can see no sign of Dale. I suppose he once again refused to accompany her here. He takes such a disapproving line over Isabella's behaviour in the War. He really seems to *hate* her for it. And he hardly knows her! It's so silly.'

Jack himself never referred to Isabella as anything other than the Contessa Lambeni. 'Ivor is far more tolerant about her. And he *fought* in the War. He even won a DSO.'

'Dale could hardly have fought in the War. He wasn't old enough.' Iris was sharp in his defence. 'And anyway a lot of American men . . .' Her attention was distracted by Pippa who, arm extended and eyes screwed up, was beckoning her. 'Pippa seems to want me for something. God knows what. Perhaps a message from Dale.'

As abruptly as he had hurried away from Isabella and Ivor, Iris now hurried away from him. Jack watched her with a sad concentration, thinking how graceful she was as she slipped through the knots of people, her long, straight blond hair glistening under now the first of the two chandeliers and now the other.

'*Bellissima*! Yes?' It was Giuseppe, who had silently moved up, glass in hand, behind him. He was wearing an Edwardian-style suit – the jacket high-buttoned, with turn-ups to its cuffs – in the check known to Italians as *Principe di galles*, Prince of Wales.

'Giuseppe! It's so long since I've seen you. I've hardly been to Doney for an age. No time and – worse – no money.'

'You know that I am always happy to treat you.'

Jack shook his head. Having seen that cramped attic room in that slummy quarter of the city, how could he now dream of allowing such a thing? 'When Audrey pays me . . .' he said.

'When the Ponte Vecchio is gold – as the Fiorentini say!' Giuseppe laughed. 'Dickens wrote a novel called *Great Expectations*, yes?'

'I trust her.'

Giuseppe briefly put a hand to Jack's cheek. '*Innocente*,' he said, with a wistful affection.

'I wish everyone didn't think I was such an innocent. I'm not, you know.'

Again Giuseppe laughed. 'It is good to be innocent. I wish I am innocent. I have not been innocent for many, many years. Not since' – he lifted an arm – 'I am *so* high in Palermo.' He lowered the arm. 'Please – come to Doney! I like to see you.'

'Until your Contessa arrives.' Jack, still smarting from that '*innocente*', was uncharacteristically bitter.

Giuseppe shrugged. 'Iris and Dale are often in Doney,' he said, not realizing how the simple statement inflicted on Jack what was almost a physical anguish. 'But I soon understand – they do not wish to be troubled by Giuseppe Valeriano. They wish to be alone together. Talking, heads close, close. Laughing. Lovers! Lucky! Florence is good for lovers.'

Jack put his hands to his ears, as though to obliterate what the little Italian was telling him. But he was telling him nothing new. 'I can't take this noise. Deafening.'

'It is the noise of *infelicità*. Happiness is quiet. Come. We will go into the study.' It was clear that Giuseppe had a free run of the house.

Drinks in hand, they pushed through the crowds and then made their way down a corridor to an octagonal room, lined with reddish-brown tooled leather, at the far end of it. Austere and sombre, with its carved, high-back chairs and its marble floor in alternate lozenges of dark-green and a purplish-red which suggested raw horse-meat, it had a view of the far-off Duomo. Jarringly out of place in this setting, a typewriter, surrounded by stacks of letters and documents, stood on a steel desk.

Jack pointed. 'That rather spoils things,' he said.

'I must work somewhere. And I must work in comfort.'

'Is that typewriter yours?'

'I use it. Isabella does not type. She sits here' — he indicated one of the chairs — 'and I sit there, and she dictates to me. She dictates remarkably. No hesitation, no error. Like her whole life. She knows what she wishes. She speaks it, she does it.'

'I didn't know you *worked* for her.'

Giuseppe smiled. 'I do many things for her. I try to be indispensable. If one loves someone and wants always to be with someone, then that is the best thing to do — to make oneself indispensable.'

Jack wondered how he could make himself indispensable to Iris.

'You've known her a long time?'

Giuseppe shrugged, as though he were not sure. 'It seems — all my life. I first met her when she was in prison.'

'In prison!'

'After the War. You know her story? I was working in the prison.'

'And you became friends?'

'I did what I can to help her. I was assistant cook in the prison. Not a good cook. But I think that I am good to — for? — her at that time. Now she remembers. She shows me *riconoscenza*.'

'Gratitude?'

'*Si*, gratitude.'

By now Jack had seated himself. On the low table beside him, some books stood in piles. One of them, slim and gilt-edged in an India paper edition, struck him as familiar. He put out a hand, looked at the title on the spine: Henry James's *Portrait of a Lady*. It had been on another table, in Doney, some weeks ago that that same book had been lying. As now, he had put out a hand and had looked at the title on the spine, while, leaning across the table to each other, totally ignoring him, Iris and Dale had conversed in short, abrupt sentences, each of which seemed to throb with a barely controlled sexuality.

Jack now opened the book and looked at the fly-leaf. *'To my wicked, wanton Dale, with all his Pippa's love.'*

What was the book doing here? Only a few minutes ago Iris had been telling him that, such was Dale's hatred of Isabella's past and so of Isabella herself, he absolutely refused to meet her. Could it be that Pippa had brought the book to the *palazzo*? Or could it be . . .?

'You like Henry James?'

'Someone once said that there were three Henry Jameses — James the First, James the Second, and James the Old Pretender. I like James the First and James the Second.'

'James is too difficult for me. But not too difficult for Isabella.'

'Well, it's her own language, isn't it?' Jack was once again staring down at Pippa's inscription.

Suddenly Ivor appeared. 'Oh, there you are! I've had enough of this. It's like a rugger scrum — except that there's no one in the least appealing against whom to rub oneself.' He totally ignored Giuseppe; Jack might have been alone in the study. 'Let's beat it. You can come back to the villa for a cold collation.'

Jack felt a surge of rebellion, as he often did in the course of their relationship. He could never account for it. 'Actually, I've got to do something else. Sorry.'

'Something else? What else?'

'Prepare for a lesson first thing tomorrow morning.'

'Oh, you're far too conscientious! I keep telling you that. . . . Ah, well, never mind. I'll give you a lift home.'

'I think I'll walk.'

'Walk!'

'I need the exercise.'

'Well, if you want a three-mile hike, good luck to you.'

Stiffly, hands to the seams of his trousers, Ivor quitted the room.

Giuseppe looked at Jack and burst into laughter. With a sense of disloyalty, Jack began to laugh too.

The obstinate, extended silences between Giles and Margot, over a meal or in the sitting-room after a meal, always disturbed Jack. But far more disturbing to him were the sounds of their angry recrimination. Sometimes these sounds even filled him with apprehension, similar to that experienced by people when they hear the first ominous creakings and rumblings of an earthquake.

As he entered the villa, he could hear them shouting at each other.

'Well, look at the report for yourself, just look at it! Anti-social behaviour. Truancy. Seems to have lost all interest. For God's sake – this is something *new*! He was never like that. It's having its effect on him.'

Paralysed, with no real wish to listen and yet unable not to listen, Jack stood, heart thumping, in the hall. His own parents rarely fought each other, and then never with this despairing savagery.

Now it was Giles: 'If the boy's behaviour has deteriorated, don't you think it might just be that you can no longer be bothered with him? Or with Prunella? You leave every bloody thing to Maria. Every bloody thing! For Christ's sake, they're *your* children!'

'I thought they were yours too.'

Jack began to slink away. It was like two dogs tearing at each other, jaws slavering. Better to leave them alone, for fear of a rabid bite.

In his room, he took off his jacket, throwing it haphazard over a chair. He kicked off his shoes, then pulled off his socks. There was still more than half an hour to go before he would have to face them over dinner. He stretched out on his bed and opened *The Ring and the Book*. There was something organized and therefore satisfying and consoling in its sequence of passionate confrontations. Not like that – that *mess* at the other end of the house. He began to read.

Suddenly he heard the door slowly creaking open. Piers,

furtive and forlorn, was standing before him.

'Are you busy?'

'Reading.'

Without a word, the boy edged towards the bed. His face, Giles's in miniature, was extraordinarily pallid; in one hand he was holding a teddy-bear which Jack had never seen before. He edged even closer. Then he sat on the end of the bed, his woeful eyes on Jack. He clutched the teddy-bear close to him, both arms around it, then toppled over, as though in a faint, until his skinny body was almost within touching distance of Jack's. He rested his head on the crook of Jack's arm.

Jack felt first an intense embarrassment, then an intense revulsion, and then an intense pity.

The two of them lay like that, silent and motionless, until Margot began calling: 'Jack! Jack! Oh, where are you? Dinner! Dinner's ready!'

∽⟡∾

19

'I thought you said that Pippa was an expert skier.'

'She is.'

'Then why does she never ski?'

Dale shrugged. 'Perhaps she prefers drinking to skiing. Drinking and reading those detective stories.'

'How can anyone so intelligent . . . ? She even *rereads* them. When we arrived she was finishing *Death of My Aunt*, and now she's started on it all over again.'

'Most of the time she's too smashed to know *what* she's reading.'

'Are we — am I — making her unhappy?'

'Pippa has been unhappy for a long, long time.'

Occasionally guilt shrivelled up and stained the edge of Iris's existence in the thin, dry air of Zermatt, just as the brilliant light, leaking through the bellows of Dale's Kodak, was found to have shrivelled up and stained the edges of the snapshots, taken at his request by passing strangers, which showed the pair of them hand in hand or arm in arm or leaning one against the other. But the guilt was transient. 'Oh, I'm so happy!' For most of the time Iris did not care if, to be so happy, it was necessary to make someone else so unhappy.

That night he lay naked beside her on her bed. Days of glaring sunlight on snow were followed by the glare, similarly exhilarating and stupefying, of the passion of nights when their bodies, rubbing against each other, seemed to Iris to scour each other like dry tinder, until she feared that at any moment they would burst into flames, scorching the bedclothes and scattering sparks upwards towards the high, glimmering ceiling. 'Does she ever guess that you're in here with me?' Iris found herself whispering, even though Pippa's suite — a sitting-room, a bedroom for herself, a bedroom for Dale, separate lavatory and bathroom — was at the far end of the corridor.

'She doesn't guess. She knows.'

Iris was glad that she had mulishly rejected Pippa's insistent offers to pay for her holiday in addition to paying for Dale's. To take a lover from Pippa was bad enough; also to take money from her would be intolerable. But there were times when to be under an obligation to Pippa could not be avoided.

'. . . While you were out, I found this scarf for you in that little shop round the corner. It's run by a Frenchwoman, you know — which is no doubt why it's full of such lovely things.'

'. . . I thought we'd celebrate — although there's nothing to celebrate as far as I'm concerned — and so I've ordered a bottle of bubbly, a Louis Roederer, extra dry.'

'. . . No, you must have them, if you admire them so much. I insist, I insist! Opals are supposed to bring bad luck to people not born in October, so since you're an October girl . . .'

Iris was learning that often the most efficient and subtle way to punish people is not to take things away from them but to give them things.

Going down to breakfast early one morning — the other two always breakfasted together in the suite — Iris was confronted in the corridor by Pippa, hair in disorder, feet bare and silk kimono edging off freckled shoulder. Where could she have been? Only later did Iris learn from Dale that, having failed to receive an instant answer to her ringing for the chambermaid, she had stormed off in an unsuccessful attempt to ferret her out. Something which she had sent to be pressed — it was odd that clothes so frequently pressed should always look so creased — had not been returned.

'You're up bright and early!'

'I never sleep late.'

'You're one of those people who seem able to survive on virtually no sleep at all. Lucky girl!'

Were the words intended to carry the implication which they seemed to carry? Iris decided that they were. 'This air's so stimulating. One never feels tired.'

'One? This one' — Pippa pointed at herself — 'constantly feels tired.' Suddenly, surprisingly, head tilted to one side, she gave Iris a smile of extraordinary warmth. She raised one of her stubby hands and then, turning it, ran it slowly down the girl's cheek.

'Well, this air and this sun have done wonders for you. Beautiful! You look beautiful!'

Abruptly she turned away and hurried off down the corridor.

After breakfast — by now Dale had joined her — Iris went upstairs, having told him nothing of what she was proposing to do, and knocked on the door of the suite.

'Yes?'

Pippa sat, still barefoot and still in her kimono, in a straight-backed chair before the table on which her breakfast, scarcely touched, had been set out. She looked up, her eyes baleful under her straggling fringe.

'Do come skiing with us, Pippa! Just this once!'

Pippa shook her head, reaching out for the glass which, now noticed by Iris for the first time, all too clearly contained her favourite drink of ouzo. 'No, my dear. You go about your businesses and leave me to mine.'

'But Dale says that you're a super skier. Far better than either of us.'

'I used to be super at a lot of things. No more.'

'Oh, please!'

'No. Madam has spoken.'

Iris told Dale nothing of this conversation; but as they walked out from the hotel into a cold which made her catch her breath, she kept thinking about it. The cruelty which she had shown to Pippa, Pippa had successfully matched.

Of all their days in Zermatt, that one, in retrospect, was to be the most marvellous. Just as, during the previous night, everything had for once miraculously 'worked' (the phrase was Dale's) in their protracted, first teasing and then tumultuous love-making, so everything 'worked' now. The lift arrived at precisely the right moment; and the snow was of precisely the right consistency. Feats which would usually have been beyond her, though not beyond Dale, were now within her power. She had the illusion that, if she so wished, she had only to raise her arms to take wing and circle the town below her. However far apart she and Dale might be positioned from each other, she felt an invisible, constantly vibrating thread between her and him.

'You were marvellous!' He hugged her to him, at the bottom of a tricky slope.

'Yes, I was, I was! Marvellous! I never knew that I could do anything like that!'

'That's all my teaching.'

Both of them burst out laughing. They might have been talking about their lovemaking of the night before.

As they approached the hotel, one of the people whom Dale had asked to photograph them, a bank manager from Seattle who had a way of singing popular songs to himself even in public, waved a hand and then hurried across. 'Your friend's had an accident,' he announced, his eyes glinting with the exhilaration which so many people experience after witnessing a disaster. 'I was the first to help her. There!' He pointed to the well-cleared steps which led down to the 'little shop round the corner'. 'She just took this tumble. Didn't even seem to slip or catch her foot on anything. Just fell. Almost all the way down.'

Under his tan, Dale had gone extraordinarily pale. His mouth was open, saliva gleaming along his lower teeth in the light of the premature sunset. 'Is she badly hurt?'

'My guess would be that she's got what's called a Pott's fracture. But that's only my guess. My sister once had a Pott's fracture when she had a fall from a horse. It looked the same this time round. Anyway, the doctor's with her.'

The doctor had already injected Pippa with what he called 'something strong' and what Iris assumed to be morphine, so that, as she held Dale's hand limply in her own, from time to time raising it to her lips or her cheek, it was with a vague dreaminess that she mumbled: 'Ironical, really. Iris goes out on the slopes, only a beginner, and nothing happens to her. I decide to take a little stroll — and whoops!' She gave a wheezing laugh.

'But how did you fall?'

Again she gave that wheezing laugh. 'Head first!'

When the ambulance had arrived, Pippa was carried down to it on a stretcher. At one point, when the two white-coated men were negotiating the lift, she let out a sudden, single, piercing scream. It unnerved Iris.

In the lift, Dale reached for Pippa's hand. When Iris was about to step in to join them, he told her: 'No room.' He seemed to be taking pleasure in excluding her. Iris ran down the stairs.

By the rear doors of the ambulance, as he was preparing to get in, Dale told her: 'I'll be back as soon as I can. But God knows how long that'll be! Don't wait dinner.'

'Oh, I couldn't possibly eat.' She looked up at him in pleading misery: 'Oughtn't I to come to the hospital too?'

'No room,' he said again. Briefly, even perfunctorily he put his lips to her forehead. 'Wait for me, there's a good girl.'

From then on Iris always seemed to be waiting for him. Hour after hour he sat beside the bed in which Pippa lay with her broken leg in traction. Sometimes he would be reading to her, sometimes he would be talking to her. Sometimes he would merely be holding one of her hands in both of his, while she lay back on the high-piled pillows, their crisp cases changed at least twice a day, with her eyes closed either in exhaustion or in sleep.

Iris would arrive to add more flowers to the flowers already massed around the bed. Dale would look up at her standing in the doorway and his eyes would narrow, his lips thin. He never said it but nonetheless he seemed to be asking: 'What are *you* doing here?' She might have been some officious stranger, blundering into a sick-room.

'How are you?' Iris would ask. Or 'How is she?'

'Darling, don't waste your time on all this dreary sick-room visiting,' Pippa urged her more than once. On one such occasion she added: 'Enjoy yourself. That's why you're here.'

But how could she enjoy herself without Dale?

When they went upstairs immediately after dinner on the second night after the accident — 'I can't stand all that blaring music and all those raucous voices,' Dale had said pettishly, although in the past he had been happy to dance on and on with Iris, even though she was drooping with fatigue and longing only to retreat with him to bed — Iris asked: 'What are we going to do now?'

To that question she wanted him to reply with a laugh, as so often in the past: 'Fuck, of course.' But now he merely said: 'Well, *I'm* going to read. Jack lent me *Middlemarch*. I doubt if I'll ever get through it, but at least I must try.'

On the third night it was she who made her way, barefoot and in nothing but a dressing-gown, along the corridor to the suite. Behind her, she heard accelerating footfalls and then a tipsy voice: 'Why, hello there!' It was the bank manager from Seattle, who had confided in her and Dale, from the next-door table at dinner that evening: 'I like the *après-ski* shenanigans far more than the actual skiing.'

'Oh, hello,' Iris said over her shoulder and hurried on. Normally she would have been embarrassed. Now she felt nothing.

She could hear him fumbling with his key in the lock to his room. 'Well, a good night to you, my dear.' There was something insolent in the way which he pointed the words.

Unlike Pippa, who always left the door to the suite unlocked, Dale had locked it. As she waited for him to come in answer to her rap, Iris hoped that no other late reveller would appear.

'Oh.' He was wearing nothing but a pair of underpants. He held the door so little open that she had to brush past him to enter. 'I'm absolutely bushed.'

Determined, she walked into his bedroom, pulled off her dressing-gown, and dropped it to the floor. She crossed to the bed and climbed on to it.

'I said I was bushed.'

'Oh, come on!' She held out an arm in invitation. 'What's the matter?'

Without answering, he came across, stooped and pulled off the underpants.

'You really want it?'

'Of course I really want it. Why shouldn't I really want it? Has Pippa's fall smashed what was between us as well as her leg?'

There was something menacing in the way he stared down at her, his long, uncircumcised penis slowly extending itself in an erection.

'If you really want it, then you'll have to have it in a totally different way.'

'What do you mean?'

'You'll see.'

It was a huge, pre-war Mercedes Benz, a glass partition dividing the chauffeur from the passengers in the rear, which Pippa hired to take her back to Florence.

'Wouldn't it be easier to take the train?' Iris asked.

'Easier, yes. But this will be more fun.'

But there was no fun in it for Iris. Although there was ample room in the back for her as well — there were even two folding seats in addition to the wide banquette — Dale told her peremptorily: 'You sit in the front with the driver. That'll give Pippa all the room she needs for her leg.'

'You'll also be able to see much more,' Pippa added. 'And the chauffeur's so handsome.'

From time to time Iris would look either in the driving-mirror or, briefly and surreptitiously, over her shoulder. She could see, but not hear, Pippa and Dale talking and laughing together. Dale leaned towards Pippa, he put a hand on her knee. She picked up the hand and laced its fingers in her own. At one moment, their lips met. Iris might not have been there. Speculating in her presence about the relationship, Ivor had said: 'People say that it's a mother-fixation. But it's not a silver cord that binds him to her, it's a golden one.' As he had said the word 'golden', he had rubbed well-manicured middle finger and thumb against each other. But Iris now knew that it was neither of these things, but something far stronger and stranger.

Through the speaking tube Pippa's voice reached her, tinny and muffled. 'Are you all right, Iris, my dear?'

'Yes, thank you. I'm fine.'

'You look as if all these hairpin bends might be making you car-sick. We'll soon stop, so that you and Dale can have some gulps of clean, invigorating mountain air.'

'What I want is some gulps of strong, invigorating coffee.'

Iris glanced sideways at the chauffeur. Yes, Pippa had been right. He was handsome, even beautiful, with that dark skin and shiny black hair and those eyes which, in certain lights – yes, at this moment, as the car devoured yet another hairpin bend – looked no longer blue but the deepest of violet. She stared in turn at his strong hands and thick, hairy wrists; at the high cheek-bone nearest to her; at his thighs. But he meant nothing to her.

She began to think, with a mixture of excitement and desperation, of all that had followed when, on that night, she had said to Dale, half fearful and half thrilled, 'What do you mean?' and he had replied 'You'll see.'

20

'In the summer, what used to be called the drawing-room of Europe becomes its railway-station concourse. But now, in winter, it's perfect, absolutely perfect.' The edges of the Piazza San Marco were blurred by the mist which, thick on their arrival, was beginning to dissipate as the sun rose higher. 'It's odd', Ivor went on, 'that when one sense suffers a deprivation, the others grow much stronger. In the fierce, clear light of summer, when all those sweaty people are tramping from one tourist shrine to another, one is hardly aware of the noise of their feet on the stones which inspired Ruskin to his greatest book. But on a late December afternoon like this don't the few feet sound loud?'

At the railway station, disdaining the common *vaporetto*, on which Jack would so much have preferred to travel, Ivor had hired a motor launch to take them to the Danieli, where he had reserved a suite similar in its accommodation to Pippa's at Zermatt.

'Happy?' he had asked when the bus-boy had left them.

Jack had looked around him with wonder. He had never before stayed in a hotel of any kind, let alone one of this luxury, only in boarding-houses. 'These must all be antiques.'

'Well, in a sense.' Ivor had laughed. 'The sort of antiques that you can see being manufactured in Venice on any walk down any little *calle*.'

Jack had gone across to the window; but the mist had made it difficult to see even the *vaporetto* station. Mysteriously amplified, plangent in its melancholy, he had heard a ship's hooter, even though the window was closed.

Ivor had come to stand close beside him; Jack had smelled that scent, pungent and lemony, which, decades later, would still have the power to evoke a long since vanished presence. 'The first time

I ever came to Venice was when I was five. We arrived at the Danieli not in a motor launch but in a gondola, and the water was so high that two gondoliers had to transport first my mother and then my father into the hotel on a throne-like chair. Then one of the gondoliers picked me up in his arms, and the other gondolier picked up my sister. My gondolier's trousers were rolled up to his knees. I can still see those muscular, hairy legs of his. I can still feel those muscular, hairy arms around me. I can still smell the sweat from his armpits and the tobacco-smoke on his breath and, in addition, a tarry smell, a smell of the sea.' Up to this point there had been a lilting poetry to Ivor's utterances; but then an awkward self-consciousness, inexplicable to Jack, had supervened. 'Perhaps that long-ago experience did more to form my essential nature than anything else that has happened in a generally misspent life. Perhaps, ever since, I have been looking – metaphorically, of course – for a pair of brawny arms and a pair of muscular legs to transport me to safety through the cold, murky sea of life.'

Now, in the middle of the Piazza, Ivor leaned on his walking-stick; it had a grimacing gargoyle, carved in ivory, for its head. Then he raised the stick and pointed with it at the bell-tower. 'That collapsed in 1902. It just tipped over and collapsed. A.E. Housman wrote an extraordinarily moving poem about it, linking its collapse with the death of his gondolier chum. Andrea he was called, the gondolier.' He began to declaim:

'Andrea, fare you well;
Venice, farewell to thee.
The tower that stood and fell
Is not rebuilt in me.

'Marvellous stuff. Far better than anything written by Wystan. And yet Wystan had the effrontery to write of Housman "keeping tears like dirty postcards in a drawer".'

'Do you mean that Housman was – a homo?'

'Well, if you must use that peculiarly unattractive solecism – the "o", incidentally, is short, not long, since the derivation is from the Greek word "*homoios*", meaning "same", and *not* the Latin "*homo*", meaning "a man" – then, yes, I suppose that one must admit – or, as I should prefer to put it, one can claim – that he was, er, a homo. No doubt about it.'

'I never knew that. And Housman's always been one of my favourite poets.'

'There's a lot you don't know, dear boy.' Then, since Jack was clearly exasperated at being told this, Ivor put an arm round his shoulder and squeezed him against himself. 'But that — that douce innocence of yours — as you must by now be tired of being told — is what makes us all so fond of you. Intelligence and innocence, they so rarely go together.'

They began to wander towards Florian, crowded in summer but all but deserted now. Ivor greeted one of the waiters by name and then told Jack: 'He was such a charming rogue, two, three years ago. But now he's acquired a wife and that paunch of his along with the wife, and he's become oh so respectable and *dull*.'

There was a piano out in the arcade and on it an etiolated young man, with straggling hair reaching almost to his shoulders, was playing a transcription of Tosti's 'Goodbye'.

'Tosti, who wrote this little number, was a great favourite of Queen Victoria. He's also a great favourite of mine. He always makes me want to cry.' Ivor seated himself at one of the outside tables. Then he pointed with the stick: 'Sit, sit!' Jack sat. 'Unless, of course, you think you'll catch cold out here.'

'Of course not!'

'I suggest that we each have an Americano. But don't misunderstand me please, as Maurice Bowra did, getting unnecessarily excited, when I made the same suggestion to him in precisely this same spot last summer. . . . Salvatore — *due Americani, per favore!*'

'*Subito, signore!*'

'I could really do without a song about a funicular when sitting in this Piazza,' Ivor complained as the pianist, long hair bouncing on narrow shoulders, now launched into a transcription of 'Funiculì, funiculà'.

But Jack was paying no attention. He was peering through the mist. 'Isn't that — isn't that' — he pointed — 'Miss Pryce over there?'

Hurrying along in flat-heeled, black lace-up shoes and a cape of navy serge, Ethel might have been mistaken for a hospital nurse on her way to an emergency.

'Ethel? Yes, I do believe it is! Why don't you ask her to join us?'

Jack hesitated. To have Ethel, whose presence always seemed to him to seep a censorious self-righteousness, join them was the last thing he wanted.

174

'Hurry, dear boy! Otherwise you'll lose her in this mist.'

As Jack proceeded to hurry, he wondered why on earth Ivor should seek out Ethel's company.

Ethel swung round as Jack called her name. Then seeing who it was, she looked far from pleased. 'Oh, Mr Prentice! I'd no idea you were in Venice.'

'And I'd no idea *you* were here. I'm in that café' — he pointed — 'with Ivor Luce, and he was wondering if you'd like to join us.'

'Ivor Luce? Are you here with Ivor Luce?'

'Yes. We arrived only this morning.'

'By sleeper?'

'Yep.'

'I sat up all night. But I feel none the worse for it. So — well, why not? In for a penny, in for a pound.'

'Ah, Miss Pryce!' Ivor rose to his feet and gave a deep, stiff bow. 'What a nice surprise! Come and sit over here and tell me everything you've been doing.'

Ethel smiled; she began to relax. 'I've hardly had time to do anything at all. As I was telling Mr Prentice, I must have arrived on the same train that you did. I'm just on my way back from the Scuola di San Giorgio degli Schiavoni.'

'Ah, Carpaccio, Carpaccio! That little dog is my favourite animal in the whole history of art.'

'Which little dog?'

'*Which* little dog? My dear, you must clearly have been distracted at some moment. *La visione di Sant'Agostino*. The little dog — a poodle by the looks of it — seems to be sharing the vision. Perhaps the picture ought to be entitled *La visione di Sant' Agostino e del can barbone*.'

'I don't remember any little dog.' Ethel was not the kind of person to pretend that she had noticed something which she hadn't.

'You'll be telling me next that you walked through this Piazza without noticing the bell-tower.'

Ethel laughed. Jack had never before known her to laugh like that: spontaneously, warmly, even joyously. 'Oh, I noticed *that*!'

'And I should jolly well hope so too. . . . Salvatore — Salvatore!' When the waiter came over, Ivor began to press Ethel to have a capuccino and 'one of those gooey cakes which are a must for any well-bred Italian woman at this hour'.

'But I'm not an Italian woman, and I'm not well-bred,' Ethel protested.

'Well, pretend that you're both of those things.'

Ethel eventually agreed to capuccino and cake.

'I'm amazed that you should have decided to take a holiday. Jack is always telling me how hard you work.' In fact, Jack had told him this only once.

'Yes, I *have* had to work hard. I have — family responsibilities.' She set down the fork with which she had been eating her éclair, as though she no longer had any appetite for it. All at once, she had lost her former air of relaxation. She looked dissatisfied, even unhappy. 'I'm here only for three days. I felt that I must have a break.'

'We all need breaks. Within reason. I sometimes think that my life is nothing more than a series of breaks. Not good.' But Ivor looked quite cheerful about it. 'It's disgraceful what they pay at the Institute. Sweated labour.'

They continued to talk, with Ethel slowly relaxing once again. Then she looked at her watch: 'Oh, heavens! I must get back to my *pensione*. I'm going to be late for dinner. It's really quite a walk.'

'Which *pensione* is that?'

Defensively, she did not name it. 'Oh, it's up beyond the Rialto. Not a very attractive area. But it does have the advantage of being cheap.'

'Why don't you let me take you out to dinner at Harry's Bar, along with Jack here?'

'Oh, no,' Ethel said, ungracious in her embarrassment, as Jack also so often was. 'Thank you all the same. You see, the *pensione* terms include dinner. It seems silly not to have dinner there, since I'm going to have to pay for it.'

Ivor shrugged. 'Well, as you wish, my dear.'

The two men watched her as she hurried off, head lowered and guide-book under arm, across the Piazza. Then Ivor laughed: 'How some people hate wasting money. My dear, dead sister was just like that. She'd endure anything in order not to have to do it. One can imagine what the poor woman will get to eat. Spaghetti in a watery tomato sauce. Tough veal. A crème caramel. And the company!'

'Why did you want her to join us for dinner?'

'Because I thought she might be lonely. It's not much fun being a woman alone in Italy. Even worse than in England. If your handbag's not being pinched, then your bottom is.'

'I think you felt her to be a challenge.'

'A challenge? How do you mean?'

Jack hesitated. Then he decided to go ahead. 'I've noticed this before about you. You sense when people don't like you or disapprove of you. And then it's a kind of game for you – to make them change their minds.'

Ivor looked piqued. 'And does Miss Pryce dislike me and disapprove of me?'

'I don't think she likes or approves of anyone very much.'

Ivor pondered, staring out over the misty piazza. Then he said: 'A tightly clenched fist. That's what she reminds me of. A tightly clenched fist. Clenched to withhold something vital. Clenched to strike out, should that prove necessary. And yes, it gave me a certain pleasure somehow to get that fist to open. Yes, yes, it did.'

'I think you also wanted, well, just to be kind.'

'Oh, don't say that! Please! People who want, well, just to be kind are usually the most awful bores.'

'You're not a bore.'

'Aren't I? I wish that everyone shared that view.'

In Harry's Bar, Jack had both eaten and drunk too much. Partly this was because Ivor had kept pressing him to do so; partly because he felt awkward when person after person – Italian, English, American, French – had come over to their table to greet Ivor and then, inevitably, to meet Ivor's protégé. 'This is a particularly charming and intelligent young English friend of mine . . .' 'Now, Principessa, you really must meet this delightful young man . . .' 'Rita, do let me present to you . . .' Jack wished that Ivor would not gush so. One elderly Italian woman, her eyes heavily shadowed with mascara, and a scar thickly but ineffectually covered with powder at one temple, had sat down for a while, deserting her own party. She had leaned across the table, her hands clasped, and Jack had felt her knee against his. Deliberate, accidental? He had not been sure. He had moved his knee away.

Now he lay out on a bed wider than any on which he had ever slept – 'Oh, dear, what a *pompous* bed!' Ivor had exclaimed when that morning they had inspected their quarters – and attempted to take in an essay by Pater on Winkelmann. Ivor had insisted that he read it: 'It's as full of inaccuracies as the fur of a Venetian cat with fleas, but it gives you a wonderful idea of what the Renaissance was all about.' He felt vaguely queasy. If he let himself fall asleep, he dreaded that he might be sick.

Suddenly, he heard his door opening. Ivor stood in the doorway, in scarlet silk pyjamas, his monogram embroidered on the pocket, and scarlet slippers, similarly embroidered. His red hair, damp from a bath or a shower, was brushed sleekly back from his freckled, aquiline face. The nostrils looked pinched, the shadows were deep under his cheek-bones.

'I saw that your light was still on as I came out of the bathroom. Can't you sleep?'

'I thought I'd read for a while.'

Ivor crossed over to the bed. 'The essay on Winckelmann?'

Jack nodded. He felt suddenly panicky, he did not know why. He wished that Ivor would leave him. 'It's difficult,' he said, not knowing whether he meant the essay or the present situation.

Ivor lowered himself on to the edge of the bed. He put up a hand and smoothed his already smooth hair. He gave a little laugh. 'You look so studious — peering down at that large book. You also look — so fetching.' Again he gave a little laugh. Then he stretched himself out on the bed beside Jack. He put a hand to Jack's chin, raised his head and turned it towards him. 'Stop reading. Look at me.'

Jack looked. Then he looked away. His panic intensified. But he still was not sure what it was that caused it.

'I suppose you realize that I've become very fond of you?'

Jack stared down at the book.

'Very fond of you.'

Ivor leaned forward and put his lips to Jack's averted cheek.

At that, as though stung by a hornet, Jack leapt out of bed. 'No! *No!*' He crossed over to the window; and again, mysteriously plangent, he heard a ship's hooter. The sound somehow pacified him. 'Please,' he said. Then: 'Sorry.'

'No need to say sorry. I'm the one to say sorry. One commits these *bêtises* from time to time. Perhaps I commit them more often than most people. But faint heart never won fair lady — or, in this case, fair gentleman.' He had now got off the bed. He walked, unhurried and seemingly unembarrassed, towards the door; then turned. 'Forgive — and forget. Yes? A miscalculation. But one of little consequence.'

He was about to leave the room, when Jack stepped forward from the window. 'Would you – should I . . . ?' He did not know how to put it.

'Yes?'

'I'd better go tomorrow.'

'*Go?* Go where?'

'Well, back . . . back to Florence. You won't want me around now.' Ivor was staring at him; he tried to stare back. 'Will you?'

'Of course I want you around! Of course!' Suddenly Ivor was laughing. 'This little setback needn't have any meaning. Why should it? You're unharmed and I'm unembarrassed. So . . . Oh, Jack, don't be so silly. I love having your eager, ignorant intelligence to strike sparks from my world-weary, knowing one. We're good for each other. We can help each other. Can't we?' His self-assurance seemed to vanish, as he asked the question. He repeated: 'Can't we?'

Jack nodded. Suddenly, he knew that they could.

'Oh, good boy! Sensible boy! I knew that you'd be good and sensible about it. I've planned a wonderful day for tomorrow. It was to be a surprise, but now I'm going to tell you all. I've ordered the launch and we're going to make the journey down the canal from Venice to Padua. Now how about that? Anna-Maria is going to give us lunch at her Palladian villa, and we're also going to look in on the Villa Barbara and the Villa Emo and . . . oh, well, you'll see for yourself.'

Alone, Jack felt suddenly elated. It was as though, totally unscathed, he had survived a potentially lethal motor-crash.

Jack was away from the Institute, with the 'flu with which he had been stricken as soon as he had returned from Venice.

In the common room, Tim puffed at one of the cheap Italian cigarettes which he seemed to buy, in preference to English or American black-market ones, merely in order to give Miss Sweeney cause for complaint. In between sips at a cup of coffee – it was so hot that it was turning her nose red – she waved a hand before her face and drew one deep sigh on another.

'And how did *you* pass your Christmas, Miss Pryce? Now that you've heard all about all my misdoings, let me hear all about all your doings.'

'I don't think my doings would be of much interest to you.'

'Oh, there you're mistaken. *Nihil humanum* . . . Please! Did you give any private lessons on Christmas Day and New Year's Day?'

'As a matter of fact, on neither.'

'So?'

'So?'

'So what *did* you do?'

'Well, if we must have this inquisition' — suddenly Ethel, previously so sharp, was smiling — 'I took myself off to Venice.'

'Venice!'

'Oh, I do so love Venice in the winter,' Miss Sweeney looked up over her coffee-cup to say. 'When we were children, my parents *would* take us to the Lido every summer. And I *loathed* it. But Venice in the winter is quite another thing . . .'

'Did you buy any Murano glass?' Mr Greville enquired, as he placed a corrected exercise book on top of the pile before him. 'Such lovely stuff.'

'No, my budget wouldn't really have stretched to that.' Ethel smiled down at the table, as though at some secret joke. Then she looked up: 'To my surprise, I ran into Mr Prentice. He was there with Ivor Luce.'

'Ivor Luce!' Miss Sweeney put down her coffee-cup.

'Doing it in style. At the Danieli. Rather different from my own little *pensione*. On the evening I met them, they were having drinks at Florian and were about to have dinner at Harry's Bar. The following day I saw them on a private launch. They didn't see me,' she added.

Mr Greville cleared his throat. 'I think that perhaps someone should warn that boy . . .'

'My guess would be that the time for warnings has passed,' Tim said. 'Anyway, why are we all being so stuffy about it? Why shouldn't the boy have a good time? What's it to do with us, in any case?'

'He's very young,' Miss Sweeney said.

'And very unworldly,' Mr Greville added.

'I don't think he's in the least bit unworldly,' Ethel said. 'He's got his head well screwed on, and he knows precisely which side his bread is buttered.'

Iris, who had been reading in a corner, jumped up. 'Oh, do stop all this! Stop it!' Her face was reddening with anger, her voice was strained. 'It's just horrible to talk in this way about a colleague.'

Ethel shrugged and pulled a face. Miss Sweeney sighed and

sipped again at her coffee. Mr Greville pretended that nothing had happened.

Tim raised his hands. Then he clapped. 'Now there's a decent, good-hearted girl!'

21

Carefully, Franco removed the bedpan from under Harry. 'Oh, do cover it with a cloth!' Karen had scolded him when, as she was waiting outside the bedroom, Franco had carried it past her. But there was no point in now covering it with a cloth. He himself knew perfectly well what it contained, and there were rarely visitors so early in the morning.

He pulled a face as he emptied the contents of the bedpan down the ancient lavatory. 'Oh, do rinse it out!' Isabella had scolded him, when, officious as always, she had looked in on him through the half-open door of the lavatory. But there was no point in rinsing it out when, in five or ten or fifteen minutes, that feeble now weirdly falsetto voice would yet again call out to him 'Franco! Franco!' As he placed the bedpan against the wall, he muttered to himself, imitating Harry: 'Drat the boy!'

Soon Signorina Audrey would arrive, as she had promised. She would be coming not merely to get Harry's luncheon, the ostensible reason for her visit, but also to scrounge her own, Franco thought cynically. Should he wait for her? No, he was damned if he would. If the *signore* needed anything, he would just have to hang on till she arrived. Spoiled he was, thoroughly spoiled. But then every *gran'signore* was like that.

'I'll be on my way now,' Franco said brusquely in Italian, on his return to the sick-room.

'Where are you going?'

'To the swimming-pool,' Franco lied. 'I must have my daily swim.'

'But Signorina Heaton hasn't arrived yet, has she?'

'She's coming. Any moment now.'

'But you know how unpunctual she is!'

Franco shrugged. 'What can I do, *babbo*? I can't hang around all morning. I must have some time off.' Selfish, utterly selfish! They were all like that. When his father had been dying, it was all his mother could do to get away to spend a few minutes by the sick-bed. And yet. . . A tenderness, unaccountable and uncomfortable, slithered through his bowels. He lowered a hand and placed it on Harry's forehead.

Having recoiled involuntarily from its roughness and damp-ness, Harry then felt remorse. 'You're a good lad,' he said, as he so often did. 'I don't know what I'd do without you.'

'Die,' was what Franco wanted to answer. But he merely smiled, touched and grateful as well as irritated.

'I can't think why Nerone hasn't been near me for three, four days.'

'Because you haven't paid his bill for three, four weeks,' Franco wanted to answer. But again he merely smiled. Somehow he would have to rustle up enough cash to pay that money-grubbing doctor. But at this time of year, with so few visitors, that would be tough.

'Have you telephoned him?'

'How can I 'phone him when we were cut off ten days ago?'

Harry covered his face with his emaciated hands. 'Oh, Lordy, Lordy!' he moaned in English. Then he went on in Italian: 'The trouble is that I've just lived too long. Far, far too long.'

He could say that again! 'Why don't you ask Signore Luce for some money? He's rolling in it.'

'Oh, I couldn't do that!'

'Why not?'

'Pride. Something which probably means nothing to a little guttersnipe like you!' Harry gave a wheezing laugh, his bony shoulders shaking, to indicate that the seeming insult was merely a joke. 'In any case, we've never really got on with each other. I've never had much use for pansies. It always made me uncomfortable when my late wife *would* insist on entertaining people like Norman Douglas.'

'Signore Douglas?' Franco remembered him. In a wood not far from Harry's villa, he had gathered around him some pubescent schoolboys, Franco among them, and had then held aloft a note of pitifully small denomination to be awarded to the boy who, in an increasingly frenzied contest, succeeded in coming first. Stingy old bugger!

'I hope he never laid his dirty hands on you.'

Franco laughed.

'Did he?'

Franco laughed again.

As he screeched round one corner after another on his Vespa, Franco deliberated where to go. Under the arches of the Piazza Repubblica used to be fine; but now there were so many plain-clothes policemen there, primarily determined to catch the boys selling not themselves but black-market cigarettes and booze. At this time of year, the Lung'Arno was out. Yes, it would have to be the Uffizi. As that English army officer in mufti had once explained to him, the love of art and the love of arse often went together. ('Arse?' Franco had queried, puzzled; and the English army officer had then laughed and, with an inelegant gesture, had indicated what the word meant.)

He knew a back way into the Uffizi, through the door to the kitchen of the employees' canteen. He could slip in without paying. Why, he could even steal a picture if he felt like it!

Because the spring had all at once taken another of its impetuous leaps towards the summer, Audrey had left both window and door of her kitchen open. As Jack approached the house, he could therefore hear Adrian booming away: '. . . Some say they do, and some say they don't. But a handsome, if louche, young man and an extremely rich, ageing queen – well, what do *you* think, my dear? I know what *I* think.'

Jack wanted to run away through the gate hanging askew from its rotting gate-post, past the Rolls-Royce parked on the verge of the road outside, and down the hill to the tram-stop, never to return. But an obstinate pride and a no less obstinate sense of duty – Audrey was expecting him, to sort out some notes for her – forced him to continue round the house and up to the front door.

'Oh, it's you!' Audrey exclaimed, as she opened the door. 'I'd totally forgotten you were coming.' She looked embarrassed, clearly asking herself: 'Could he have heard us?' She was not herself malicious, and Adrian's malice was one of the reasons why she had never really taken to him. His hypocrisy was another. *An extremely rich, ageing queen. . .* ! The description was as apt for him as for Ivor.

'Is it inconvenient? Would you like me to come another time?' Jack now felt an increasing reluctance to come face to face with Adrian.

'Good heavens no! We've oodles to do. I've got Adrian here. He popped in just now – chiefly, I suspect, because he wanted to kill some time while Luigi is having his hair cut. I ask you! Fancy waiting around for one's so-called driver while he's having the full treatment at one of the most expensive barber shops in Poggio Imperiale! Anyway, I'll get rid him, tell him we've things to do.' She knew that, seated in the kitchen with a cup of coffee, Adrian could probably hear what she was saying. If he could, she was glad of it. Ivor and the boy might or might not be having an affair, but of one thing she was sure: the boy, unlike Adrian's little *numero*, was totally unmercenary.

Like Audrey, Adrian was also embarrassed at being confronted by Jack. He, too, was asking himself: 'Could he have heard us?' But he concealed his embarrassment more successfuly than she had done. 'I was going to give you a ring. Giles and Margot are coming to a buffet lunch next Sunday, and I was wondering if you'd like to come too?'

Clumsily Jack lied. 'Well, as a matter of fact . . . some friends . . . we'd planned to go into the country.'

'Oh, that's sad! I know that on this occasion Ivor can't be among those friends, since he's already accepted to come to me.'

Jack wished that he had not started to blush. 'No, these are two girls staying in Florence at the present.' Extemporizing, suddenly he had thought of Pat and her sister Flora. He must get in touch with them.

'Two *girls*! . . . Ah, well, never mind. Another time. You didn't by any chance happen to see if Luigi – my driver – was sitting in the Rolls?'

'The car was empty.'

'He *must* be back by now,' Audrey said, eager to get rid of Adrian and to push on with her work with Jack. 'Unless he's having a permanent wave,' she added.

Adrian looked at his watch. 'I told him to be sure to be back by eleven. I have to pick up Adriana at eleven-thirty.'

As Adrian walked off down the drive, Audrey turned to Jack and said in a deliberately loud voice: 'How can that Adriana woman *not* know the score? His *cover-girl* he calls her behind her back to his chums. Either she's a fool, or she's decided to pretend to be one.'

After they had worked together for several minutes – Audrey was even more impatient than usual, at one point scolding Jack for muddling up some papers which, in fact, she herself had muddled up – she broke off: 'I still owe you money.'

'Oh, please don't worry about it, Miss Heaton.'

'Easier said than done! Of course I worry about it. How could I not worry about it? All my life, I've had an absolute horror of being in debt to anyone, anyone at all. There was a time when the mere thought of a mortgage or a bank-loan . . . Anyway, I've had an idea. Perhaps, as an interim measure, I could pay you in kind.'

'In kind?'

'Come with me.' She got up, stiffly because in the spring her arthritis was always most acute, and beckoned imperiously. 'Come!'

Jack followed her down the corridor, into the room which had once been Johnny's. As always, the bed was made, with a pair of black silk pyjamas laid across its counterpane, and a pair of black velvet slippers standing on the worn Chinese rug beside it.

'Last night I decided that it was pointless to keep all these relics. She remains, and my love for her remains. But all this' – she waved a hand in an inclusive gesture – 'all this doesn't have to remain. It was sentimental of me to think that it had to remain. I was doing a Widow of Windsor.'

'Widow of Windsor?'

'Queen Victoria, my dear. After the death of her beloved Albert. . . . Oh, in some ways you're so well educated, and in others . . . It's not just you, it's your whole generation. That Crediton girl had never even *heard* of *I Promessi Sposi*. I ask you! The greatest of Italian novels and one of the greatest novels ever written. Anyway . . . ' She pulled open the doors of the heavy mahogany breakfront wardrobe to reveal the men's suits, trousers and sports jackets hanging in profusion. 'Take your pick of anything you fancy!'

Jack was aghast. 'Oh, but . . .'

'No need to be worried about size. Johnny was about your height and build, give or take an inch or two. And I have this wonderful jobbing tailor. Even the Corsini use him.' She pulled at a sleeve of a tweed hacking-jacket. 'This would be fine for you. Very *sportif*. Johnny ordered it from Hawes and Curtis on our last visit to London, and she wore it only once or twice.' She pulled the jacket off its hanger and held it out. 'Try it on,' she ordered.

'I don't really think . . .'

'Try it on!'

It was a surprisingly good fit. 'Mastroianni will have no difficulty in putting up those sleeves half an inch. Johnny had these extremely long arms,' she added, as though to have extremely long arms were a physical attraction. 'Yours are rather short, aren't they? I've noticed that before.'

'But are you sure . . . ?'

'Certainly I'm sure. I told you. Last night, I suddenly said to myself: "Now, Audrey, this has gone on long enough. Get rid of all that stuff, clear out that room. Then find yourself a lodger, to help with your day-to-day expenses." You might be that lodger!' she cried out, the thought suddenly coming to her. 'Why not?'

Oh, God, God!

'Now how about that?' she pursued.

'It's a terrific idea. But I have to be near the Institute. And in any case — I couldn't upset Margot and Giles by leaving them.'

'I'd charge you less. Those two rook you!'

How did she know what he was paying? Had she asked them? 'Well, let me think about it.'

'There *is* the Credition girl. That Pensione Dante is a dump. Johnny used to say that it ought to be called the Pensione L'Inferno. Ah, well! Anyway . . .' She pulled open a drawer. 'Underwear? Silk. All in A1 condition.'

Jack shook his head. 'Sorry. Somehow — wearing someone else's underwear . . .'

'It's all been washed!' Audrey said indignantly. 'And Johnny was *scrupulous*. Absolutely scrupulous.'

'I'm sure. It's just that I have this totally irrational feeling. When my grandfather died, I just couldn't bear to wear his overcoat. And it was a nice overcoat. And I needed a new one. My parents were furious with me.'

'Well, then, how about these cuff-links? You can't object to cuff-links.'

'I never wear shirts with cuffs.'

'Then you ought to. For formal occasions. I'm surprised that Ivor has never told you that those *cricket* shirts of yours are just not right for a luncheon or a dinner party. Or a cocktail party, for the matter of that. Anyway . . . there are piles of the most beautiful formal shirts here. You can just take your pick. Johnny always went to Cole's — unless she went to Sulka, as she did on rare occasions. What's your collar size?'

'Fifteen.'

'Well, that's fine. In her later years Johnny went to fifteen and a half. A half is as good as makes no difference. You'll probably put on weight with that passion of yours for *pastaciutta*.'

What passion was she talking about? Only on one occasion, having overslept and so having missed breakfast, he had eaten more of her overcooked lunch-time *pastaciutta* than he would normally have done.

Eventually he was landed with the hacking-jacket, two pairs of cuff-links, two striped shirts with inordinately high collars, a silk cravat in a paisley pattern and the black silk pyjamas. All these things Audrey stuffed into an outsize Gladstone bag, also once the property of Johnny.

'Well, that's to be going on with,' she said.

Did this mean that she would not now be paying him? Jack was too embarrassed to ask.

When he arrived home, he opened the Gladstone bag — it had been a terrible nuisance to everyone when he was getting on and off the crowded tram — and removed its contents, throwing them haphazard across the bed. Could he ever bear to wear them? He stared down at them; then decided he couldn't. Out in the corridor, Maria was on her hands and knees scrubbing the tiles. She was singing to herself, happy again, since she now had another boyfriend, the delivery-boy from the butcher's. On an impulse Jack went out and called her.

Shyly she edged into the room.

He pointed at the clothes and asked, in the halting Italian which made her smile or even sometimes giggle, whether she would like them for *il suo amico*.

'*Per Alfredo?*' She was astounded. It was the first time that Jack had heard his name.

'*Si. Io non ho bisogna.*' Oh, if only he could speak the language as Iris now spoke it!

Maria let out a scream of delight. She picked up the jacket and examined it. She looked at the label on one of the shirts, although it could mean nothing to her. She put the cravat round her own neck. '*Tutti?*'

'*Tutti. Perché non?*'

Overwhelmed, she suddenly leaned forward, put her arms around him and, head on his shoulder, hugged him to her.

He smelled that feral odour, similar to that of the huge tabby cat which would often stalk across the garden and then bound through the window, to settle on his bed. He felt extraordinarily excited by it. He in turn hugged her, then clumsily, screwing his head round, attempted to put his lips on hers.

She gave him a push; pulled free; burst into laughter. 'Non, non! Malvagio! Malvagio!'

Malvagio? He had no idea what it meant. But clearly she was not really annoyed. He reached out to grasp her hand. But with another laugh and another cry of 'Non, non!', she was gone.

Soon he could once again hear the swish, swish of her brush on the tiles, and that high, slightly husky voice of hers singing 'Volare'. The sound of the brush, the sound of her singing and that feral odour still in his nostrils now filled him with a profound sense of well-being. He picked up now one item of clothing and now another, folded it carefully, and placed it in the bag. No doubt she would return for them.

But what would Audrey think if she saw a butcher's delivery-boy in Johnny's hacking-jacket? The thought had suddenly come to him.

He smiled to himself, as he clicked the Gladstone bag shut.

In the olive grove above Florence, the young, pink American, a doctor at the nearby base, raised the kidney bowl in his rubber-gloved hands. The stainless steel of the bowl glinted in the sunlight. He smiled at Franco and then, as though partaking of some obscene sacrament, sipped from it. 'The elixir of life,' he sighed.

Franco stared, lips curled back in disgust. Pazzarello! Stomache-vole!, he thought and almost said.

Partly because of that disgust and partly because of all the outstanding bills piled on Harry's desk, Franco brutally demanded 'More', when the American held out some dollar notes. Again he demanded: 'More.'

The American shrugged his shoulders, drew a deep sigh. After he had twice added to the sum, he said in Italian: 'Basta, basta.' Then, with amazing agility for someone seeming so feeble, he raced towards his car, jumped into it and drove off, leaving Franco first to gag on the dust of its passage and then to shout incoherent abuse after it.

It was a long walk to the nearest bus stop; and a long wait once he had got there. But Franco was pleased. In his trouser pocket he had enough notes — his hand kept seeking them out — to pay Nerone, to pay Anna, to pay the electricity bill, and to buy *babbo* some of that Ben-ja he so much liked.

Karen had gone to Sweden, Mervyn explained, to attend a family wedding. 'It's all quite dotty, really. She's constantly saying how much she hates the country and hates all her relatives there. But one of them has only to get married, christened or buried, and she's at once dashing over to Cook's. The odd thing is that, where our children are concerned, nothing will budge her. Last month our eldest, Cressida, had to go into the London Clinic for a gall-bladder operation. Did Karen rush over to help out with the offspring? You bet she didn't. Two months before that the wife of our youngest, Damon, went and pupped again. Was Karen on hand? Of course not. But just because the son of some distant cousin is to be christened, she makes that long and expensive journey, leaving me here to my own devices.'

The upshot of all this was that Mervyn begged Iris to spend the evening with him; and, touched by his abject pathos, she decided that for once, after many refusals, she would accept.

'It's the couple's evening off, so they've left us a cold spread. You don't mind, do you? Olga's tarragon chicken is really rather delicious, and I've got a Verdicchio dei Castelli di Jesu of which even Ivor has approved.'

As they sat facing each other at either end of the long, narrow table, he asked, 'So what have you been doing with yourself?'

'Teaching.' She smiled.

'And being taught?'

'Being taught?'

He drew the corners of his mouth downwards, and shrugged his shoulders. 'I gather that you have two excellent teachers in Pippa and the Somers boy.'

'I can't imagine what it is they teach me!'

'The art of living, perhaps?'

'I shouldn't have thought that Pippa was an expert on that. Her way of living often seems to lack any artistry at all.'

'I hoped at one time that *I* should be your teacher,' Mervyn said with a heavy, yearning melancholy.

'You have been. I've learned a lot from you.'

'I find that past sense terribly depressing.'

'I'm sorry. I didn't mean it to be.'

A long, oppressive silence followed. Then he said: 'Talking of teaching, how is your chum Prentice getting on?'

'Oh, he's a far better teacher than I am. For one thing he's been properly educated, and for another he's terribly conscientious.'

'I was not really enquiring about his abilities as an employee of the Institute.' He smiled across at her, as he raised some chicken to his mouth. He chewed, swallowed. Then he said: 'I was really enquiring about the *éducation sentimentale* which he is receiving from our Ivor.'

'I know nothing about that.'

'You know that they're friends.'

'They seem to have hit it off. Why not?'

He sighed. 'Are you really so innocent? Or are you pretending to be?'

'I know what people are saying. I find it rather — disgusting.'

'In many ways Florence is an extremely provincial place.' When, head bowed over her plate, Iris made no response, he went on: 'The whole affair appears to have caused something of a stir in the common room. Miss Sweeney came to see me about it.'

'Miss Sweeney! What on earth has it to do with her?'

'She's the senior member of the staff, isn't she? So presumably the others chose her as their spokeswoman. But quite what she expected me to do . . . I can hardly read the boy a lecture on morals. After all, he's not breaking the laws of this country. None the less, if an employee brings the Institute into disrepute . . .'

'Aren't I also bringing the Institute into disrepute?' Suddenly she looked up, in defiant challenge.

'You?'

'Isn't there also gossip about me and Dale? I bet there is!'

'For a young girl and a young boy to have a, er, liaison is rather different from a young boy and a middle-aged man having one. Isn't it?'

Iris threw down her napkin on the table as she jumped up. 'I'm sorry. I think I'm going.'

Mervyn hurried after her as she made her way, high heels clicking on the marble flags, down the corridor to the lift. 'My dear, my dear! Come back! Don't be so silly!'

Fortunately the lift was already on the floor. She wrenched open the door and got in.

'Iris!'

As the lift began to descend, she could see his face through the glass, at first level with hers, then increasingly above it. He looked agitated; woebegone; shocked.

As Iris walked down the ill-lit corridor to the Pensione Dante, the front door opened and there, illuminated by the light behind them, were Ethel and Guido. As though fearing that, on his departure, he might slip into the room of some other guest to filch something, Ethel always saw Guido out.

'Now you really must get a move on,' Ethel was saying, in the abnormally loud, carefully enunciated voice which she assumed for her pupils. 'The exams are drawing near, and the way you're going I'm afraid you're most unlikely to pass.'

Guido laughed. 'I will pass, I will pass. Do not trouble!' He put a hand on Ethel's shoulder; then hastily withdrew it when he saw Iris approaching.

Iris had no desire to speak to Ethel after the mischief she had made about Ivor and Jack; so she merely nodded first to Guido and then to her, before slipping past them.

'There was a telephone call for you a moment ago,' Ethel called after her. 'Signora Martinucci was looking for you.'

'For me?' Could she have missed Dale? Oh, hell. She had not heard from him for almost a week. When she rang the *palazzo*, either Pippa or the manservant always told her that he was out.

'From Mervyn, I gather.'

'Oh. Thank you.'

'I thought you were having dinner with him.'

How on earth did Ethel know that? Without saying anything further, Iris hurried along to her room.

She was stepping out of her dress, when Signora Martinucci knocked on the door. '*Telefono, signorina! Telefono*!

Dale!

But of course it was Mervyn again.

'I just rang to see if we were still friends.'

'Of course we're still friends.'

'Fancy running out on me like that!'

'I'm sorry. I was just fed up with all that . . .'

192

'I do admire your loyalty. That's one of the things I like about you. You're a' — he gave a tremulous little laugh — 'sweet girl, you know.'

'Thank you.'

'I mean it. You — you will have dinner with me another evening, won't you?'

'Of course!'

'Karen's away for the whole of this week. Shall we fix a day now?'

'Let's talk about it tomorrow.'

'Oh, that sounds unpromising! But never mind. As you wish, my dear. . . . Anyway, I can take it that I'm forgiven?'

'There was nothing to forgive.'

22

'But what I don't understand, my dear, is *why* you should want to go to work in Rome. After all, you have your family here – and all your friends here.'

Hearing Miss Sweeney say this to Violetta, Jack wondered whether she was being malicious or naïve.

With the tense self-composure which she had shown throughout this farewell party for her, Violetta explained in her excellent English: 'One gets in a rut. When that happens, the best thing is to get out of it.'

'The name of the rut is Giles,' Tim said *sotto voce* to Iris, who was standing beside him.

'Sh!'

It was Giles who was giving this farewell party in the Institute common room. He had invited Karen and Mervyn; but, having decided that 'it's really not quite our sort of thing,' (as Mervyn had put it to Karen), they had made the excuse that they were obliged that evening – 'such a bore, but there it is' – to attend a recital by a visiting English pianist.

'Where's Mrs Conquest?' Miss Sweeney had asked of Giles on her arrival.

'Margot? Oh, she has to be with the children. It's Maria's evening off, and the woman who usually comes in to take her place is away on holiday.' Giles's face looked grey and greasy, and there was an expression of shrinking pain on it. Seeing him as she had come into the room, Iris had wanted to put her arms around him in comfort, even though they had never really hit it off.

'Do you think that Margot gave him an ultimatum?' Tim now asked.

'Sh! For God's sake!'

'Signora Alberoni is talking so loudly' — this was an Italian member of the staff, noted for her exuberance — 'that no one can hear us. I'll ask the question again: do you think that Margot gave him an ultimatum?'

'I've no idea at all. How should I know?'

'I didn't ask you what you knew, I asked you what you thought.'

Suddenly there was a sound of clapping behind them. It was the porter, an elderly man so distinguished-looking, with his silvery wings of brushed-back hair and his neatly clipped moustache, that on one occasion a visiting English diplomat from Rome had assumed him to be the Director of the Institute. Swaying from side to side and occasionally also tilting his body backwards and forwards, he was already drunk — as, with alarming abruptness, he would become on rare and always unforeseeable occasions.

In the English acquired when he had been head porter in a London hotel in the years between the wars, he now intoned: 'Mr Director of Studies, ladies, gentlemen!'

'Oh, stow it!' Tim muttered, grabbing on tiptoe for yet another canapé as a waiter swept past with a high-raised tray.

But the speaker was clearly not prepared to stow it. 'I do not keep you long. But this is an occasion when I wish to speak something about our Signorina Violetta. The name is *attissimo*' — he thought for a moment, swaying so violently now that it seemed certain that he would topple over — 'most *apt* for her. Signorina — Miss Violetta — *is* a violet. Beautiful. Soft. Gentle. Shy. We all love Miss Violetta. Yes?' He looked around the company and again demanded: 'Yes?'

'Yes,' Tim said. 'Definitely. Quite right.'

The porter scowled across at him, guessing correctly that he was making fun of him. 'Now Miss Violetta leaves us, and leaves the Institute for which she works three, four years. Why? Why?' Suddenly he appeared to be on the verge of tears. 'Why?' he repeated with even more emphasis. 'Mr Director Conquest, why, why, why?'

Giles stepped forward. His face glistened with an extra-ordinary pallor; but whether as a result of strain, embarrassment or anger, it was impossible to say. He stood in front of the porter, the rim of his half-finished glass of red wine touching the bottom button of the embroidered waistcoat which he tended to wear on such occasions. ('So common,' Ivor had commented on it to Jack.) 'I think that what our Vincente is trying to do is to propose a toast to our guest of honour. So that you all do not have to stand here listening to him until the cows come home — make a note of that idiom, please, those of our Italian colleagues who are unfamiliar with it — I shall now propose the toast myself.' He raised his glass high. 'To Violetta. May she have all the success that she deserves in her new job with the British Council in Rome! They are lucky to have got her — just as we are unlucky to be losing her.'

'To Violetta!' Mr Greville cried out, raising his glass.

'To Violetta!' everyone now joined in, with the exception of the porter who, glassy-eyed and intermittently hiccoughing, had sunk down on to a sofa beside Miss Sweeney.

'Speech! Speech!' Tim cried out. 'Violetta, speech!'

'Oh, leave her alone, do!' Iris was furious.

'Come along, Violetta!' Ethel called. She and Violetta had never liked each other. 'Do your stuff.'

Violetta stepped forward. Her lower lip was trembling, and she bit on it as though to stop it from doing so. Then, her eyelashes fluttering behind her huge glasses, she began abruptly: 'I have nothing to say. Nothing. Except to say, "*Grazie mille. Grazie per tutto.*" She turned to Jack with a smile that was little more than a twitch. 'Do I have to translate for you, Mr Prentice?' His slowness in learning Italian had by now become a joke.

Jack shook his head.

'You have all been very kind. Very good. You have forgiven my mistakes. You have made me one of yourselves. I shall miss . . .' Her voice faltered. She gulped. She was all too clearly about to burst into tears.

It was Iris who saved the situation. She stepped forward; put an arm round Violetta's shoulders; then said to her in the most conversational of tones: 'Violetta, I'm going to be in Rome for part of the Easter holidays. Is there any chance of our meeting?'

Gratefully Violetta smiled. 'I will give you my address and telephone number. Please call me when you arrive.'

Giles began to mop at his forehead with a far from clean handkerchief.

Iris and Jack, both of them slightly drunk, left the party together. Although he was host, Giles had left long before them, explaining that he must return to Margot and the children. 'You take your domestic responsibilities so seriously,' Tim, also slightly drunk, had commented, while splashing yet more of the acrid red wine into his glass.

'I could do with a walk,' Iris said.

'Me too. It was so fuggy in there.'

'If the spring is already so hot, what will the summer be like?'

They began to stroll towards the Lung'Arno.

'That was all so sad,' Iris said. 'Do you think we'll get ourselves into messes like that?'

'Bound to.'

'I sometimes hate the idea of marriage. All those responsibilities – and duties and obligations. Poor Giles!'

'Poor Violetta!'

'Why can't married couples just say to each other: "Sorry, that's it. It was nice knowing you but now . . ."?'

'Children are the problem. Usually. They certainly are for Giles.'

'Do you want to have children?'

'Of course.' That she should put that question suddenly filled Jack with an extraordinary excitement. 'Don't you?'

She shrugged. What sort of father would Dale make? Pretty poor, she decided.

'I wish I saw more of you.'

'We see each other every day! Except at weekends. And even at weekends we often run into each other.'

'I mean . . .' He felt terrified; but he forced himself to continue. 'I mean like this. The two of us alone. Together. Not in that ghastly common room, with everyone watching and listening and making bitchy comments.'

She said nothing. He edged closer to her, finding an excuse in the narrowness of the pavement. But although he longed to take her arm, he did not dare to do so.

'Oh, they've lit the Loggia! Dale said they were going to do so.'

Dale? How had Dale been able to foretell that? Jack felt a brief, murderous hatred.

Iris wandered towards the Loggia, and Jack followed behind her. 'Mervyn was telling me of all the uses to which the Loggia has been put over the ages. It was originally built merely to provide a covered space so that public ceremonies could be conducted without the fear of rain. Less than half a century after it was completed, it provided a refuge for old men in the heat of the day. Later, it was a market. A doss-house. A place of assignation. Still is,' she added, pointing to a small, stocky figure which neither she nor Jack recognized as Franco's, approaching, unlighted cigarette in hand, an ageing, balding tourist.

If he had not been so drunk, if she had not spoken of the Loggia as a place of assignation, if that spring night had not been so oppressively hot . . . He was often to attempt to weigh these imponderables. As it was, he suddenly stepped forward; put both his arms around her as she stood with her back to him; and then, turning her round, made a clumsy attempt to kiss her.

She drew back her head, so that his lips grazed her cheek. 'Sorry. I'm sorry, Jack.'

'Have I done the wrong thing?'

She laughed at the naïveté of the question. 'No, of course not! It's just that . . . well, I like you a lot but . . .'

'Dale?'

What business had he to ask that question? She stared coolly at him.

At once he realized, with panic, that he had annoyed her. 'Sorry. Forget I asked that.'

She leaned forward and gently kissed him on the forehead. 'I must go home,' she said.

'Then I'll see you home.'

'No, no! You live in the opposite direction. Just see me to the tram.'

'I wish I were going to Rome with you.' He wanted to ask if she was going with Pippa and Dale, but restrained himself.

'What are you going to do over the holidays?'

'I've no idea.'

Had Ivor proposed nothing? Perhaps Jack was now avoiding him because of the gossip.

The tram clattered round a bend and past them. 'That's my tram! I'll make a dash for it.' She was off. He watched as, swift and graceful, she ran after it and managed to catch it. Then he continued to watch as, swaying now to one side and now the other, it lurched on, its arms scattering sparks, to disappear round a corner.

*

Two stops later, Iris dismounted from the tram on an impulse. It was only five minutes' walk from here to Pippa's *palazzo*. Jack's mention of Dale had aroused in her an extravagant longing to see him again after — what? — six, seven days. Her footsteps quickened.

The door was opened in answer to her ring not by the manservant but by his wife. 'La Signorina Crediton!' She recognized Iris. She smiled in welcome.

Then, behind her, Pippa had suddenly appeared, her hair tousled, her face and neck mottled with purple, and a glass in her hand.

'What sort of hour is this for a visit?' she demanded in slurred, truculent tones.

'I'm sorry, Pippa. I was passing, and I wanted to say something to Dale.'

'You wanted to say something to Dale? Or you wanted to do something with Dale? I must say, you have a cheek! You have a fucking cheek!'

Then Dale was also there. He grabbed Pippa's arm, just as she was advancing on Iris, and jerked her back.

'Leave me alone! Just bloody well leave me alone! If this shit-faced bitch thinks she's going to prance round here and appropriate you, she's got another think coming to her.'

'Pippa! Pippa! Stop it!'

Appalled, the servant had slunk back into the shadows. Now she scurried off.

'Sta-a-ap it! Sta-a-ap it!' Pippa gave a crude imitation of Dale's American accent. Then she rushed on: 'I don't have to stop doing or saying anything I want to do or say. This is *my* house. Got it? *My* house? And you're just here on sufferance.'

'Come on, Iris, let's get out of here.' Dale grabbed Iris's arm with the same violence with which he had previously grabbed Pippa's.

Then Pippa was screaming after them: 'Don't bloody well bother to come back! See what that whore of yours can do for you! See if she can pay all your bills and get you out of all your scrapes! Just see!'

Windows were thrown up; passers-by stopped in their tracks.

Dale flagged down a taxi, and pushed Iris into it before giving directions to the driver. She was trembling so hard that even her teeth were chattering. It might have been not an unusually warm day of spring but an unusually cold day of winter. He put an arm round her. Then he began to laugh. 'Don't let it worry you! Sweetie, she's drunk. *Drunk.*' His lips were now against her cheek.

'How could she have spoken to me like that?'

'She's constantly speaking to me like that. It means nothing, absolutely nothing. In fact, she's really rather fond of you.'

'Fond of me! That was a nice way of showing her fondness!'

For a while they sat in silence, hands clasped.

Then she said: 'Where are we going?'

'Don't you know where we're going?'

'Why are you just sitting there like that?'

'Where else should I be sitting?'

Suddenly tender, Margot walked over to the armchair in which Giles was slumped, leaned over, crossing her arms around him, and then put her lips to his cheek. 'The novel,' she said. 'Get on with the novel. Why not?'

'Because it's no bloody good. For all these years I've tried to persuade myself that I'm another Proust or Musil, but I'm fucking well not.' He had never before used expletives like 'bloody' and 'fucking' while talking to her. That he should now do so was as much of a shock as his repudiation of the novel to which she, as much as he, had made so many sacrifices over so many years.

'You'll feel differently about it tomorrow,' she said in exactly the same tone of voice that she used to the children when they were panicky or fractious. But, usually efficacious in their case, it failed to be in his.

'Oh, no, I won't. I was looking through it last night – after the party – and it was as though, all the time that I'd been slaving away at it, I'd been suffering some kind of blindness. I can *see* when other people's novels are no bloody good. Why couldn't I see that my own novel was no bloody good either? It's so – pretentious . . . so derivative. . . so self-conscious in its desire to be experimental. . .'

'Every writer goes through periods when everything he does seems to have no value.'

'But I'm *not* a writer. That's what I realized yesterday evening.'

Was he having some kind of nervous breakdown, Margot wondered. It was so totally unlike him to do nothing but sit in an armchair and pick at the frayed fabric of one of its arms, while staring either down at the watch on his wrist or out through the window into the garden. When the children had come into the room to ask him whether he could mend their diabolo, he had shouted at them: 'Oh, for Christ's sake, beat it!'

'Oughtn't you to be going to your meeting with Mervyn?'

'I've no desire to see Mervyn. None whatever. He's a lazy, conceited bastard.'

'But he wants to see you. He's leaving for Portofino tomorrow. Remember?'

'Well, good luck to him there!'

But slowly, as though he were still convalescing from some serious illness, he levered himself up from the chair, hands to its arms, and limped to the door. She went after him.

'Darling.'

'Yes?' His tone was harsh.

'Things will soon seem better. You'll be back working on the novel. I know you will. You've had too much to do these last months.'

He slipped away without another word or even glance.

It was the first time that Giles had ever asked Jack to go for a walk with him. There had never been any intimacy or even, Jack sometimes thought, friendship between them, but merely the relationship of two colleagues who have nothing but their shared work in common.

They strode out for most of the time in silence. Jack let Giles choose the route; but, threading through narrow, dingy streets, with nothing of interest to be seen except a cat delicately picking at some morsel in a gutter, a group of children playing what appeared to be an Italian version of hopscotch, and two stout women, shopping-baskets piled around them, arguing vociferously and all but coming to blows, it seemed totally devoid of plan or purpose.

Then, suddenly, a square, a dry fountain at its centre, struck him as familiar. Yes, of course! This was the square in which he had once glimpsed Giles and Violetta sitting on a bench; and over there was the tall, narrow, peeling house, in which Giuseppe had his cramped eyrie. Jack all but blurted out: 'I once saw you and Violetta sitting on that bench.' Then he realized how cruel that would be. Had Giles intentionally come here? Or had he done so merely by accident?

To Jack's amazement, Giles now crossed over to the bench and sat down on it. Jack placed himself at the other end. The sun glinted on an empty Coca Cola bottle which someone had chucked into the basin of the fountain. From the open window of one of the houses came the crudely amplified sound of a voice singing 'Volare' on the radio. It made Jack think, with a mingling of longing and regret, of Maria scrubbing away at the floor of the corridor outside his room. If only he could be more masterful, decisive, successful!

Giles was stroking the back of the bench, as though to make sure that it really existed outside his imagination. His eyes, squinting at the upended Coca Cola bottle, looked dazed, as though with a fever. His right knee jerked up and down.

'People who talk about the beauty of Florence can never have visited a quarter like this. Imagine living here!'

'Where I live in England is even less attractive.'

Jack might not have spoken. He realized that nothing that concerned him, nothing at all, was of any interest whatever to Giles.

'It's not just the gloom of these houses. It's the feeling of deadness — utter deadness.'

'I don't get that.' Even as Giles had been speaking, a woman had been vigorously shaking a carpet out of a window high above them.

'Deadness,' Giles repeated.

Eventually they continued their walk, out eastwards to an area in which a few turn-of-the-century villas, standing in their gardens, were surrounded by concrete or brick apartment blocks, stark in their utilitarianism, building sites or rubbish-tips. Now Giles was looking sharply around him. Perhaps, after all, this walk did have a purpose?

'No, it's not that street. It must be that one. God — this neighbourhood is even worse than the one we've just left.'

They had now turned up a dirt road, little more than a path between low thorn-bushes, with the sun in their eyes and a taste of dust on their tongues. Ahead was a white bungalow, standing in one corner of a field in which two goats were tethered and some leghorns were disconsolately pecking for food.

'Have you ever been here?'

Jack was amazed by the question. Why should he ever have been there?

'It's where Miss Sweeney's younger sister lives. Signora Bottone. She made a misalliance with a *contadino*. She runs the local society for animal protection. It's Karen Le Clerq's main interest — along with flower-arrangement. Karen's idea of protecting animals is either to sterilize them or — as she would put it — to put them to sleep. She bought the society a van in which Signora Bottone's husband — that's the *contadino* brother-in-law of whom Miss Sweeney is so ashamed — whizzes about the city rounding up any stray dogs or cats. Karen doesn't, of course, herself perform either the sterilization or the putting to sleep. She leaves that to a vet. Nor does she herself ever keep any animals.' He was speaking with a derisive bitterness which he had never before displayed to Jack.

Signora Bottone, dressed in some baggy slacks and a blouse torn under an armpit, looked so like Miss Sweeney that she might have been mistaken for her twin. Unlike Miss Sweeney, she spoke an English that had something vaguely but indisputably foreign about it. What was it, Jack pondered, as he listened to her. A sing-song lilt? The openness of the vowels? The avoidance of all abbreviations, so that she said 'it is' instead of 'it's' and 'did not' instead of 'didn't'?

'I have heard about you,' she said to Jack, after welcoming them into the sparsely and cheaply furnished space, a single worn rug on its floor of marble chippings, which did service for living-room, dining-room and study. 'From my sister.'

'Miss Sweeney was very kind to me during my first weeks at the Institute,' Jack replied, saying no more than the truth. 'I'd never taught before. I was always going to her for advice.'

'My sister likes to give advice,' said Signora Bottone, who had all too often been on the receiving end of it. 'We knew Ivor Luce when he was a child,' she went on, making Jack wonder, in embarrassment, by what train of thought she had come to this declaration.

He almost said: 'Oh, but he seems so much younger than you both.' But instead he asked: 'Was that in Florence?'

'Of course. In Florence. Where else? We all grew up together — until my two sisters and I were sent to school in Montreux and he and that sad little sister of his were sent off to England — he to Harrow, she to Cheltenham Ladies' College. I always remember a birthday party of mine, a fancy-dress birthday party. Ivor came as a maharajah, wearing a turban on which his mother had pinned *real* jewels. Can you imagine it? She was like that. Spoiled those two endlessly. And totally feckless.' She turned to Giles: 'Would you like to see the dogs first, or would you like some coffee?'

'Let's see the dogs.' Giles's face now had the same grey, shiny look as at the party; the eyes still had in them that same expression of shrinking pain.

'Very well.'

They followed her out through a back door into a yard with a high barbed-wire fence around it. In narrow runs, each with a shelter constructed out of corrugated iron at its far end, innumerable dogs were crowded. When they saw the three humans, some of the dogs rushed to the fences to press their often emaciated bodies against the wire; some retreated into the shelters in panic; and some set up a deafening barking in the middle of their runs.

'We try to operate like the Battersea Dogs' Home. Karen — Mrs Le Clerq — drew up a kind of charter for us, roughly based on their procedures. Each dog here is kept for a week to be claimed by its owner. If it is not claimed, then we give it another week for someone else to take it. After that. . . .' She shrugged.

'Awful,' Jack muttered.

She looked at him sharply. 'What did you say?'

'I don't think I could bear. . .' He broke off.

'*Someone* has to do it. The alternative would be for these poor creatures to roam the streets, half-starved and often sick.'

'Wouldn't that be preferable to death?' Jack wanted to ask.

Giles inspected the cages, from time to time going down on his hunkers to talk to some dog which he particularly fancied. 'Do not put your hand through the mesh,' Signora Bottone warned him more than once; until, having yet again disobeyed this injunction, he was suddenly bitten. The dog was a fox-like black-and-white mongrel with a peaked, puzzled face and an inordinately long tail.

As he wrapped a handkerchief around his bleeding forefinger — 'It is lucky she did not take it off,' Signora Bottone told him before she rushed off to fetch some disinfectant and sticking-plaster — Giles turned to Jack: 'That's the one. That's the one I want.'

Jack was amazed. 'After she's *bitten* you?'

'Oh, she was just frightened. Unsure of herself. Here was this strange giant pushing his finger through the mesh. People have probably ill-treated her in the past.'

'And you plan to take her home?'

'Of course. That's why we came here — so that I could find a dog to take home.'

He spoke as though he had long ago revealed to Jack the object of their walk.

'She is rather a little dear,' Signora Bottone said, as she attached a lead to the dog. 'But just a bundle of nerves. Do be careful, won't you? And be careful of her with the children.'

'She won't be any trouble.' Giles spoke with total self-confidence.

'She is only a mongrel, you understand. We do have that pedigree German shepherd — and of course that lovely little Peke.'

'This is the one for me.'

'Well, if she is the one you have *really* set your heart on. . .'

'We'll call her Perdita.'

'Yes, that is a nice name. An appropriate one. . . . Oh, how kind of you!' Giles had handed her some notes, telling her: 'That's towards the expenses of the home.'

As they walked back, Giles was totally absorbed in the dog. 'Sit!' he would order her in English. At first, having issued the command, he would have to push down her rump; then, quite soon, she would sit of her own accord. 'Cross!' he would call; and, wagging her tail, she would scamper across the road with him often in the face of oncoming traffic. 'Good girl! *Good* girl!'

At one moment he remarked to Jack: 'Isn't she amazingly intelligent and companionable?'

That apart, Jack might not have been there, for all the attention that Giles paid him.

23

〰️

'I don't know why I came out in this thing. It's so hot!'

The 'thing' was a mink stole, which Isabella now negligently chucked over the back of a chair. She had swept into Doney, one hand patting her hair into place; had looked around her, clearly for Giuseppe; and then, failing to find him, had come over to the table at which Iris, Dale and Jack were sitting. Often in the past, having entered the bar in similar fashion, she had totally ignored them.

'Has my *nano* been in?'

She put the question to Jack, who had no idea what a *nano* was. Iris, who knew that a *nano* was a dwarf, was the one who therefore answered: 'Not while we've been here. And that's been for the past hour or so.'

'How you young people fritter away your time!' Without asking if she might join them, Isabella then pulled out a chair from under the next-door table and placed herself on it. A hand went down and began stroking a shin with a dreamy absorption.

'These two have been teaching almost continuously from nine this morning until five this afternoon,' Dale protested. 'And I've been at my easel for most of the day.' He all but added: What do you ever do except fritter away your time on bridge parties, cocktail parties, shopping expeditions, and visits to the hairdresser?

'I don't know what's happening to him. These last weeks he's been so unreliable. Never around when I want him.'

'Perhaps he's writing an epic poem,' Dale said. 'It can't be easy to be both a poet and a *cavaliere servente*.'

'Byron managed it in Venice,' she retorted drily. 'So why not Giuseppe in Florence? In any case, he's not my *cavaliere servente*. Just a chum, who's kind and sympathetic and helpful. If also —

sometimes — a bore,' she added.

Both Iris and Jack were embarrassingly aware of the hostility, seething like some malodorous cauldron, between Dale and the Contessa.

As though in an attempt to make that cauldron boil over, Dale was soon asking Isabella, after she had ordered a Negrone for herself and another round of *espressi* for them: 'Did you ever imagine that one day this city would have a Communist deputy?'

'No, frankly, I didn't,' she answered coolly. 'But then nothing surprises me any longer. I never imagined that one day there would be a brothel for American and British officers in a street as respectable as the Via Parione. I never imagined that one day there would be male tarts picking up some of those officers in broad daylight in the Loggia dei Lanzi. Nor indeed' — her beautifully modulated voice suddenly acquired a vulgar edge to it — 'that an apparently well-bred, well-educated American would think nothing of becoming a gigolo in order to avoid doing an honest day's work.'

The casual insult make Iris flush with anger and Jack squirm in his chair from embarrassment; but, gazing steadily at Isabella, Dale merely laughed. Isabella held his gaze; then she laughed too.

'Why do you dislike me so?' she asked.

'*Do* I dislike you? I'm not sure. Anyway — you dislike me.'

'Not at all. But there are certain aspects of your life which I can't help — despising.'

'Couldn't we change the conversation?' Iris said.

'Why should we?' Again Dale laughed. 'Home truths is an interesting game. Let's go on playing it for a while.' He leaned across to Isabella: 'And what precisely are these aspects which you despise?'

She shrugged. 'I despise people who waste themselves,' she said. 'You're not getting any younger. How can you bear to waste your best years on that dreadful woman?'

'In fact, she's not dreadful,' Dale said quietly. 'In many ways she's really rather admirable. Courageous. Loyal. Generous.' The implication was that Isabella was none of these things. 'In any case, didn't you waste your best years too?'

'*I?*' She was genuinely astonished. 'My first twenty-five or so years in Italy were wonderful. *Wonderful*. What's followed since the end of the War — well, that's another story.'

Jack was suddenly so much interested that his habitual shyness when in the company of this beautiful, elegant, arrogantly outspoken woman suddenly vanished. 'But how could those years have been wonderful?'

'Why not?'

'Well . . .' Now his courage was ebbing as rapidly as it had surged forward. 'For an Englishwoman . . . living in Mussolini's Italy . . . the War . . .'

'I didn't say that those twenty-five or so years were *easy*! Of course not! For much of the time they were bloody difficult! But they weren't wasted! All the time I was *alive*!'

'Did you ever meet Mussolini?' Iris asked with feigned innocence, eager to see how Isabella would react to the question.

'Well, of course I did! Of course! My husband was one of his most trusted advisers.'

'And did you like him?'

'*Like* him? How could I have *liked* him? If he hadn't been Il Duce I'd never have dreamed of allowing him into my house. But one doesn't have to *like* that sort of man, for God's sake. He was coarse, crude, even brutal. But if you'd known Italy before he came to power . . .'

'You mean before he made the trains run on time?' Dale asked.

'How many politicians have succeeded in making the trains run on time? In itself that was an achievement. But he did so much, much more, that's what outsiders fail to realize. The defeated never get a fair deal from history.'

'And what precisely was this much, much more?' Dale enquired, tilting his chair back and gazing at her through narrowed eyes.

'Oh, you people are all so ignorant. Ever heard of the draining of the Pontine Marshes? No, of course you haven't. Well, that achievement was symbolic of everything Mussolini did for this country. He drained the marsh which Italy had become. And just as the Pontine Marshes then began to grow crops, so Italy once more began to be fertile.'

'Perhaps some people would consider the castor-oil bottle to be a better symbol of his achievement. The final product – *shit*.'

Isabella laughed. It amazed both Iris and Jack that, so far from showing any resentment, she should react as though Dale were joking with her. That he was not, in fact, in any way doing so was clear from his expression, as of some snarling dog constantly jerking forward in an effort to break free of its leash and so to bury its teeth in an enemy. 'Well, I must love you and leave you. Although, in your case' — she turned with a seemingly friendly smile to Dale — 'that cliché is perhaps just a wee bit insincere. If my little hunchback friend drops in, tell him that I couldn't wait any longer and that I'm far too busy for the rest of the evening to see him.' She raised a hand in farewell; some half-dozen bracelets jangled against each other. 'Goodbye. I'll take care of the bill on the way out, so don't let Lauro charge you twice. He has a way of doing that.' She leaned forward and tweaked the mink stole off the chair; then threw it across her shoulders.

Intently, in silence, Dale watched her as she first paid the bill and then, in a pair of those extravagantly high-heeled shoes which added at least three inches to her stature, swept out through the swing doors. He sighed. 'Style,' he said. 'Real style. What poor, dear Pippa lacks. But what you' — he turned to Iris — 'will certainly acquire.'

'Thanks! I was hoping that I had style now.'

He shook his head. 'Not yet. Far too impetuous. Far too careless. Far too emotional. But it'll come, you'll see. . . . In your case, Jack, it's never going to come. Never, I can promise you that. But don't look so crestfallen. You have all kinds of qualities already — all of them far more important than style.' He glanced at his Rolex watch, a Christmas present from Pippa; then turned to Iris: 'We ought to be going. It's past seven o'clock.'

'Oh, are you going somewhere?' Jack asked.

'Yes, I'm taking Iris to see *Casablanca*. Incredibly she's never seen it. Of course it'll be the dubbed version. I love it when Humphrey Bogart speaks with an almost falsetto Italian voice.' Dale made no suggestion that Jack should go with them. Iris almost did so; then decided, with a pang of guilt, that she would much prefer to have Dale wholly to herself.

'See you tomorrow.'

'See you.' Jack was forlorn.

'Perhaps Giuseppe will turn up.'

'Perhaps.'

But Jack knew that he wouldn't. It was one of those days.

As, in the dimming light of the early summer evening, Jack wandered along the Lung'Arno, knowing that he would annoy Margot by yet again arriving late for supper and yet somehow unable to hurry, he passed a couple seated, arms around each other, on the stone balustrade separating street from river below it. Seeing him approach, the woman jerked her head sideways and away and simultaneously withdrew herself from the man. It was Ethel, Jack realized with amazement. The man was that pupil of hers, whose name he did not know. Clearly she had not wished him to see them.

Being so young, he thought of Ethel as far too old to be sitting like that in the embrace of an Italian at least ten years her junior. Only the previous year he had been both disconcerted and shocked when, returning home unexpectedly from Oxford one late Sunday afternoon, he had surprised his parents in their bedroom. 'Who's that?' his mother had called out in alarm, as he had let himself in. Then she had called: 'Your Dad and I have just been having a shut-eye.' A shut-eye! He knew that he was being foolish but the idea of two people in their forties having that kind of shut-eye on a Sunday afternoon struck him as both undignified and squalid. It now struck him as similarly undignified and squalid that Ethel and her pupil should be publicly embracing each other.

He paused. How beautiful it all was! The Arno glistened, like the trail of a giant slug, between its darkening banks. A troop of ragamuffin children, returning from a swim, were wading along through its shallows, from time to time stooping to splash each other with water. The blood-red of the sky was bandaged with ragged strips of cloud. On the Ponte Vecchio the crowds were tiny, black silhouettes. He drew a deep sigh. Years later, he decided, when he had forgotten most things else about his time in Florence, this would be what he would remember. How lucky Dale was to be able to capture something of it in paint; how lucky Giles was to be able to capture something of it in words.

As he thought of Giles, he all at once saw him, down below him by the river. He, too, would be late for supper, so that Margot would be even crosser. He was throwing a white rubber ball for the mongrel. He would lift an arm in a pretence of throwing, and the dog, wagging that inordinately long tail of hers, would then leap around him with a series of shrill barks. At last, in a wide arc, he would throw the ball. The dog would race off, would seize it in her jaws, and would then race back to drop it at his feet. 'Good girl! *Good* girl!' From time to time Giles would bend and pat her, and she would then attempt to lick his face. Jack had never seen him so happy since that day when Margot had discovered about his affair with Violetta.

Now the ball, misthrown, had ricocheted off the parapet over which Jack was leaning, to fall into the river. Dauntless, the dog plunged into the water and paddled across. Smiling, hands on hips, Giles waited for her return.

'Oh, Giles, it really is too bad! I promised Maria that she could go off at eight-thirty to see her boyfriend.'

'Sorry, darling! Sorry!'

'I'm cross, Giles. I'm cross.'

But he was not really sorry; and she was not really cross.

It was odd, Jack thought, that Margot should have been so upset when Giles had spent so much of each of his evenings with Violetta instead of with her, but that she should really be not in the least upset when he spent so much of his evenings with the mongrel. With the dog he was now totally infatuated. Early in the morning he was out taking her for a long walk in the Cascine, before he set off for work. He was constantly talking to her in a ludicrous baby-language. At each meal, he fed her titbits from his plate. She slept on his bed, making Margot complain that the snoring and grunting kept her awake and that, in any case, she could not stand the smell.

As they started on their spaghetti — Maria had scampered in with it, her face flushed with annoyance at a delay which might mean that she would miss her delivery-boy — Margot said: 'Oh, darling, do please have a word with Piers before he goes to sleep. He simply will not listen to me. He's become so disobedient. Anything I tell him . . .'

But Giles was not listening. Bending down sideways in his chair, he was passing a thread of the spaghetti, dripping *sugo*, to the slavering animal.

24

Franco awoke, head pounding when he raised it off a hard, square pillow streaked with hair-oil. Something was amiss. He scowled as, hand to forehead, he tried to think what it was. He looked at his watch. After having spent most of the night at and around the Piazzale Michelangelo, he had returned home after three; so that it was hardly surprising that it was now almost ten. But the lateness of the time wasn't it. No. What was amiss was that, for once, he had been able to sleep without that intermittent ringing of the handbell or that croaking, falsetto: 'Franco! Franco!' from the room next door. Staggering up in a half-sleep, he would ask crossly 'What is it?'; or, even more aggressively, 'Well, what is it now?' Then Harry would gasp: 'Some water — some water with ice in it. My throat is absolutely parched'; 'The light's coming through the curtain. Now that we have these early summer dawns, you really must learn to pull the curtains properly'; or 'I'm afraid I've been a naughty boy again. It just happened in my sleep.'

But for once there had been not a sound; everything had been as silent as the grave.

As silent as the grave. As the phrase came into his mind, Franco leapt off the truckle bed, stooped to pick up the underpants lying on the bare floor, and struggled into them. Then, shouting '*Babbo, babbo!* Is everything all right?', he rushed through the half-open door into Harry's sickly-smelling room.

The emaciated old man, lying on his back, with his mouth open and his eyes closed, looked as though he were merely asleep. There was no sign of any struggle with the demon of death. On the sheet beside him — he must have thrown back the blanket, since that night of early summer had been a hot one — lay the unfinished box on which he had given up working several

212

weeks before, even though he had insisted that both it and his paints and his brushes should not be removed from the top of the bedside table, since 'I might eventually summon up the strength to get back to it.' A brush rested between thumb, finger and forefinger of the hands which, so white and delicate, always aroused Franco's admiration — the hands of a *gran'signore*, Franco used to think. There was a dark red stain, not of blood, as Franco first thought in horrified revulsion, but of paint on the sheet. *Poveretto*! He must have been trying to work when it had happened.

The boy looked down with pitiless curiosity. He had never supposed, after the prolonged agony of his father's death, that anyone's going could be so easy. Not a sound! Not a movement! Well, all his life *babbo* had been blessed. Even at the close, when his work was confined to painting the boxes and there was no more money, there were always rich friends like the Contessa Lambeni and the Milord Inglese to give him money, to pay his outstanding bills or to send him presents. And there was always also — he gave a bitter grimace — a poor servant like himself to attend on him for nothing. *Drat the boy*! He muttered it under his breath; then he burst into laughter.

As he continued to stare down, suddenly and alarmingly he felt a strange thing happening to him. There was an excruciating tightness in his chest and down the sides of his throat; and then, as though a vessel had all at once exploded within him, to release the inexorably mounting pressure, he felt the tears pressing up under his eyelids and then rolling down his cheeks. He threw himself, in a wild desperation of grief, on to the body; he put his lips first to a cheek, which felt as stiff and cold as cardboard, and then to a mouth totally unresponding to his own. He wailed: '*Non! Non! Babbo! Babbo! Senta! Senta, babbo!*'

Eventually he became still and silent; but for many seconds longer he lay across the corpse. Then, totally composed, he got off it. His whole body and even his face ached, precisely as they had done when, taking a corner in the Cascine at a dangerously high speed, he had caused his Vespa to skid and topple over, spilling him across the gravel of the woodland path which he had been cruising in vain.

He tiptoed to reach down from the top of a wardrobe an ancient rucksack in which, when he was still mobile, Harry would store his things before setting out on one of his painting expeditions. In the rucksack, trapped in a hole in the canvas lining, he found an ancient Mars bar. He examined it in wonder. Had it been there since before the War? Slowly he unwrapped it, dropping the paper to the floor. The chocolate had a white, mould-like bloom on it. Franco raised the bar to his mouth; almost bit into it. Then, with a grimace, he threw it down. He began to hurry about the room, picking up things at random – a travelling clock, with Harry's family crest embossed on its cracked, green shagreen; some nail-scissors; some coins, American, English, Swiss, Swedish, hoarded at the back of a drawer; two silver photograph frames, from which he extracted and tore up the faded photographs of Harry's dead wife and dead mother; gold studs for shirts of a kind which Franco himself never wore, gold cuff-links, a gold wedding-ring, worn thin on one side; a portrait miniature of a bewhiskered man in a high cravat; a silver-topped, cut-glass bottle which, when he opened it and sniffed, smelled dusty and bitter.

He returned to the bedside. He braced himself. Then he leaned forward and raised the stiff, cold hand nearest to him. He undid the crocodile-leather strap of the Longines watch, which in those last months it had been his duty to wind every morning ('I just don't seem to have the strength in my fingers,'), and then, grimacing once again, tugged at the signet-ring in an effort to remove it. When the bone of the little finger creaked in its socket, he could not go on. *Drat the boy!* Again he repeated it to himself. His mouth bunched itself tightly and then burst open in a sound half titter and half wail.

Rucksack on back – he had also stuffed into it what few things he himself possessed – he wandered from long-deserted room to long-deserted room. Anything of any value, apart from some pieces of furniture and some large pictures, had been sold weeks, months, even years ago. But he put a silver cigarette-case into one pocket and a silver match-case into another, and then added a Waterman fountain-pen, supposing its rolled gold to be gold through and through.

The Vespa barked into joyous life. He would have to buy some petrol; but in his pocket he had the notes earned that previous night at and around the Piazzale. They had been intended to pay off Harry's new debt to Dr Nerone, but that *succhiasangue* could now wait. Forever, perhaps.

The Vespa jolted over one clump of weeds in the drive and

then over another. Franco could hear *babbo's* voice, complaining to la Signorina Audrey: 'I don't know what the wretched boy *does* all day — or night. Just look out of the window at the drive. It's a disgrace, an absolute disgrace. Oh, drat the boy!'

Suddenly as he sailed down the main road to the city below him and then on — where to? Roma? Venezia? Napoli? Milano? — Franco felt the tears, briefly scalding and then drying in the wind of his passage, coursing down his cheeks.

Iris had been to lunch with Isabella Lambeni. Uneasy, as she always was in the presence of this woman who at once attracted and repelled her, she had drunk and eaten too much, and had emerged into the hot afternoon sunshine feeling vaguely sick and headachy.

'Come and make a fourth at vicarage bridge,' Mervyn suggested.

'But, Mervyn, she doesn't *play* bridge,' Karen told him crossly. Iris yet again wondered: Why couldn't he remember? She had told him that she did not play bridge on a number of occasions. He had even volunteered to teach her.

'Well, come back with us anyway.'

Iris shook her head. 'I feel I must have a walk, if I'm to survive that huge lunch.'

'Well, you did seem to be making what our Miss Sweeney calls "a good knife and fork".'

'Why don't you both come for a walk with me?' Iris suggested. 'It's such a lovely afternoon.'

Mervyn longed to accept. He imagined the two of them, strolling hand in hand, on some hillside slope or through an olive-grove; stopping to examine a view; sitting on the grass under a tree... Oh, what was the use! 'How about a walk, Karen?'

'How can we go for a walk? You've asked Mimi to play bridge.'

'We could put her off. We haven't got a fourth.'

'Ivor'll play. He's always willing to play. Ask him — before he gets into his car.'

Mervyn looked at Iris, raised his eyebrows and pulled down the corners of his mouth ('What's to be done?' the expression asked of her), and then hurried off.

'I wish I could get you interested in the Animal Welfare

Society,' Karen said. 'Don't you like pets?'

'Pets? No, I don't like pets. I like animals, but I don't like pets.'

Karen, incapable of appreciating the distinction, looked bewildered. 'It's so easy to fritter away one's time in Florence.'

The observation reminded Iris of Isabella's remark in Doney about how she, Dale and Jack frittered away their time.'I don't have much time to fritter away. I teach twenty-eight hours each week. That's a lot, you know.'

As she climbed up a steep, stony path towards Poggio Imperiale, Iris suddenly thought that she would go and see poor old Harry. At Isabella's luncheon Adrian had said that he really thought that the poor old boy was on his way out; and Ivor had then remarked: 'That little rascal Franco must be cheating him right and left.' She would buy him some groceries at that dusty, crammed little *spezieria* at the corner below his drive; some flowers, too, if she could find a shop selling them.

It was odd, she was often to think later: even as she had walked towards the front door, the bag of groceries under one arm and a hand clutching a huge bunch of flowers, she had known, known with absolute, devastating certainty, that there was not a soul in the house. None the less, although the front door was ajar, she had gone through the motions of ringing at the bell and then calling: 'Franco! Franco!' before going in.

She set down the bag. Then, still clutching the unwieldy bunch of flowers, she walked down the corridor to the sick-room, calling, with mounting apprehension: 'Mr Archer, Mr Archer!'

She put her head round the door; then dropped the flowers to the ground and hurried over to the bed. 'Mr Archer!' But she knew already that there was no point in calling his name again. Between his lips and nose a motionless blue-bottle might have been mistaken for a mole. She had never before seen a dead body. She stared at him for several seconds. Then she hurried out of the room to the telephone in the hall.

But many weeks before it had been cut off; as had Audrey's, from which she got no answer but a continuous, high-pitched buzz when she called from the *spezieria*.

Fortunately Audrey was at home, and Jack was with her, working through a pile of papers on the kitchen table, while the afternoon sunlight slanted through a window on to his close-cropped hair.

In the sick-room, Audrey repeated over and over again, 'Poor old chap, poor old chap,' as she stooped over Harry's body and first touched his forehead, as though to see if he were running a fever, and then held his unyielding hand in her own. She looked up, her pale-blue eyes suddenly filling with tears: 'He was really my oldest chum. I never imagined . . . I always thought that I'd be the first . . .' But how could she have thought anything of the kind when, still so robust, she had tramped over on her visits to this visibly dying old man? Suddenly, her eyes narrowed; she stared down at the wrist of the hand in her own. There was a grey, greasy circle on the reddish-blue skin.

'His watch!' she cried out. 'His watch has gone!'

She whirled round; then saw the jagged pieces of the torn-up photographs on the floor by the dressing-table. She pointed: 'What are those doing there? Oh, the frames, the frames! The frames, the silver frames, have gone!' She hurried round the room, pulling open drawers and cupboards. Then, followed by Iris and Jack, she entered the other rooms of the house.

In the drawing-room she let out what was almost a scream. 'The silver cigarette-box and the match-box! They were engraved. Mappin and Webb. Wedding presents from Johnny and me. That boy – it must be that boy! Where is he? What's happened to him? He must have looted the house and gone.'

Feverishly she now pulled open drawers and cupboards, rushing from room to room. In the hall, she fumbled with the key of a closet and eventually got it open. She stared, open-mouthed, at the shelves.

Ranged on them were innumerable of Harry's boxes. 'But he was supposed to have sold all these!' she exclaimed, hands on hips. She swung round to Iris and Jack and repeated, as though it were they whom she was accusing of some misdemeanour: 'But he was supposed to have sold all these! To that rogue on the Ponte Vecchio! I just don't get this.' She put a hand to her forehead, as though in an attempt to relieve an agonizing headache. 'I just don't get this *at all*. How did the poor old chap live if these were not sold? Where did the money come from?'

Neither Iris nor Jack had an answer.

'Anyway, we must get on to the police! At once! The boy must be caught. Jack . . . Oh, no, it's no use sending you to telephone. It's unlikely that any of them speak English and no one's going to understand your Italian . . . Iris, it'll have to be you. Could you run

– *run*, dear – to that little store round the corner and put through a call? I don't know the number, but they can get it for you.'

After Iris had hurried off, Audrey turned to Jack: 'I wonder who's the executor. And I wonder if he left a will. Well, we'll find out in due course.'

25

Workmen and nobs sweat, people like us perspire, young girls glow. Who had once said that to him? Jack could hear the cooing, lubricious voice, but could not put a face or a name to it. A don? A schoolmaster? A clergyman?

As she looked up, surprised and pleased, from the chipped crockery, rusty tools and misshapen shoes and boots spread out on a frayed strip of carpet in the hot sunlight of the flea-market, Pat was glowing.

'Fancy seeing you here!'

'Fancy seeing *you!*'

'Oh, I often come here on Saturday morning in the hope of finding a book bargain. I've actually found one only once. What are you here for?'

'Presents. For the family, when I return home next week. I wanted to take them something different from the junk in the souvenir shops.'

'Well, you can take your Dad a pair of old riding-boots' – Jack pointed with the toe of his shoe – 'and you can take your Mum that fish-kettle over there.'

Pat laughed. 'No. I'm going to give up. It's too hot for me. How can you bear to wear that tweed jacket and those flannel trousers?'

Ivor had asked Jack the same question the evening before; and, when Jack had replied, 'I've got nothing else,' had offered, as he had offered on their first meeting and many times subsequently: 'Oh, do drop your silly pride and let me take you to my tailor and treat you to a suit. Not that incompetent little man whom all the Corsini and all the English and the Americans patronize. This one is really good. He could run you up something light in a jiffy.' Jack had shaken his head; then, ungracious in his embarrassment, had muttered: 'Oh, no. Oh, no thanks.'

'I'd take off the jacket, but my wallet might fall out,' Jack now said.

'Why carry a wallet?' Suddenly an idea came to her. 'Why not give the wallet to me? I can put it in my bag, and you can then carry your jacket. How about that?' Clearly she envisaged their spending the day or at least the morning together.

Obstinately he shook his head. 'It's fine.' There was a tear where the left sleeve of his shirt joined the shoulder, and he did not wish to expose it. Maria, who washed his clothes along with those of the rest of the family, had repeatedly promised to mend it for him but had never done so. Nor had she kept her promise to darn some of his socks. Did she expect him to pay her or at least tip her for such small services? He wished that he knew. Perhaps he should ask Margot or Giles: but the former was constantly busy, now that she had received promotion at the Consulate, and the latter had become increasingly remote in recent weeks.

'One can at once recognize the young English in Florence. The girls wear sandals and peasant straw hats, and the boys wear Harris tweed jackets and grey flannel trousers. Don't be the sort of young Englishman one can recognize at once.' She was laughing at him, but without any malice.

'Where's your sister?'

They had begun to stroll away from the flea-market.

'Flora? Oh, she left ages ago. Only a few days after that meeting of ours in the Cascine. We thought you'd get in touch, but you never did.'

'I meant to. Sorry. Too busy. We're terribly overworked – and they pay us a pittance. One of our teachers – Miss Pryce – thinks we ought to go on strike. But what would be the use? They'd just sack us. There are plenty of English swanning about who'd love to take our places.'

'You should become a nanny! I've had virtually nothing to do – there's an old family retainer to look after the children in addition to myself – and there are virtually no expenses. They even take me to the theatre and to restaurants with them.' She looked around her, at the tall, ochre houses already baking in the sun. 'Where are we going?'

'I've no idea.'

'Oh, let's go to the sea! It's so hot. We can hop on a train. There must be a train.'

'Won't it be awfully expensive?' It was near the end of the month, and he had virtually no money left.

'I can lend you some money if you're broke.'

'I never borrow money. I hate doing it.'

'Oh, come on!' Then she stopped in her tracks and turned to him: 'I have an awful feeling that you're *thrifty*. Oh, don't be thrifty, Jack. Thrift is supposed to be a virtue in Edinburgh, where I come from, but I do so hate it.'

'I'll try not to be thrifty. But thrift is also supposed to be a virtue where *I* come from.'

In the train she talked to him animatedly for a while, leaning forward as she did so, one hand brushing away from her face the coarse, blond hair blown across it by the wind buffeting through the wide-open window beside her. Then, suddenly, she rested her head against the wooden slats of the third-class carriage, closed her eyes, and at once fell asleep. Jack gazed at her. With her clear complexion, her capable hands and her sturdy body in its simple white cotton dress, she transmitted, even in repose, an abiding impression of physical and mental well-being and strength. Maria transmitted the same sort of impression.

She opened her eyes, startled. 'Have I been asleep?'

He nodded. 'You've missed some really spectacular scenery.'

'Oh, why didn't you wake me? The trouble is that I got to bed awfully late last night. This weird American — an army doctor — invited me to a dance at the base. I can't think why, since he seemed to be totally uninterested in me. I didn't get home until after two. And by then he'd made me drink far too much bourbon.'

'Pippa drinks bourbon. When she's not drinking ouzo.'

'Pippa?'

'Oh, you've not met her. Just as well.' Jack had felt a puritanical shrinking from Pippa, her face blotched, her breath laden with alcohol fumes and her talk peppered with four-letter words, on the two occasions when he had met her with Iris and Dale.

At Pat's urging, they jumped out of the train at random as it briefly made a coastal halt.

'We've been awfully extravagant, buying tickets to Viareggio and then getting off here,' Jack said.

'But here's going to be so much nicer than Viareggio. You'll see. You don't want an Italian Blackpool, do you?'

'I've never been to Blackpool.'

'Well, neither have I for the matter of that.'

221

They walked through the little town, which looked as though it were about to slip off the cliff-top on which it was balanced on a tilt, to cascade into the sea. Then they took a steep path, and finally scrambled over rocks. From time to time Jack chivalrously extended a hand to assist Pat over some particularly tricky obstacle; but, robustly independent, she rarely took it.

The cove which they eventually reached was totally deserted. As they had descended, they had seen beyond it a wide stretch of beach brilliant with umbrellas and bathing-huts and people confetti-thick. 'How lucky for us that the Italians are so gregarious.'

'It'll solve the question of bathing-costumes,' Pat said. 'I've just realized that we never thought of them.'

'We can't bathe in the nude!'

'Can't we?' She began to undo the belt of her dress.

'Someone might come — at any time. Someone might even see us from a passing boat.'

'In that case, let them! Good luck to them.'

Reluctantly, his face reddening with embarrassment and his back to her, Jack stripped off to his underpants. Oh, golly! They too had a hole in them. He turned. She was now in knickers and brassiere. He could see a pinkish corrugation round her waist, where her plaited belt must have bitten tightly through the thin cotton dress. He looked away.

'Oh, what droopy drawers!' she cried out.

His shame increased; but, as he hobbled after her over the shingle, he also felt breathless with a mounting excitement.

She was as good a swimmer as he was. Out and out they swam; then they floated side by side, looking up at a sky cloud-streaked here and there as though a child had faintly scrawled on it with a white crayon.

'Wonderful,' she said.

'Yes, wonderful.'

'One feels so cramped in Florence. I get this sense of innumerable identities pressing closer and closer on me until, well, I feel I'm just going to pass out — as I almost passed out in all those crowds in the Duomo during Midnight Mass at Christmas.'

'I went to St Mark's in Venice for Midnight Mass.'

'In Venice! You spent Christmas in Venice! Wasn't it terribly expensive? Everyone says it's far more expensive than Florence.'

'It wasn't cheap!' He all but told her that he had been Ivor's guest – 'There's this rich man, and he asked me to accompany me as his, well, kind of secretary,' – but it would sound too odd, he decided, and did not do so.

'I meant to go to Venice before returning to England. But somehow . . .'

'You'll come back to Italy, won't you?'

'Not in the immediate future. I want to get on with my training as a physiotherapist. But some day . . .'

Suddenly, she struck away from him, scattering water. He floated on for a while, feeling more contented and peaceful than for a long time. Then he followed her back to the shore.

They were lying side by side; he was almost asleep. He felt her hand closing on his forearm. She gripped it more and more tightly. When he opened his eyes and turned his head, she was smiling at him. 'Droopy drawers,' she said. She laughed. Then she rolled over towards him, to lie on her side, her other hand under a cheek. He could see one nipple through the sodden brassiere. She raised the hand which had been gripping his forearm, and then placed it on his cheek. He shifted and moved his mouth up to the palm of the hand, kissing it. It tasted salt.

With a sigh, she again rolled over, until their bodies were touching. Then she put her mouth on his. He had never before been kissed by anyone like that; it was as though she were repeatedly sucking the life out of him and then restoring it. *The kiss of life.* The phrase suddenly came to him. The kiss of death, the kiss of life. Her hand went down.

'Do you mind?'

He shook his head, their mouths once more glued together. How could he mind? How could he possibly mind? He felt for the nipple through the brassiere. She laughed, relinquished him, sat up. 'Let me get this bloody thing off.'

'Oh! Mightn't someone . . . ?' He broke off. He no longer cared about someone or anyone.

Now, her naked breasts above him, his finger-tips rotating at the nipples, she was kneeling between his wide-spread legs. Her head went down, the coarse, blond hair screening her face. 'Oh . . . Oh . . .' Then he closed his eyes. His breath came faster and faster.

'Now we must eat something!' She was pulling her dress on over her head. 'Swimming and sex – both give me an enormous appetite.' She crossed over to him, fastening the belt. 'Was it all right?'

'Super. Oh, Pat . . .' He said nothing more; he could only think of clichés.

She smiled at him, teasingly. Then she asked: 'Was it the first time?'

He nodded in acute embarrassment.

'And you're what — twenty-two, twenty-three? Oh, how marvellous!'

Was she being sarcastic? But she seemed to mean it.

'I did it for the first time when I was thirteen,' she went on. 'One of my uncles. My aunt had just died and I suppose that he . . .' The casual revelation seemed to cause her no pain or guilt. But the thought of that uncle filled him with disgust.

Hand in hand, he now dragging her and she now dragging him, they trudged back up the precipitous path to the village. At one point they met an old peasant, his round, yellow, pitted face like a huge sponge, who was descending, remarkably agile, with a tiny child of indeterminate sex held in the crook of a bare, muscular, hairy arm.

After he had passed them, Jack said: 'That was an odd look!'

'What look?'

'That man's. He glared at us.'

'Rubbish!'

'Perhaps he could see us from up above.'

'You're suffering from guilt, that's what's the matter with you. He looked at us with curiosity, nothing more. Perfectly natural. Two foreigners in a place where probably no foreigners ever come.'

Was he suffering from guilt? Perhaps he was; perhaps this malaise which he was now experiencing — an ache at the back of the legs, a vague throbbing of the temples, a disinclination to talk — was merely a sympton of it.

In the town, Pat said: 'That trattoria looks all right.'

'Won't it be terribly expensive?'

'Are you worrying about money?'

'Have to.'

'I told you — I can make you a loan. Or, better still, I'll treat you.'

'Oh, I couldn't possibly let you . . .'

'Why not? Oh, for God's sake! Don't be so conventional!

You're terribly conventional, you know. If I have money and you haven't, why shouldn't I pay? Perhaps next time – if there *is* a next time – you'll have money and I shan't. That's the sensible way to look at it.'

But he found that he could not look at it like that. None the less, he eventually followed her into the cool of the trattoria.

As she wound some spaghetti round and round a fork, Pat looked up and said: 'You've grown awfully quiet.'

'Have I?'

She nodded, placed the spaghetti in her mouth, and then wiped her top lip with the back of her hand. 'Perhaps you're suffering from the *post coitum* thing.'

'The post-coitum thing?'

'*Post coitum Omne animal triste est*,' she quoted.

'Oh! Yes, of course. . . . Did you do Latin then?'

She laughed. 'Only *amo, amas, amat* – that kind of stuff. But I once knew someone who quoted that to me, and it stuck in my mind.'

'Someone? You mean – someone with whom you made love.'

'That's my business!' She laughed, baring strong, previously white teeth now stained with tomato sauce. 'Isn't it?'

'I suppose so.' But he felt, irrationally, that it was also his business. For a while he was silent, irritated that, unlike her, he had difficulty in preventing his spaghetti from slithering off his fork. Then he said: 'I suppose you've had lots of – lots of boyfriends?'

'Do you mean lots of sex?' That was what he meant; but her teasing frankness now made him blush. 'I told you – that's my business, not yours.' She leaned across the table. 'You know, for someone doing it for the first time you were really rather good.'

'Really?'

'Really!'

He could not help feeling gratified – even though he wished that she would not speak so loudly (might not there be someone in the trattoria who understood English?) and be so brutally direct.

She put out a hand and touched his cheek. 'I now wish I wasn't going back to England. But we'll meet again, won't we?'

He nodded. 'Of course.'

'Won't we?' She repeated it, as though doubting his assurance.

'Yes, yes!'

Again she gave her loud, carefree laugh. Then she began to sing in passable imitation of Vera Lynn, nasal and plangent: 'We'll meet again, don't know where, don't know when . . .'

Customers looked round; some of them smiled.

'Sh! Sh!' Jack hissed, raising his coarse napkin to his mouth, as though to hide behind it.

After he had eaten a lonely supper of *vitello tonnato*, salad and grapes that evening — Margot and Giles had gone out to dinner, having asked him, in Maria's absence, to keep an eye on the children until their return — Jack lay out on his bed in nothing but those 'droopy drawers' of which Pat had made fun, a hand shielding his eyes from the soft evening light through the window, and began to relive that experience on the beach. It was as if some grainy, sepia film were flickering before him. Then, suddenly, colour first seeped and then flooded into it. The film now accelerated, now slowed down, and now froze for seconds on end. He saw that pinkish corrugation around the slender waist; that nipple hard against the sodden pink material of the brassiere; that coarse blond hair screening Pat's face, as she knelt between his wide-spread legs and worked away at him. Then, all at once, as though by trick-photography, Pat was no longer Pat but Iris: the hair wavier and softer; the legs longer, less robust; the hands delicate. . . Oh, yes, yes, yes!

It was at that moment that the dog yelped and yelped again. Hell! What was going on? He sat up, supporting his body on an elbow; then, at yet another yelp, scrambled off the bed, thrust his bare feet into slippers, and reached for the woollen dressing-gown so totally inappropriate in weather like this. The last thing that Giles had said to him had been: 'And you will keep an eye on Perdita as well — won't you?'

He peered out of the window into the garden. He could now hear, gratingly shrill, the excited voices of the children. He should have seen that they had gone to bed long ago, he thought guiltily.

'Got her!'

'No, you bloody well didn't!'

'Did!'

'Hit the tree!'

'Well, how about that?'

'She's over there now! Beside the shed.'

He rushed out. 'What the hell d'you think you're doing? Leave that dog alone! Go on! Beat it! Get back into your room and start getting undressed!'

As though aroused from sleep-walking, the two children stared at him in dazed bewilderment. Piers let a stone fall from his hand. Then Prunella emitted a whimper and raced past Jack, into the house. As Piers followed her, Jack, his indignation suddenly blazing into fury, put out a hand and slapped him hard across the head. The boy, amazingly, uttered not a sound at the impact.

Jack advanced through the dimming garden towards the terrified dog. Her back against the fence, she growled as he approached her. Then she bared her teeth, snarling. 'Good dog,' he said. 'Good dog.' Unlike Iris, he was fond of both dogs and cats, having been brought up with them. But, sensing Giles's possessiveness, he had given this dog no attention.

He continued to advance. Then he put out a hand. 'Good dog! Come on! Come!'

The dog came. She leapt at him, fastening her teeth in his thumb.

The following morning, a Sunday, Jack went along to the sitting-room to see if the paper were there. He tried to spend at least half an hour each day reading it, in an effort to improve his Italian.

The door was ajar; and he assumed – since Margot and Giles had failed to appear for breakfast when, tousled and constantly yawning, Maria had served it to him – that the still curtained room was empty. It was only as he was walking across it to the table on which papers, magazines and books were untidily stacked, that he heard the muffled sobbing, not unlike the amplified sound of the dripping of a tap.

Then he saw Giles. He was sitting, barefoot and in his pyjamas, the dog laid across his knees, with the fingers of one hand deep in her coat, while the other hand covered his eyes. For a moment, Jack imagined that the dog, her body totally motionless, was dead. Then, as he stared at her, she let out a faint growl, and her eyes briefly shifted.

'Is something the matter?'

Giles did not answer. The sobbing continued.

'Giles . . .' He took another step forward. 'What's wrong?'

One hand still covering his eyes and the other hand still playing with the thick fur of the dog, Giles cried out in the fretful, panicky voice of a child: 'Oh, fuck off! *Fuck off!*'

'As you wish.'

Even as, retreating, he said the words, Jack realized how ludicrously inadequate they were.

26

Audrey slipped into her mouth one of the *langues de chat* which Iris, guilty that she had allowed so many days to pass without a visit, had brought to her.

'The same thing happened to another Felix,' she said. 'Except that he was *Félixe*.' She gave the name an exaggeratedly Gallic pronunciation. 'Félix Faure. He was President of France when he collapsed and died on top of his mistress. It's surprising that she didn't herself collapse and die under all that inert blubber. With our poor Felix — Felix Luce — there was mercifully no danger of that. He always was *wee*. Although rumour has it that in one respect . . . After all, he did have that huge nose.'

She reached for the champagne bottle between them and splashed some more of its contents into the Waterford glass, the last of a set of twelve, which she had insisted that Iris must have while she herself drank out of a cheap, coarse tumbler.

'I'm celebrating,' she had greeted Iris. 'My ship has come home. Well, not precisely a ship,' she had amended. 'More a lifeboat. But at last I've got *Time and Tide* to pay up for that piece of mine which was reproduced in the *New York Times*. If *Time and Tide* waits for no man, I told them, this woman is sick to the back teeth of waiting for *Time and Tide*.'

Since Audrey at once spent any money which she received, however small the sum, Iris doubted whether there was much left over from the *Time and Tide* cheque once the champagne had been bought.

Audrey sighed: 'Those who live by sex have a way of dying by sex. So for Felix to kick the bucket like that was really rather apt. But what a shock for Ivor! And how disgraceful of that Communist rag to splash the truth all over its front page! Why not just say that he died in bed — without saying *whose* bed?'

229

'I never met him.'

'Just as well. He certainly wouldn't have been able to resist you. And you'd have had an embarrassing and strenuous time resisting him. Why, he once even had a go at *me* – which suggests that he was either abnormally conceited or abnormally unobservant. Johnny was furious, I can tell you.' Again Audrey poured champagne into their glasses. 'Ivor will be richer than ever now. Well, good luck to him! He's one of the few rich people who know how to spend their money. Not like Pippa – now splashing it around on good-for-nothings and now hoarding it as though bankruptcy were imminent. How can you bear to wear that silk scarf in this weather?' she suddenly demanded, pointing at it. 'It's very pretty with that dress of yours, but even so . . .'

Iris's hand went to the scarf in embarrassment. 'I have a sore throat,' she lied.

'Well, I'd have thought that a good gargle would be more effective than wrapping it up like that.'

'I have gargled. And the chemist gave me some lozenges.' Once one had told one lie, it was surprising how easy it was to follow it with another.

'Get the doctor to prescribe some penicillin.'

'Oh, it's not as bad as all that. And I couldn't face those injections every four hours.'

'Johnny hated injections. She'd pass right out. Odd, really, when she was so dauntless in every other respect. One of those silly psychoanalysts – a disciple of Freud – told her it was all to do with her terror of the penis. That's how he put it – "*The* penis". So I asked him, "Which penis are we talking about? Do you mean yours?"'

Soon after that, Iris said that she must leave: after the weekend the Cambridge examinations would start, and she must have a word with Tim about the orals which they would be conducting together.

'Oh, I do hate to lose you so soon!' Audrey sighed, putting an arm around Iris's waist, as she walked with her to the door. 'Have you decided whether you're going to stay on in Florence or not?'

Iris shook her head. Since Pippa had not decided whether she was going to stay on in Florence, Dale had not decided; and since Dale had not decided, she herself had not decided. 'I don't know if I'm really cut out for teaching. Not like Jack.'

'But there are all sorts of other things you could do here.' What were those other things, Iris wondered ruefully. 'You're such an asset to our little colony. And it does so need new blood. The old crowd is thinning out so fast — Harry only a few weeks ago, now Felix.' She laughed. 'Perhaps I'll be the next one for whom the bell tolls.'

Suddenly Iris felt a surge of admiration for this gallant old woman, living on without her partner of half a century, without even a part-time servant, without money. 'Of course you won't! You're tough, very tough.'

Audrey smiled in pleasure. 'Yes, I *am* tough. Durable. A survivor. That's the most important thing about me.'

For once, when she felt Audrey's lips on her own in a farewell kiss, Iris experienced no inward shrinking.

As she walked down the overgrown drive, she put a hand to the silk scarf round her throat and then eased its constriction with a forefinger. Could the old girl have intuited — there were often times when she seemed to have almost magical powers of perception — what the scarf concealed? Iris now pressed her hand against her neck, activating its soreness with a mixture of excitement, annoyance and dread. Again she pressed.

. . . 'Take care! Stop it! *Stop!*' He had been holding her by the throat with one hand, while the other hand had clasped a wrist, now similarly bruised, so that she had been obliged to wear not merely the scarf but a dress with long, buttoned sleeves for her visit to Audrey. She had been terrified both by the dazed, demented expression on his face, and by the extraordinary strength of someone who, until then, had always struck her as frail. She had tried to kick out, her body heaving from side to side, and had then extricated her other hand from under him, to lunge at his face.

'Bitch!' At that he was laughing. Then, all that demonic fury suddenly ebbing from him, he had collapsed, a dead weight, on to her.

. . . *A dead weight*. Suddenly she thought of the two Felixes, each dying in the arms of his mistress at the moment of consummation. How lucky that Dale had not died on top of her! That would really have given all the Florentine cats a bowl of cream to slurp over.

She smiled to herself; then laughed aloud. *Langues de chat*. Had she unconsciously chosen those particular chocolates because of what they symbolized?

As he carried the tea-tray out to the Chinese-style pavilion in which, their jackets off and the sleeves of their shirts rolled up, Ivor and Jack were lolling in deck-chairs, the expression on the face of Aldo, the red-haired manservant, was one of stunned distraction. His mouth was pulled to one side, almost as though he had suffered a stroke; his short eyelashes kept fluttering up and down. With unusual clumsiness, he tipped the tray to one side as he stooped to rest it on the table, with the result that, had Ivor not deftly put out a hand, at least one of the Spode teacups would have crashed to the floor. 'Scusi, signore! Scusi!' He exhaled his apologies on what was almost a sob.

As, head bowed, Aldo walked slowly back to the house, Ivor said: 'It's extraordinary — he really does seem genuinely to be grief-stricken by my father's — our father's — death. And yet the old boy behaved appallingly to him — as he did to all his by-blows. Fancy employing your own son as a manservant. I ask you!' He raised the lid of the teapot and sniffed: 'Such is his grief, he seems to have brought breakfast tea instead of Earl Grey. Ah, well! No matter.' He began to pour out the dark-brown liquid. 'Yes, Aldo actually sobbed when he heard the news. And there was I, totally dry-eyed.'

'Don't you feel anything — anything at all?'

'Of course I feel something. Incredulity to begin with. Then relief. Then excitement. Euphoria.' Quizzically he stared at Jack. 'Does that shock you?'

'Yes. A bit.'

'What shocks you is not that I feel those things but that I admit to feeling them. But, as you must know by now, dear boy, for good or for ill I like to tell the truth. My father was an absolute old horror. He was a Fascist and, like most Fascists, he was also a bully. He behaved abominably to me and my sister and even more abominably to my mother. Now — I'm rich!'

'Weren't you always rich?'

Ivor laughed gleefully, throwing back his head. 'Not *stinking* rich! Not until now. My mother left me a certain amount of money, but most of it was in trust for my father's use during his lifetime. He had virtually no money of his own. That poor Lisa, with whom he spent his last hours – or hour, probably, since even in old age he was extremely nippy on the job – will get nothing. Or jolly little. And Aldo and the rest of the poor bastards. . .' He sighed. 'Well, for them I suppose I'll have to do *something*. Won't I?'

'Yes. Yes, you must.'

'That's enough about death. It's a subject that has always absolutely terrified me. I can't bear to think about it – which is something I tend to do more and more, as my fifties advance . . .. Tell me – have you decided whether to stay on in Florence or not?'

'Probably not.'

'Oh, dear!'

'It's such a dead end. I'm not getting anywhere. Am I?'

'Does one have to get *somewhere*? Is that the purpose of life?'

Jack frowned in thought. Then: 'Yes, I think it is,' he at last said hesitantly. 'One must have *some* destination.'

'Oh, yes, yes, I suppose you're right. But I've never had any destination, not really. My life has just been one long pleasure cruise – swanning from port to port.' He leaned forward, clasping his hands together. He put his head on one side; he smiled winningly. 'Join me on my pleasure cruise.'

Jack averted his gaze, stricken with embarrassment and, to his surprise, also with guilt. 'Oh, Ivor . . .'

'Forget I said that! You've got your own life to lead. Of course you have! Why should you want to lead – or share – mine? Of course not. Out of the question. You must go back to England, get your doctorate, become a distinguished fellow of some grand Oxford or Cambridge college. Yes, yes!' He sounded sniffy and sarcastic. But then, with genuine warmth, he continued: 'But whenever you feel like it – whenever you want a pause in the hot race of life – you will remember that this house is here awaiting you – and this sentimental old friend is also here? Won't you?'

'Of course I'll remember. Thank you.'

'Good boy!' Ivor leaned forward and playfully pinched Jack's cheek. Then he withdrew: 'Oh, God, I shouldn't have done that to you! That's what my father was constantly doing to any woman he wanted to make!'

Legs outstretched before him and hands deep in his pockets, Tim sat opposite to Iris in the otherwise deserted common room. Both of them had a free period.

He rested his head on the grease-stained back of his rickety armchair, closed his eyes, and then opened them again.

'Oh, I do wish you hadn't mentioned the exams to me. I just don't feel strong enough, not after the night I had. I got awfully drunk in that little *bettola* above which I live. Then someone began talking about the death of Ivor's father – what a way to go! – and someone else said that he'd often seen him going into a knocking-shop in the Via Parione. A knocking-shop in the Via Parione! In my ineffable innocence I'd never known that such an institution existed – so conveniently near to this ghastly place, too! So I upped and toddled off there. The Spider Club. That's what it's called. There was this iron spider's web in place of the usual grille – through which first a shrivelled hag and then a bully-boy with an American accent peered at me before granting me admittance. Packed to the rafters and groaning at the gunwales with British and American servicemen. There was this one bint I rather fancied – gi-gant-esque boobs she had, and I rather go for boobs. You can divide the male sex into leg men and tit men. Except that I'm both. Well, the hag asked me for a down payment, but I just hadn't got that sort of lolly on me – not after a day at the races. So we haggled for ages – until, in desperation, I offered to deposit my watch with her. A twenty-first birthday present from my godless godfather. Whether I'll ever be in a position to redeem it . . . And, until I do, I'm going to be even later for my classes than in the past. Anyway' – he leaned forward, suddenly eager – 'this girl – just let me tell you about her!'

'No, I'd much rather you didn't.'

'But you cannot imagine how she –'

'Oh, do shut up, Tim! It's all so unutterably squalid.' But Iris was laughing as she said this. 'The life you lead!'

'And what about the life *you* lead, my pet? I don't disapprove of that. Or the life that our Jack leads. I don't disapprove of that either – now do I?'

'Let's talk about those orals.'

'Those *orals*! Iris – in your demure, well-bred way, you really are a terribly shocking girl!'

'You know perfectly well what I mean. You and I are listed as taking some of the orals together. And I've no idea what on earth is expected of us. Have you ever done them before?'

He nodded. 'Yep. I'm a real pro at them by now. But I refuse, I absolutely refuse to ask the sort of questions which people like our Ethel and Miss Sweeney ask.'

'Such as?'

'Well, you know the sort of thing. What part of Florence do you live in? What's your hobby? Do you go to the opera? Where are you planning to spend your summer holiday? The same old questions, endlessly repeated. Anyone with any sense gets the answers off by heart. No good, no bloody good at all. We've got to take them by surprise.'

'How?'

'By asking the sort of questions for which they *can't* prepare of course! Odd questions. Unexpected questions. Have you ever visited the Spider Club? – if it's a man. Have you ever worked in the Spider Club? – if it's a woman. That kind of thing.'

'I'm not sure if I'll be much good at thinking of questions like that.'

'Leave it to me! I'll draw up a list of questions. How about that? But not now, not now . . .' He put a hand to his forehead. 'If I move at all, I have this peculiar sensation that my head is on a spring. Like a jack-in-the-box. Oh, I do wish that I had a box – a very deep, a very dark box – into which I could vanish!'

'You'll really draw up a list?' By now Iris had learned that Tim made many promises which he never fulfilled.

'Of *course*, my pet! Have you ever known me to let anyone down?'

'Often.'

'Beast!'

Yet again Jack ate breakfast alone. This time Maria was light-hearted, whisking around the table on her sturdy, bare legs, her breasts out-thrust, and at one moment, when he stooped to pick up a teaspoon dropped by her, pinching him on the back of the neck and then bursting into peals of delighted laughter when she heard his 'Ouch!'

'Has the signora had her breakfast?' he asked her in Italian, to be told that Margot and Giles had already been served it in their room. Could it be that, for some reason, they wished to avoid him? Jack's previously sunny mood darkened at the thought.

After breakfast, he hung around for a while, so that he would not offend Giles by setting off for the Institute alone. The robust American woman whose turn it was to take the children to school eventually arrived, firmly told Piers to 'stop that whining at once' (he was complaining that Maria had borrowed a propelling pencil of his and had failed to return it), jerked Prunella's straw hat lower down over her forehead, and then admonished both of them: 'Make it snappy! I'm not going to have my kids arriving late yet again because of you two!'

Soon after that, in her dressing-gown, her hair hanging in a plait down her back and her face greasily pale in its total lack of make-up, Margot appeared.

'Are you off?'

'I was waiting for Giles.'

'Well, don't.'

'Isn't he coming to the Institute?'

'No. Not today.' Her upper lip twitched. She rubbed at an eye with the back of her hand. 'He's not well.'

'Oh, I'm sorry. Is it the usual?'

Now that the summer had come, many of the English and the Americans intermittently suffered from what Ivor called 'a touch of the della Squercias'.

'I suppose you might call it the usual.' Again the upper lip trembled; she put a hand to it to stop it from doing so. She was in danger of bursting into tears. 'He's in this ghastly depression. I can't go to the office while he's like that. I've just telephoned to tell them. Not that my being with Giles helps him at all. In fact, I sometimes wonder if I don't make him worse.' She stared woefully down at her slippered feet. Then she gave herself a shake. 'At all events . . he wants you to do something.' She inserted a hand into a pocket of her dressing-gown and pulled out two large keys on a ring. 'I've already rung Ethel Pryce to tell her to take charge of the examinations. And I've also rung Mervyn, of course. Not that he'll do anything useful — just make himself a nuisance. These are the keys to the safe and the papers are all in it. Give the keys to Ethel. Miss Sweeney and Mr Greville will both be furious that Giles has asked Ethel to take over. But she's efficient, she isn't afraid to boss people around, and she knows the drill. Either of those other two would just get things into a total muddle.'

Jack took the keys from her and put them into his trouser pocket.

'Now for heaven's sake don't lose them. If you do, we'll really be up the creek.'

236

'Of course I won't lose them.'

'Sorry. Don't be offended. My nerves are all on edge. They're short-handed at the Consulate, and once the tourists begin to pour in, there's endless bother with lost passports and lost travellers' cheques and lost loved ones and people being arrested for getting drunk or shop-lifting or failing to pay their bills. I ought to be on duty. Particularly as I got that promotion only last month. Oh, dear! Life is *not* easy just at present.'

'Give Giles my good wishes. Tell him I hope he'll be better soon.'

'I'll tell him. But he won't take it in. He takes nothing in at present. Just sits staring at the wall or out into the garden, with that wretched dog on his lap.'

As Jack walked out briskly to the Institute, he at first felt harassed and depressed; then, as so often, the beauty of the city, glowing in the early morning light, raised his spirits. He began to whistle to himself: 'Volare', the song which Maria was constantly singing at her work and which he was constantly hearing on the wireless.

Suddenly, from behind him, he heard someone take up the song: not whistling it but singing it in the punishingly slow, slurred voice of a reveller lurching home in the early hours. He turned. Good God! It was Giuseppe, huddled in the entrance to the Banca Toscana, his misshapen back propped against its still unopened bronze door.

'Giuseppe!' Jack turned; then hurriedly retraced his steps. 'What are you doing up at this hour?' It was Giuseppe's boast that he never got out of bed before eleven, although he claimed often to read and write in bed long before that.

Giuseppe looked up with eyes red-rimmed either from lack of sleep or weeping. The knot of his tie had slipped down to the third button of his shirt, and the shirt itself, a blue-and-white striped poplin with a high, stiff collar, was grimy. There was a jagged tear at one shoulder of the Edwardian-style jacket, the collar of which had somehow got turned up. For many seconds he stared up at Jack, as Jack stared down at him, shocked by the dirtiness and dishevelment of someone usually so elegant and spruce. Then, in a hoarse voice, the words slurred as when he had taken up the song, Giuseppe said: 'I am going home. But the walk is long.'

'Why not take a taxi? Or a tram?'

Giuseppe looked down at his outstretched legs with a frown; then put his hands into the pockets of his trousers and pulled out their linings. '*Niente.*' He left the linings dangling out, as he gave a high-pitched giggle. '*Niente affatto.*'

'Oh, Giuseppe!' Jack knew that he would be late unless he hurried; but he could not leave the little man, drunk and penniless, in a street in which many people would certainly recognize him. 'Where have you been? What have you been doing?'

'I have been to the — the' — for a moment he frowned in an effort to remember where he had been — 'to the — the Spider Club. You know the Spider Club?'

Jack shook his head.

'*Bordello.* Very fine.' Again he gave the high-pitched giggle. 'Very expensive. I do not have enough money to pay for so much *sciampagna*, so they catch me' — he illustrated the words with a gesture — 'like this, and throw me away.'

'Well, let me give you the money for a taxi.' His impatience to resume his journey to the Institute made Jack unusually peremptory.

Giuseppe began to protest at the offer; but with a 'No, no! I insist,' Jack stooped, put an arm under each of his armpits and then, with a grunt, jerked him up to his feet. Giuseppe swayed forwards and backwards and all but fell over. Jack put out a steadying hand to his shoulder. He winced at the pressure on the finger bitten by the dog.

There was a taxi passing, and Jack flagged it down. Then he not so much pushed as bundled Giuseppe into it, before handing the driver a note and some coins. It was probably far too much, but he did not have the time to haggle.

Giuseppe was slumped so low on the back seat that as the taxi drove off he was totally invisible.

What on earth had reduced him to such a condition, Jack wondered as he set off, at a jog-trot, for the Institute. Giuseppe was usually so fastidious in both his appearance and behaviour. It was difficult to imagine him consorting, like some latter-day Toulouse-Lautrec, with prostitutes and pimps.

'Yes, poor Margot rang me at the *pensione*,' Ethel said, when Jack handed her the keys to the safe.

The authority so recently conferred had already changed her, so that her colour was high, her eyes bright and her voice commanding as, a few minutes later, she gave instructions about the invigilation of the forthcoming examinations to the staff already gathered in the common room. 'Now listen carefully to this, please, Miss Crediton and Mr Prentice,' she paused to say at one moment. 'You are not familiar with the procedures and it's essential that you should both get them right.' 'Do please attend, Mr Harris,' she told Tim at another moment. 'I don't want you to come back to ask me about all this when I've already explained it all.' Miss Sweeney, offended that it was not she who had been asked to deputize for Giles, at one moment ventured, 'Miss Pryce, dear, I don't think that's quite clear,' to receive the snappish reply: 'It should be perfectly clear to anyone of any intelligence. But, in case it isn't to you, by all means let me repeat it.'

Having finished this repetition, Ethel gathered up the papers spread out on the table before her, pushed back her chair and rose. 'Well, I think that wraps it all up — unless, of course, there's someone else for whom things are not quite clear.' She looked around the assembled company. 'No?' No one spoke; no one looked up at her. She was aware of their hostility, but so far from this daunting or depressing her, it produced in her a mounting exhilaration. She glanced at her watch. 'Then, in that case, those of you who are invigilating should be at your posts in precisely eleven minutes. Right? Miss Crediton and Mr Harris — you're neither of you on until this afternoon, are you? But I'd be grateful if you'd remain in the Institute — the lunch break apart. Something may crop up. One must be prepared for every emergency.'

'It is precisely because Miss Crediton and I want to be prepared for every emergency that we're going to spend at least part of the morning going through our questions for the orals.'

Ethel gave Tim an indulgently patronizing smile. 'Oh, yes, I remember. You're planning to *stray from the beaten track*' — the words had been his — 'in the sort of questions you put to your candidates. Well, I wish you both — and them — good luck.'

'How she'd love to be Director of Studies,' Mr Greville exclaimed when the door had closed behind her.

'She is Director of Studies,' Miss Sweeney answered bitterly. 'To all intents and purposes. In her own estimation. For the time being.'

*

'How about this? "Explain to someone who has never made an omelette how to set about doing so."'

'But some of them may never have made an omelette themselves. Have you ever made an omelette?'

'Well, no,' Tim replied. 'But then I'm a man. That one's for the women.'

'Some of these women can never have made an omelette,' Iris said. 'They have servants to make them for them.'

'Well, we can try it on some woman who looks obviously plebeian. . . . The next one I have is: "If you had to go to Paris, would you choose to go by car, by train or to fly?"'

'That's not going to test anyone's conversational skills. The answer could be a monosyllable.'

'Initially, yes. But then the question follows: "What's your reason for saying that?"'

Iris shrugged.

'Okay?'

'Hm. All right.'

'I wish you'd think of something.'

'"If you were conducting this oral examination, what question would you ask yourself?"'

'That sounds altogether too metaphysical for the Italians. It would be fine in Germany.'

'Are you going to ask your question about the Spider Club?'

'Dare I?'

'Better not. Ethel would certainly disapprove if she heard of it.'

Jack had arrived back home, sweating profusely from the walk through the oppressive heat of the late afternoon, and had stripped off his shirt in order to change into a clean one for dinner. There was a knock at the door and, before he could call out, Margot had entered.

She looked everywhere but at him as, in an agitated voice, one hand fiddling with her reddish hair where, loosened from its usual bun, it came to a fox's brush at the back of her neck, she said: 'Oh, Jack. Jack, I know I'm being a fearful nuisance — or Giles is being a fearful nuisance — when you've only just got in after a hard day of invigilating. But he's worked himself into this state. Even more of a state than usual. Totally irrational. But there's just no way of arguing with him. He's immune to argument, totally immune.'

Jack had by now slipped his clean shirt over his head and was doing up the buttons. 'What's the trouble?'

'It's some — some papers.' She was clearly embarrassed. 'They're in the drawer of his desk at the Institute. He's afraid' — the colour mounted into her cheeks — 'that Ethel might, er, look at them. He doesn't want her — anyone — to read them.'

'Oh, I don't think Ethel would start opening his drawers or reading his papers.'

Margot drew a deep sigh; then crossed to the window and gazed out into the garden. 'No, of course not. That's what I keep telling him. But, as I said, he's worked himself into this terrible state of agitation.'

'Didn't he lock the drawer — if the papers are so important to him?'

'I'm sure he did. But he insists that he forgot to do so. Oh, he's not himself. Not at all himself. Maria produced a really delicious *bollita mista* for lunch — she really excelled herself — and he hardly ate a mouthful. One of his favourite dishes too.'

'So what do you want me to do?' But Jack had already guessed.

'Well, I know this is asking an awful lot . . . but could — *could* you bear to go back to the Institute and make sure the desk drawer is locked? I've got the key to it here.' As she had done that morning, she produced a key-ring from a pocket. 'This is the one. The smallest of all.'

'But *I* might read the papers!' Jack laughed, so that she would know that he was joking.

'He trusts you. He says you'd never do anything like that.'

'Why doesn't he trust Ethel?'

She shrugged. 'Search me. Pehaps because she's a woman. He has a pretty low opinion of women at present.'

As Jack was about to leave the house, Giles appeared, the dog beside him. Stubble darkened the lower half of his face and his eyes also seemed to be far darker than usual. His hand was trembling as it rested on the back of one of the two chairs in the hall. 'Sorry about this,' he said in a soft, toneless voice, totally different from his usually loud, robust one. 'But I don't want those letters to get into the wrong hands.'

Letters? Margot had spoken of papers.

'Just lock the drawer. It's the second down on the left — as you're facing the desk. No need to open it.'

It was as though he were now distrustful of Jack, as well as of Ethel.

Jack nodded. 'I'll just lock it . . . How are you?'

But Giles had already shuffled back into the bedroom, the dog at his heels.

On his hurried walk back to the Institute — his fresh shirt now grew as damp as the one for which he had exchanged it — Jack puzzled over the discrepancy between Margot's 'papers' and Giles's 'letters'; then he eventually decided that it was Giles's version which must be the right one and that the letters must be ones written to him by Violetta from Rome.

There was a strong smell of liquor on Vincente's breath when he came to the door of the Institute in answer to Jack's ring. He was still in the dark-blue trousers of his uniform, but had removed its jacket and dark-blue tie, as well as the stiff collar of his shirt.

'*L'ufficio è tuttora aperto,*' he told Jack, adding: '*La signorina Pryce è la.*'

Jack assumed that Ethel was still dealing with the examination scripts for that day. He had heard Miss Sweeney and one of the Italians on the staff offer to help her, and her brisk: 'No, thank you. I can manage quite well on my own.'

Jack knocked on the door of Giles's study. Ethel's voice called out in response: 'Vincente?' Clearly she assumed that it could only be the porter.

'It's me.' Jack walked in.

Ethel looked up at him, her mouth open. He had never before seen her look like that. She might have just been caught shop-lifting.

'Sorry.'

She had begun to scrabble together the papers on her desk. Under her agitated hands, Jack made out one of the strong, brown manilla envelopes which arrived at the Rome Embassy from Cambridge by diplomatic bag and were then brought to Florence by courier. Jack also made out an examination paper. Why on earth was she in such a state? Presumably she was merely tidying up from the examinations of the day now over.

Then a suspicion came to him; and the suspicion, however hard he tried to resist it, became a conviction. But there was no evidence, no evidence at all.

'Yes?' Her tone was now peremptory. 'I thought you'd gone. I thought everyone had gone.'

'I had gone. Then I came back. An awful nuisance.' He tried to speak as though that suspicion and that subsequent conviction had never in turn slithered, snake-like, into his mind, to coil there venomously. 'Giles wanted me to lock one of his drawers.' How on earth was he to explain why Giles wanted him to lock that bloody drawer? He could hardly say: 'Giles wanted me to lock the drawer because he was afraid that you would read some love-letters in it.' Inspiration came to him: 'He's got some money in it. And he doesn't want to put temptation in the way of the cleaner.'

'Well, lock it then.'

He pulled the key-ring out of his trouser pocket, slouched over to the desk, and then fumbled repeatedly to insert the key, without success.

'Give it to me.' She had risen; she was standing over him. He handed her the key. 'You were putting it in the wrong way,' she said scornfully. She still looked extraordinarily pale. She turned the key, then handed it back to him.

'Alma is completely honest,' she said of the cleaner.

'Yes, I'm sure she is. But Giles was afraid . . .'

'It would have been more sensible to have asked you to remove the money and take it back to him. Wouldn't it?'

'Yes, I suppose it would.'

'What exactly is the matter with Giles?'

Jack shrugged.

'Margot said it was overwork.'

'Yes, I suppose it is. He does work awfully hard. And then there's his novel.'

'Oh, his novel!'

She gave a contemptuous laugh.

The heavy Parker fountain-pen — was its case made of gold or rolled gold? — glinted on the table after the candidate at the viva, a spruce, plumpish young man with a comically inaccurate command of English, had risen to his feet.

'You've left your pen behind,' Tim called after him as, hand to door-handle, he was about to leave the room.

'*Signore?*'

243

'Your pen!' Tim pointed. 'You don't want to leave your beautiful gold pen.'

'*Ma...*' The young man hesitated; he almost said something. Then he shrugged and, reluctantly, returned to the desk, picked up the pen and clipped it into the breast-pocket of his elegant grey silk suit. '*Grazie, signore.*'

'*Prego.*'

After the young man had closed the door behind him, Tim burst into laughter: 'Well, that was a neat way of attempting a bribe!'

'Oh, I don't imagine...' Iris demurred.

'Of course! Don't be silly! Why otherwise should he take a fountain-pen out of his pocket in the course of a viva, place it on the table in front of him and then leave it there?'

'Perhaps I should have accepted it. I need a new fountain-pen.'

'I could have flogged it – or exchanged it for the watch I left at the Spider Club. Ah well!' He turned to her. 'Why *are* we English so honest? The Italians manage so much better by not being so honest.'

Iris at once recognized the candidate who, awkwardly muscular, next swaggered in. It was Ethel's pupil, Guido.

Tim looked down for his name on his list. 'Ah, Mr Antonini! Come and sit down here opposite to us.'

Guido gave Iris a nervous smile and a nod. He placed himself gingerly on the edge of the chair; then leaned forward, legs wide apart, one elbow on the table and chin cupped in hand.

'You start,' Tim said *sotto voce* to Iris. He pushed his list of questions towards her.

Hurriedly she looked down it. Then, choosing at random, she asked: 'Can you tell me about any foreign literary figure who made his – or her – home in Florence?'

'*Scusi?*'

'You mustn't speak in Italian,' Tim said. Then, since Guido merely frowned in puzzlement, he added: 'No Italian, please.'

'*Scusi?*'

Tim looked over to Iris, raised his eyebrows and shrugged his shoulders. Iris repeated her question, extremely slowly.

'Ah!' Guido looked suddenly relieved. Then he closed his eyes and started: 'Yes. There is Robert Browning. A great – ah – English poet. He and his wife – ah – Barrett Elizabeth Browning live in Pisa, in Rome but, specially, in Florence. In Florence they

244

take up residence in Casa Guidi' — eyes still closed, he frowned in concentration — 'stone's throw from Palazzo Pitti. Barrett Elizabeth Browning write poem — ah — title "From Casa Guidi Window." Yes?' He opened his eyes. Tim merely stared at him, with no response to the question; Iris nodded. 'Barrett Elizabeth Browning die in' — he closed his eyes again, his face was once more contorted in a frown — 'in, in 1861. Of *tuberculosi*.' He opened his eyes, looked first at Tim and then at Iris as though to gauge their reaction, and then smiled in relief.

'Thank you, Mr Antonini.' Tim was severe. 'Now would you like to tell me how you would set about changing the tyre of a car after a puncture?'

'*Scusi?*'

'No Italian, *please*! You must only speak English. We are testing your command of English.'

Taking pity on him, Iris repeated the question.

Once again Guido relaxed. Once again he closed his eyes and, chin on palm and brow corrugated as though in a struggle to recall something inefficiently committed to his memory, he stammered out an answer.

The same happened with the next three questions put to him, two by Tim and one by Iris.

'That will do,' Tim eventually said. 'Thank you.' His tone was chilly.

'I may go?'

'You may go.'

Guido smiled in relief, got up and hurried out of the room, without another word to them.

'Well, what do you make of that?'

'He didn't do too badly.' But Iris knew that something had been wrong.

'He didn't do too badly! He did far too well. He must have somehow got hold of that piece of paper.' He indicated the sheet of ruled foolscap between them.

'Oh, I don't think . . .'

'Of course he did!'

'But how?'

'I don't know how. That's what we must discover. I left that sheet in a drawer of my desk. Someone must have got at it.'

'But who?'

Iris did not really need to ask that question. Appalled, she had

245

already guessed the answer.

'Well, it *could* have been Antonini himself. Or it could have been Vincente — after all, he goes round the building each night to turn out lights and lock doors. Or it could have been one of the cleaners. But somehow I don't buy any of those possibilities. Nope. I've got a hunch that one of our colleagues . . .'

Iris was often later to wonder if she ought to have told Tim that she suspected Ethel of being the culprit; just as Jack was often to wonder if he ought to have told Tim and Iris of coming on Ethel in Giles's study, with the open envelope of examination question-papers before her on the desk and the door of the safe ajar. Tim told Miss Sweeney. It was Miss Sweeney who told Mervyn.

'I really hate to blab on a colleague in this fashion. It's honestly not at all my style.'

'You've done absolutely right, Miss Sweeney. Absolutely right.'

'It's kind of you to say so, Mr Le Clerq. I've been tussling with my conscience all through this long summer day.'

'Of course it may only be a coincidence or a happy fluke that this young man — not a very bright young man, by all accounts, a labourer — should have done so remarkably well. But I must certainly investigate the matter further. I must have a word with Miss Crediton, Mr Prentice and Mr Harris. And then I must have a word with Miss Pryce herself. The last is an interview which I certainly do not relish.'

'What could have persuaded her to do anything so foolish?'

'*If* she did it. We mustn't, er, prejudge the issue.'

'No, of course not . . . But *if* she did it . . . Miss Pryce has always seemed to maintain the very highest standards. I should never have imagined for one moment . . .'

Mervyn sighed. He was going to be late for Isabella's party if this woman rabbited on and on. 'Well, yes, it's certainly all *most* bewildering.' He rose to his feet. 'So . . . I must thank you for coming. You musn't reproach yourself with any thought of disloyalty. You've done your manifest duty, Miss Sweeney. You owed it to the Institute to tell me what you have.'

'Well, that's certainly how I regarded it myself. But no one likes a sneak . . .'

246

'Now put the idea that you've been sneaking right out of your head! Please! I beg of you! . . . Can you see yourself out? I must dash and change.'

Ethel scrambled over a pile of masonry on her way to the Institute. Although it was the hottest day so far of that summer, she felt that at the centre of her being there was a huge block of ice. Then the ice began to thaw, and its cold was seeping outwards, along all her arteries. She was shivering as she halted, leaned over the parapet separating the street from the river, and gazed down at the glinting thread of water weaving between stretches of cracked mud. When Mervyn had told her over the telephone that morning that there was 'a little difficulty in connection with the Cambridge examinations' which he wished to discuss with her as speedily as possible, she had at once known its nature. How could she have ever supposed that she — and, even less likely, Guido — would get away with it? This was the question which, as she had lain out on her bed, a handkerchief drenched in eau-de-Cologne pressed to her forehead, she had repeatedly asked herself, without finding any answer. No one who knew Guido could possibly imagine that his translation of a by no means easy text could be so proficient; or that he had ever heard of the Brownings or knew such English words as 'wrench', 'pump' or 'pressure gauge'. Of course it had been particularly unfortunate that Iris had been one of the two examiners at his oral, since she, unlike Tim, had met Guido. But even if it had not been for that piece of bad luck . . .

As she continued to stare down at the river, a recollection suddenly came to her from the last Easter vacation, which she had spent, alone as always, by Lake Como. Lying out one evening on the balcony of the small room which she had rented in a house on a hillside behind Bellagio, she had heard a loud explosion. Then, getting up and going to the rail, she had seen flames spurting from a motor-boat in the middle of the lake. Red, orange, yellow, white: the flames were so beautiful as they were reflected in the darkening water that for several seconds she had had no thought for the passengers on the boat, all of whom must presumably have perished in the conflagration. Then, as the flames had subsided as quickly as they had burst outwards and upwards, she had heard the raised voices of the other occupants of the house, the cries in the narrow street below her, and the frenetic ringing of the bell of an ambulance hurtling down the road to the lakeside.

The next morning she herself had taken the *vaporetto* from Bellagio to Como. It had been full of noisy school-children, all of whom had suddenly crowded the railing farthest from her, pointing and shouting. But there was nothing to be seen but a few charred pieces of wood, a floating rubber cushion, and the iridescence of oil spreading in concentric circles over the tranquil water.

Why should that recollection have come to her now? And why should she derive comfort from it? Had her love-affair with Guido been something as brief, beautiful and disastrous as that conflagration?

As she walked on, she felt none of the shame and apprehension of the whole morning until now. She was amazed. What had come over her? Always ruthless in self-analysis, she told herself: 'What I'm feeling is satisfaction – quiet satisfaction! But why, why?' Then she found her answer. She had done something extremely perilous to help Guido and so to demonstrate to him the depth of her love. If she was sacked – as she was now certain that she would be – then that demonstration would be even more effective. The rest – the gossip, the disgrace, the financial problems, the difficulty of finding another post in Italy – mattered hardly at all.

Mervyn was amazed by the calm way in which Ethel admitted that, yes, she had opened the question-papers, yes, she had looked at Tim's notes for the viva, and yes, she had passed on the knowledge so acquired to her private pupil, Signore Antonini.

'But how could you have done such a thing?'

In answer, Ethel merely shrugged and gave a small smile, her eyes gazing down at the hands clasped tightly in her lap.

'Was it a question of money?' Mervyn knew about the sister whom Ethel gallantly supported in a home. If it had been a question of money – a bribe offered, which in her penury she had been unable to resist – then he was in a mood to grant her a reprieve.

'Money? No. Certainly not!' Now she looked up. She gave a dry laugh. 'Signore Antonini owes me for his last four lessons. He certainly couldn't afford to bribe me.'

'Oh, dear!' Mervyn now felt genuinely sorry for her. He smiled ruefully, leaning towards her across the desk. 'Well, what am I to do?'

'Sack me, of course! What else can you do? If you didn't sack me, the scandal would involve not only me but you — and the Institute.'

'Oh, dear!' He pondered on that. Then he said: 'But why should anyone know?'

'Everyone knows everything in Florence.' She all but added: 'After all, everyone knows that you're absolutely gone on the Crediton girl.'

'I take your point. Hm. Yes.'

'It's all so tragic.'

'It's not tragic at all. Just a little sad.'

Ethel lay sprawled across her bed; Iris sat at the bottom of it. From time to time Ethel dragged deeply at the cigarette which she was holding between thumb and forefinger. Iris had never seen her smoke before.

'I wish I'd not been involved.'

'Involved? How involved?'

'In that viva. And I wish that Jack hadn't been involved. He oughtn't to have said anything about finding you in Giles's study.'

'Even if you'd both kept silent, the result would have been the same.' Ethel ground out the cigarette in the ashtray on the pillow beside her.

'I don't see that.'

'Of course it would have been the same. There just aren't any secrets in this awful place. Everyone knows everything.'

The two women looked at each other. They were closer than ever before.

'What are you going to do now?'

'Leave Florence in the first place. I can't hang on here. In any case' — for a second it seemed as if she were about to lose her composure — 'there's really no longer anything for which to hang on.'

Iris wanted to say: 'But what about him?'; but she could not bring herself to do so. Although she and Ethel were closer than ever before, they were still not that close. Instead, she asked: 'Where will you go?'

Ethel laughed. 'I've no idea. No idea at all. Perhaps I'll return to Palermo. I used to teach there. Gossip from Florence is unlikely to travel that far. And if it does, people there will probably take no notice of it. Florence is almost a foreign country to them. But there are other possibilities. Greece. Turkey. Cyprus. "The world was all before them, where to choose . . ." It's rather an exciting feeling. I'll manage. I always do.' Suddenly she leaned forward, stretched across the bed, and grasped Iris's hand. 'Don't worry!'

'It's good of you, Ivor, to intervene on that silly woman's behalf. But I really don't see how I can do any differently.'

'Disqualify lover-boy. Administer a stern rebuke to her. And then forget the whole business.'

Mervyn laughed. 'You're far more kind-hearted than most people realize! But it's all too obvious that you've had absolutely no experience of running anything in the whole course of your life. How *could* I keep her on after she's proved herself to be so totally dishonest? It's out of the question.'

'She was only dishonest because she was in love with the boy. Most of us would be prepared to commit that sort of dishonesty to keep — or win — someone with whom we were in love.'

'Speak for yourself! One must have some code of morals. . . Anyway, who told you she was in love with him?'

'It's obvious, isn't it?' In fact, it was Iris and Jack who had told him, when begging him to make this intervention.

'Yes, I suppose it is . . . Well' — Mervyn sighed — 'this is the sort of thing no teacher lives down.'

'It's almost as if she *wanted* a disaster.'

'Unconsciously, people often do.'

27

Miss Sweeney dipped a ladle into the Victorian silver punch-bowl which old Anna, their one surviving servant, had spent most of the morning polishing with hands crooked with arthritis. She raised the ladle to her mouth, sipped, sipped again.

'All right?' her older sister Maud asked apprehensively.

'Well . . .' Miss Sweeney wrinkled her nose. 'I wonder if you haven't overdone the slices of peach.'

'I used the same quantities which I always do.'

'Perhaps the peaches weren't quite ripe. There's a rather *tart* flavour.' With a splash she let the ladle fall back into the bowl. 'Well, never mind! They'll just have to like it or lump it. And there's always the iced tea.' It was Miss Sweeney who prepared the iced tea.

The sisters were giving their annual garden-party, as their parents and paternal grandparents had done each summer before them. It was harder work now, without the four servants and the additional hired help; and it had become an increasingly ruinous drain on their dwindling resources. Should they go ahead, they had asked each other, as they had asked each other each year since the War had ended. Each hoped that the other would say: 'Oh, let's drop it.' But neither of them did. It had become an annual rite for them, like their journeys to the English Cemetery to leave flowers on family graves which went back to the early nineteenth century.

'I really wonder if we shouldn't have asked Ethel Pryce.' When their mother had become an ailing and fretful widow, Ethel's Italian grandmother, then also a widow, had devotedly served her as something between companion and lady's maid. Ethel herself appeared disinclined to remember the connection; but the three sisters remembered it — often remarking to each other or

251

even to Ethel that Tina had been a saint, an absolute saint. Had Tina not been such a saint, they would have enjoyed even less freedom than they had done during those years of semi-servitude and strain.

'Oh, Maud, please! *Please*! We've been into all this at least a dozen times already! I didn't invite Ethel firstly because I thought it would embarrass her to meet people, and secondly because I thought it would embarrass people to meet her. Everyone in Florence seems to have heard of that awful business.' That everyone seemed to have heard of it was, in part at least, due to Miss Sweeney herself.

'By asking her we'd have shown that we, well, still had faith in her. And respect for her. And liking.'

'I still have *liking* for her. But whether I still have faith and respect . . .' Miss Sweeney suddenly noticed that the silver slice for the largest of the cakes was shamefully tarnished. 'Anna! Anna!' she called, to arouse the ancient servant, who was sprawled, exhausted, her shoes off and her skirt pulled up to her waist, on the bed in the tiny little room off the kitchen which she had inhabited for almost half a century.

Ivor sat stiffly on a canvas chair, his hands crossed over the head of the stick upright between his legs and his face shaded by the wide brim of a panama hat. ('This is a *real* panama hat,' he had told Jack. 'I bought it in the year before the War when I actually sailed through the Panama Canal.')

He raised the stick and pointed it at the house. 'So sad to see the house in that condition.' Shutters sealed off the windows of an upper storey no longer used. Frayed net curtains in other windows swayed back and forth in the breeze of early evening. In one of these windows, one of the lodgers, not deemed worthy of an invitation to the party, stood, hands on ample hips, looking down, with a small child, only her eyes and the top of her head visible, looking down beside her. The stucco was peeling and cracked, and an overgrown rose, blown askew by one of the winter gales, trailed across and down from the porch. 'Old Bill Sweeney kept it in perfect condition. He was one of the first do-it-yourself men. I remember how amazed we once were when we arrived here for dinner and he was repairing the bell. We left that sort of thing to servants — of which he had some four or five, not counting two full-time gardeners.'

Now he pointed with the stick in the direction of the garden on the edge of which they were sitting. 'And that garden! The two old girls do their gallant best with it, but before the War . . . There were so many rare shrubs, brought from every corner of the globe. What's happened to them? God knows! And in those dear, departed days we didn't drink this sort of muck.' He tipped his glass forwards and peered at the residue of peach, apple and banana at its bottom. 'Not this — this fruit-salad. We drank champagne. Or real Russian vodka. Or real Scotch whisky.' He sighed. 'Bit by bit, they've had to sell off the land. In a few months they'll have half-a-dozen brand-new houses and a block of flats on their doorstep. What would Tchaikovsky have made of it all? You know, in the '60s of the last century he lived just a little further up the hill. Number 64 it was. I always think that I have something in common with Tchaikovsky. Temperamentally I mean. But when I once told B.B. that, he said that I had far more in common with Ouida. Rather unkind, really. Eh?'

Iris stood alone, examining the Edwardian bronze statue of a naked woman with over-short legs and over-ample bosom, which stood in the centre of a pond over which a corrugated, yellowish-orange scum extended like long-soured clotted cream.

Suddenly, from the other side of a straggly hedge, she heard a male and a female voice. The male voice was Mervyn's; the female, that of Audrey's American friend, Eva.

'To administer a slap on the bottom is one thing,' Mervyn was saying. 'But to break a woman's nose is another. That's really not quite cricket. Is it?'

'Knowing nothing about cricket, I can't say whether it is or not.' Eva laughed. 'But that boy always struck me as something of a savage under all that elegance and charm. What I just cannot understand is why Isabella should have absolutely refused to have him prosecuted.'

'Perhaps she got a kick out of it all? By no means impossible. Who knows? That Fascist husband of hers may well have given her a taste for that kind of thing.'

As she eavesdropped, Iris felt a chill creeping over and then settling on her like a North Sea mist. Against her will, she had surmised something. Oh, she must be wrong, she must!

'Miss Crediton! Good afternoon!'

'Good afternoon, Mr Greville.'

'Gorgeous afternoon!'

'Gorgeous.'

'Can I get you a refill? Your glass is almost empty.'

'No. No, thank you.'

'Unfortunately this cup' — as Ivor had done, he peered down into his glass, with an expression of vague distaste — 'isn't *quite* what it used to be. But these days, what is? What is?'

'You seemed to have some difficulty in escaping from the Dowager Duchess,' Tim said. 'The Dowager Duchess' was how he referred to Ivor, when not calling him 'the Fairy Queen'. He sipped at his cup, then pulled a face. 'Ugh! This tastes as though it were the syrup left at the bottom of a can of peaches.'

'It's all right. Not bad.'

'My dear Jack, it's become only too clear to me in the course of the past year that you know absolutely damn all about food or drink.' Suddenly Tim straightened up. 'Now who's that over there? Interesting, interesting. Know her? I like those bedroom eyes.'

'Isn't she the wife of the new chaplain?'

'*Is* she? Even more interesting. I must try to get myself introduced. No use asking the Sweeney — she'd know what I was after.'

'Do you really need an introduction?'

'No, on second thoughts, I don't . . . Oh, gosh, there's Pippa passing. But no sign of Dale. Not surprisingly.'

'Why not surprisingly?'

'Well, you've heard the latest, haven't you?'

'No.'

'If you went up into the Whispering Gallery of St Paul's, you'd be the only person to claim that he couldn't hear a sound. Dale beat up the Fascist Contessa. But whether out of an excess of sexual ardour, political conviction or just plain jealousy, no one is sure.'

'Dale beat up Contessa Lambeni?'

But with a muttered 'I'm off,' Tim was threading his way through the crowds to where the new chaplain's wife was stooping to talk to an old woman in a wheel-chair.

*

254

'Thank you, dear,' Audrey said, taking from Iris the glass which she held out to her. 'And if you could just snatch one of those sausage-rolls . . . Thank you. There's something very English about eating sausage-rolls and drinking iced tea at an afternoon party. In the old days . . .' She drew a deep sigh. 'But what's the use of thinking of the old days? We now have this brave, new world, and we have to make the best of it. Don't we?' Miss Sweeney's older sister was repassing with the plate of sausage-rolls. 'Lovely party, Maud!' Audrey called out to her.

Maud limped back. 'I have a feeling it's going to be the last.'

'The *last*! Oh, but I always think of each of your garden-parties as an epitaph to the year.'

'An epitaph!'

'Oh, you know what I mean. Don't misunderstand me. Each pulls all the threads together, it's somehow a summary. A summer summary,' she quipped. 'After it, the rich of the community take themselves off to the sea or the mountains – or abroad. And we poor folk retreat into our houses and close the shutters. No, this mustn't be the last of the garden-parties, my dear.'

'Too much effort, not enough money.'

'But the garden-party is as much of an institution as the Maggio Musicale,' Audrey again protested. Then as Maud moved off to offer the sausage-rolls to other guests, she added, to Iris: 'And it seems to go on for quite as long.' She looked up from her chair, into Iris's face: 'Something's on your mind.'

Iris shook her head. 'No, nothing. Nothing.' She forced a small laugh.

'Well, don't tell Auntie Audrey about it if you don't want to. But my guess would be that it's all something to do with an assault on . . . Oh, good heavens, there she is. Oh, how brave!'

Isabella was crossing the lawn, her sharp heels piercing the yellow turf. She looked as elegant as ever, but for the plaster which covered her nose like a visor and the purple-brown bruise under one eye.

Audrey called out: 'Isabella! Isabella!'

But Isabella ignored her. She had seen Ivor.

'My dear, what a scrape to get yourself into! I once had my own nose broken – it's been slightly crooked ever since, as you may have noticed. But that was in London. And my assailant was a labourer from Donegal. What came over you? And, even more interesting, what came over him?'

'Ivor, I do not – repeat, do not – want to discuss the subject. Let's leave it like that.'

'*We* may leave it like that, but *la tutta Firenze* is certainly not going to do so.'

Isabella's right hand, encrusted with its rings, moved up to the visor. The tips of its elongated fingers rested on it. She drew a deep sigh, her eyes fixed on the rose trailing over the porch of the house. 'So much hatred. Hatred of me, of course, and of everything for which he thinks that I stand. Hatred of Pippa and that Crediton girl. But, above all, hatred of himself. Smash, smash, smash. It doesn't really matter if it's my nose, or civilized society, or he himself which gets smashed in that all-embracing hatred.'

'What's happened to him now? Is he in jug as he deserves to be?'

Isabella shook her head, still staring across at the rose.

'Didn't you call the police?'

'Giuseppe did. He was in the house at the time – doing some work for me in the study. He must have heard my screams. Perhaps – who knows? – he even saved my life. The boy looked as if he could have done anything, anything at all to me.' Again she drew a deep sigh: '*But* . . . I told the police that I'd slipped when he'd done nothing worse than given me a push. I told them that I didn't want to bring any charges.'

'But why, why, why? Are you completely crazy? I suppose you were frightened of a possible scandal?'

'I couldn't care a damn about a scandal. No, put it down to self-hatred, if you like. The same kind of self-hatred as his. If one hates oneself, then one believes that any punishment which comes one's way must be deserved.'

'But why should you hate yourself?'

'My life hasn't been wholly admirable.'

'Which of our lives has been, my dear?'

'Poor little Giuseppe. The whole incident upset him terribly. After the doctor and the police had gone, he completely broke down. Cried and cried and cried. I've never seen him like that. He kept saying that he'd kill Dale.'

'I hope he tries to do nothing so foolish.'

'Oh, what an idiot I am! I should never have told you all this. Now, please, please, Ivor, do *not* start your usual gossiping to what you call *la tutta Firenze*.'

Jack was talking to Margot when Karen approached.

Totally ignoring him, as she so often did, Karen asked Margot: 'Giles with you?'

'No, I'm afraid not.'

'I was hoping he would come. Oh, my dear, what a time you're going through!' She placed a plump, white hand on Margot's arm. 'What exactly started him off?'

'Started him off?'

'Something usually triggers a breakdown.'

'Perhaps it was too much work.' Margot was thinking of how often Giles had had to cover for Mervyn.

'He's never been able to deputize. That's what's been the trouble.'

'Maybe.' Margot was thinking of how easy it had always been for Mervyn to deputize.

'He could hardly have chosen a worse moment, Mervyn says. Just as the Cambridge exams began. If he hadn't been off, then that wretched Miss Pryce wouldn't have got up to those tricks.'

'Poor Ethel.'

'*Poor* Ethel! That woman should be thoroughly ashamed of herself.'

'I think she is.'

'You've no idea what Mervyn has gone through because of her. He's had the most terrible insomnia.'

Iris tried to avoid Pippa; but eventually Pippa cornered her as, one of the first guests to leave, she was saying goodbye to Maud.

'Iris! I've not had a word with you.'

'Oh, hello, Pippa.'

For once, Pippa had not been drinking; the glass in her hand contained iced tea. She looked neat, composed, almost happy. 'Dale asked me to give you a message.'

'Oh. Yes?'

Looking at Pippa, half in apprehension and half in hatred, Iris marvelled at the unusual clearness of her complexion, the unusual gloss of her hair. She had even made up her eyes and her lips, so that she now looked many years younger.

'He asked me to say *au revoir* to you. Or was it *adieu*? Anyway, he's gone. Somewhat abruptly.'

'Gone?' Iris had a sensation of falling, falling endlessly. She put out a hand to the table beside her and leaned all her weight on it.

'I thought it a good idea for him to visit his parents. In Tulsa, Oklahoma. Florence didn't seem the right place for him at this moment. One wouldn't want him to do any more . . . damage.'

'How long is he going to stay there?'

'Two, three weeks. But what you really mean is — is he going to come back? No, I hardly think so. As your Miss Pryce knows, Florence is not a place in which to live down a scandal. Here she'll always be the woman who cheated in order to enable her lover to pass an examination, and poor Dale will always be the man who beat up his lover in a fit of . . . well, what? Boredom, I shouldn't be surprised.'

Without a word, Iris turned and hurried off.

'What's the matter?'

Having overtaken her as she hurried down the hill, Jack had been horrified to find Iris, a handkerchief pressed to her mouth, in tears.

'Nothing! Nothing!'

'But tell me, Iris . . . What is it? What's happened?'

Iris hurried on; and stricken by her wild, gulping sobs, Jack hurried after her. 'Is it because of Contessa Lambeni and Dale? Is it? Don't listen to all this gossip.'

She turned. 'It's not gossip! You know it's not gossip!'

Part of him grieved for her; but part of him felt exhilarated (he acknowledged it later, with disgust) that everything between her and Dale must now be over. He put out a hand; rested it tentatively on her shoulder; then pressed the shoulder firmly.

'Oh, leave me! Can't you leave me alone?'

Now she began running down the hill.

He stood and watched her running.

28

Iris was standing at her bedroom window, staring out at the roofs of the Pitti Palace, when Signora Martinucci arrived to summon her to the telephone. The Signora screwed up her eyes against the glare beating up through the open shutters; then hurried forward from the doorway and, as Iris was leaving the room, slammed shut first the one and then the other.

It was Mervyn.

'Oh, Iris . . . I hope this isn't an, er, inappropriate moment. Karen has one of her committees – her Animal Welfare nonsense. And so I was wondering – why don't you pop over for a cup of tea and a chat? Or if you preferred we could take a taxi up to Fiesole, to escape at least some of this ghastly heat.'

'Oh, I'm sorry, Mervyn.'

'Can't you really manage it, my dear?'

'Not really. I've things to sort out.'

'*Things*? Do you mean actual things, or do you mean – ?'

'Actual things. Of course. What else? Even in less than a year and even when living in this *pensione*, I've collected so much.'

'You have indeed. So many hearts!' Iris said nothing. 'Iris! Are you still there? Are you still there?'

'Yes, I'm still here.'

'Couldn't you possibly leave the sorting out until the evening? You'll find it so much easier when the temperature's dropped a little.'

'No, I want to get it all finished now. Sorry, Mervyn. Sorry.'

'You don't sound it. Ah, well! The thing is I must see you before you go. I have this – this, er, little keepsake for you.'

'Keepsake?'

'A drawing. Of a young girl. There's a certain, er, fugitive likeness between that young girl and you. A combination of

259

beauty, sweetness and strength. In an uncharacteristically generous mood, B.B. once ascribed the drawing to Tiepolo, but I'm afraid it's just *'Scuola di'*. Still, it's an attractive little work — picked up in Piacenza for the, er, proverbial song. Shall I send it round or shall you — as I hope — be able to call round for it here before your departure?'

Iris thought of all his many kindnesses to her. It was cruel to show her exasperation at a love she could not possibly return. 'Of course I'll call round. I want to say goodbye — and to thank you for all you've done to educate me during this past year. But you must keep the drawing. I — I don't deserve it.'

'Of course you deserve it. In any case, it's nothing. Or almost nothing,' he added, since it had a certain value and it was a wrench to part with it. 'But I do wish you hadn't thanked me for *educating* you. It's as though I'd been nothing more to you than a schoolmaster.'

'You've been much more than just that.'

'Oh, Iris, Iris!'

Back in her room, Iris felt restless. She threw herself on her bed; crossed to the window once more to fling back the shutters, so that the afternoon sunlight splashed, scalding, over her; again threw herself on the bed. Eventually she got up. She would have to go for a walk.

As she approached the lift, it creaked and groaned up to a halt, and Guido stepped out. In khaki shorts and ragged vest, his shoes, bare legs and hands grey with plaster, he had obviously come straight from the building site. He smiled at her, the beads of sweat on his wide, sunburned forehead glinting under the feeble light above him. The rest of the corridor, its windows shuttered, was almost dark. *'Buonasera, signorina.'*

Because Ethel had once reprimanded her: 'Oh, do speak English to him — he's never going to make any progress if you use him to practise your Italian,' Iris replied: 'Good afternoon.'

But it was in Italian that Guido went on: *'La Signorina Pryce è a casa?'*

Again Iris replied in English: 'No, she's away. In Bologna. She's gone for an interview for a job at the University.'

'She is not here?'

'I'm afraid not.'

'When she comes back?'

His English seemed to have become even worse since the

débâcle of the examination. Iris shrugged. 'I don't know. She didn't seem to know herself. There was some talk of another interview in Milan. Milano,' she added.

He fumbled in a pocket of his shorts, and pulled out a crumpled airmail envelope. He held it out. 'Please give to the *signorina* when she comes back. *Il mio obbligo*. I owe. Money. For last four lessons.'

Iris hesitated. It struck her that Guido's *obbligo* to Ethel was for far more than four lessons.

'Please!'

Reluctantly, she took the envelope and put it in her bag.

He smiled at her; then clashed back the grill of the lift. '*Prego!*'

Having pressed the button, he gazed across at her and beamed. Iris looked down. She had always found the lift irritatingly slow. Now it seemed even slower than ever.

'*Dove va, signorina?*'

'A walk.'

'A walk? I come? Yes?'

She shook her head decisively. '*Grazie.*'

'Why no? Why?'

'Because . . . Oh, because I want to be alone. And because . . .' It was useless to talk of loyalty to Ethel.

'Yes, I come,' he insisted. '*Si, si!*'

'Sorry. No.'

He shrugged his muscular shoulders; then laughed, in no way offended. '*Va bene! Va bene!* As you wish, lady. Maybe – another time?'

Striding out alone, down a long street empty of any sign of life other than an emaciated cat scavenging in an overturned dustbin outside a shuttered trattoria, Iris wished momentarily that she had agreed to Guido's suggestion that he should join her on her walk. Perhaps his presence would have provided some distraction from the almost physical pain which kept surging through her, insistent wave on wave. As it was, the only thing was to walk faster and faster in the vain hope that, by exhausting herself physically, she would also somehow exhaust that pain as well.

Suddenly, the recollection came to her, with extraordinary vividness, of Isabella stepping out across the Sweeneys' lawn, with that visor covering her smashed nose and in the certain knowledge that everyone was staring at her and gossiping about her. What courage! Iris wished that she could summon up a similar courage, but knew that it was beyond her. *Smashed. Smashed. Smashed.* She found the word repeating itself on and on within her, until, weirdly, it had all at once become destitute of all meaning.

Faster and faster she walked, her feet and legs aching and the sweat pricking through her forehead and trickling down her backbone. Except when an old man wobbled towards her on a bicycle, a woman emerged from a doorway dragging a small, whimpering child, and she heard loud, insistent coughing from behind a shuttered ground-floor window, she seemed, at this hour of siesta, to be passing through a city of the dead.

She had thought that she had been walking aimlessly, choosing now one turning and now another at random. But here, amazingly — tall, narrow houses, their ochre stucco peeling and fissured, reared up around a parched fountain — she was all at once in a piazza familiar to her. So often Dale had helped her out of his car in this piazza and then, his arm around her, had raced with her to that door — yes that door over there — as though, famished, he could not wait another moment to devour the banquet awaiting him. 'Suppose someone sees us?' she would often ask; and he would reply: 'So what? Does it matter?' He was right. It hadn't mattered, it hadn't mattered at all.

The stone of the bench on which she had seated herself burned through the thin, flowered cotton of her dress. But she was indifferent to its heat. She stared, eyes narrowed, at the empty Coca Cola bottle glinting up at her from the dry basin of the fountain. One winter's evening, because they had arrived early and the Signora had failed to answer their repeated, impatient ringing of the bell, she and Dale had sat huddled against each other on this same bench, their bodies shivering. Oh, how happy, how happy she had been!

Our nest. That was how he had talked of it. *Our nest.* But the nest had been fouled. Disgustingly, nauseatingly.

She jumped to her feet. She wanted, against all reason, to see that nest for the last time. She wanted to ring the bell, to climb the stairs, to greet the Signora, to enter the room . . .

But, as she began to walk towards the house, she heard the sound, as of a child's croup horrendously amplified, of a distant klaxon. She turned her head in the direction from which it was coming. A police-car slewed round the corner and shot towards the house. Now there was the frenetic ringing of a bell, and a high, rectangular white box, an antiquated ambulance of the Misericordia, jolted and swayed over the cobbles.

Motionless, Iris stood and watched. She felt as if, victim of some hideous assault, she were gasping for life, and that that police-car and that ambulance had been summoned here for her.

Dark, undying pain.

Jack knew that he should be packing for his departure the following morning. But, instead, he lay out on his bed, staring up at the ceiling. *Dark, undying pain.* He savoured the words, as though they were a chunk of black, bitter chocolate, just as he savoured the emotions of jealousy, loss and hopeless yearning which had prompted the remembrance of them. It had been stupid, stupid, stupid of him to have experienced that exhilaration when Iris, ineffectually struggling to choke back her tears, had run away from him down the hill. If, indeed, she had lost Dale – something of which he could by no means be certain – there was no hope, no hope at all that now, at long last, she would turn to him. 'Of course, she married him on the rebound . . .' He could hear his mother saying this, in knowing self-satisfaction, of one of his girl cousins. A ball ricocheted off a wall into the hands of a bystander, hitherto excluded from the game, who had never expected to catch it. There was no such chance, however, of his catching this ball. 'I like you. I like you a lot.' It was the comforting cliché used over and over again to rejected suitors. What it really meant was: 'Sorry, sorry, not a chance in hell.'

Dark, undying pain. Again he said the words over to himself, struggling to remember: Tennyson, Browning, Arnold?

He was aroused by a knock. He sat up, swung his legs down from the bed. 'Yes? Come in!'

It was Maria. She was carrying a large cardboard box, which she now extended to him. *'Ecco!'* She smiled.

'Che cosa?' he asked, in the Italian accent which always made her either grin or giggle.

This time she giggled: *'Il postino,'* she answered.

Who could have mailed him a parcel of this size?

He attempted to unpick the string; then dug out from his suitcase the nail-scissors which he had already packed. He scrabbled away the tissue paper; stared down in amazement. Neatly folded, innumerable ties, row on top of row, filled the box.

They were of every fabric, every colour, every pattern. There were ordinary ties, bow-ties, ties abnormally narrow, ties abnormally wide, cravats, stocks.

He knew now who had mailed the parcel, presumably as a parting gift. But why, why?

Later that day, his packing completed, Jack walked down the corridor to the sitting-room to fetch the local newspaper. He went out of habit. He no longer needed to improve his knowledge of Italian.

Giles was seated at the desk under the window. As Jack entered the room, he looked up with a sharp intake of breath. 'Did you want something?' He was once more his old self and not as he had been the previous day, whimpering to Margot that no, no, he couldn't possibly face all those people at the Sweeney party.

'Only the paper. Sorry.'

'Well, take it then. It's over there.' He pointed. The dog lay at his feet.

As, paper under arm, Jack emerged from the sitting-room, he came face to face with Margot. 'Oh, you didn't disturb him, did you?'

'I didn't realize he was in there.'

'He's writing again. Isn't that marvellous? He's been writing all today. He says it's just racing along.'

'Yes, that's marvellous.'

The paper spread out before him on the bed, Jack was glancing over a page when suddenly, down in the left-hand corner, his eye was caught by the headline: *Suicido o omicidio*? The brief paragraph related how *il poeta* Giuseppe Valeriano had been found by his landlady hanging by a tie from a beam in his attic room. The police were investigating.

'I just cannot imagine why he should have done such a thing,' Jack said over dinner. Just as the dog-bite had throbbed on and on in his finger, so the mystery of Giuseppe's death had become a constant throb within him.

'Or why someone else should have done it to him,' Margot said.

'It couldn't have been murder. How could it? He sent me all those ties of his.'

'Unless the murderer sent them to you,' Giles put in.

'That's nonsense. No, he must have killed himself.'

'Over Isabella?' Margot suggested.

'Having learned that she was having an affair with Dale?' Giles said.

Jack frowned. 'I wish I knew.'

'You'll never know. Never exactly. That's where I have the advantage over you. I know the exact truth about every one of the characters in my novel. Every single one.'

Giles smiled down at his plate in contentment.

29

Rucksack on back and lugging a suitcase pressed on him by Ivor, Jack made his way up the platform. Ivor had offered to see him off, but Jack had said no. Ivor had then offered to send the car and chauffeur to take him to the station, but Jack had said no to that, too.

He was still thinking, with a bleak sense of loss, of Giuseppe Valeriano. Although he had spent far less time with Giuseppe than with Ivor, now in death the little poet seemed far closer to him than Ivor did in life. On top of the wardrobe rested the bulky cardboard box crammed with the ties. He had shrunk from placing even a handful of the least flamboyant of them in his suitcase. Delighted, Maria would find them and regard them as the tip which Jack had failed to give her. Some of the ties her boyfriend would wear when he took her out or when he went to church; the rest would end up dangling from wire coat-hangers in the flea-market.

Iris was leaning out of the window of one of the carriages. Jack looked up, she looked down.

'Oh, hello, Iris.' He put down the suitcase. His arm was aching and his hand felt chafed. 'I'd no idea you were travelling today.'

'Nor had I — until yesterday afternoon. I was planning to leave on Monday. Then I suddenly thought, why on earth am I staying here? So I rushed over to Cook's and managed to get a sleeper.'

'First class.'

She shrugged and smiled. Her eyes were stricken; there were dark rings around them. Then she said: 'You will get in touch, won't you? You've still got the address I gave you?'

He nodded. 'Yes. Yes, of course.' But he knew that he would never get in touch. 'Well, that's the end of a chapter,' Ivor had remarked to him the previous evening, when they had said goodbye. 'But of course there'll be another chapter for us,' he had added. In the case of Iris, no such other chapter would follow. 'Well, my seat is somewhere up near the front of the train.'

He picked up the case and began to trudge on.

Iris leaned farther out of the window and shouted: 'Let me stand you dinner in the restaurant car.'

But Jack did not hear her.

So often, during the past year, Jack had stood watching as Iris had moved away from him: carried off by a tram, a car or taxi; hurrying along a street or into a lift or down steps; sucked into another group at a party; obeying some summons from Dale.

Now it was she who stood watching; and it was he who moved away from her.

·Francis King

The Woman Who
Was God

'A Gothic creation of power and brilliance, full of bizarre episodes that crash the weird and the ordinary against each other' *Observer*

'He couldn't have died in that way!' A mother feels these things: Ruth St Just might not understand why her son Jim had joined a religious 'community' on the tiny African island of Ellamore, or even why he had gone abroad in the first place. But she was convinced that when he plunged to his death on the jagged rocks of that foreign shore, it could not have been an accident.

The Foreign Office didn't see it that way. No matter how much this obsessive woman badgered them, investigations would go no further. Despairing of the evasive and obstinate official channels, Ruth takes matters into her own hands. She sets off on a personal mission to Africa, determined to expose the sordid truth behind the sinister sect and the mysterious, charismatic woman who reigns over it, and to uncover, among her bizarre band of misfits and eccentrics, the disturbing circumstances that led to the death of her son.

'Essential reading – this novel will resonate in the mind for a long time to come' *Financial Times*

'Francis King, one of the finest contemporary novelists, is prolific, fluent, judicious and moving. He leads us through the novel as an initiate would lead us through a maze' Melvyn Bragg

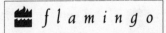

Francis King

Visiting Cards

'Francis King's brilliant comedy will crack the ribs' · *Observer*

An embarrassing mix-up over his name led to unknown writer Amos Kingsley's election to the presidency of the World Association of Authors; but it was his previously unrevealed talent for compromise that kept him in the position.

He soon runs into deep trouble, however, when the annual WAA congress in Malindi erupts over the issue of the imprisonment of three Malindian writers. While his fellow delegates indulge in the traditional conference pursuits of drinking, plotting, in-fighting and infidelity, Amos must find a way to appease the warring factions without offending their hosts, and without losing his job.

'Francis King turns his sense of humour riotously loose at the expense of literary conventions . . . masking his disgust, born of experience, at the futility and squalor of these charades, he directs his snowball with deadly accuracy, inserting a few razor blades meanwhile' *Guardian*

'Brilliantly funny, serious in its muted way, and totally successful in demolishing the humbug, the phony and the inflated' *Financial Times*

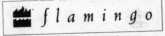

flamingo

Francis King

Punishments

'*Punishments* once again demonstrates that he is a master.'
Observer

Summer, 1948: Michael, an attractive young English medical student, is eager for experience as he travels to the German university town where he and his friends will stay in the homes of local undergraduates.

He is prepared for the desolate landscape, even for the hunger of the people. But does the cheerful friendliness of their welcome mask any antagonism? How do the Germans cope with their guilt, if indeed they feel any? Michael, after all, cannot forget the bombing of London and Coventry, or the concentration camps. For their part, how do the young German students suppress their memories of horror?

As Michael struggles to understand what is going on beneath the surface, and as he comes to realise why he is both attracted to and repelled by Jurgen – he begins to understand that these few weeks will change him for life . . .

'One of his tautest plots . . . alive with period detail and vividly exhuming an era, King's reconstruction of a Germany demoralised and bankrupted by military defeat frequently calls to mind Christopher Isherwood's depictions of Berlin after the First World War.' Peter Kemp, *Sunday Times*

'So good and so disturbing . . . reading Francis King closely, as he deserves, is both rewarding and punishing: he forces you to perform your own acts of darkness . . . marvellously described.'
Victoria Glendinning, *The Times*

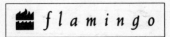 *flamingo*

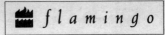 *flamingo*

Flamingo is a quality imprint publishing both fiction and non-fiction. Below are some recent titles.

Fiction
☐ The Things They Carried *Tim O'Brien* £4.99
☐ Matilda's Mistake *Anne Oakley* £4.99
☐ Acts of Worship *Yukio Mishima* £4.99
☐ My Cousin, My Gastroenterologist *Mark Leyner* £4.99
☐ Escapes *Joy Williams* £4.99
☐ The Dust Roads of Monferrato *Rosetta Loy* £4.99
☐ Dirty Weekend *Helen Zahavi* £4.50
☐ Mary Swann *Carol Shields* £4.99
☐ Cowboys and Indians *Joseph O'Connor* £5.99
☐ Ordinary Love *Jane Smiley* £4.99

Non-fiction
☐ A Stranger in Tibet *Scott Berry* £4.99
☐ The Quantum Self *Danah Zohar* £4.99
☐ Ford Madox Ford *Alan Judd* £6.99
☐ C. S. Lewis *A. N. Wilson* £5.99
☐ Meatless Days *Sara Suleri* £4.99
☐ Finding Connections *P. J. Kavanagh* £4.99
☐ Shadows Round the Moon *Roy Heath* £4.99
☐ Home Life *Alice Thomas Ellis* £3.99

You can buy Flamingo paperbacks at your local bookshop or newsagent. Or you can order them from Fontana Paperbacks, Cash Sales Department, Box 29, Douglas, Isle of Man. Please send a cheque, postal or money order (not currency) worth the purchase price plus 22p per book (or plus 22p per book if outside the UK).

NAME (Block letters)_____

ADDRESS_____

_____

_____